UNIX
SHELL PROGRAMMING

RELATED TITLES

C Programmer's Guide to NetBIOS
W. David Schwaderer

C Programmer's Guide to Serial Communications
Joe Campbell

Programming the Apple® IIGS in C and Assembly Language
Mark Andrews

QuickC™ Programming for the IBM®
Carl Townsend

Understanding C
Carl Townsend

Turbo C® Developer's Library
Edward R. Rought and Thomas D. Hoops

Programming in C, Revised Edition
Stephen G. Kochan

Programming in ANSI C
Stephen G. Kochan

Advanced C: Tips and Techniques
Paul Anderson and Gail Anderson

Portability and the C Language
Rex Jaeschke

Topics in C Programming
Stephen G. Kochan and Patrick H. Wood

UNIX® Networking
Stephen G. Kochan and Patrick H. Wood, Editors

UNIX® System Security
Patrick H. Wood and Stephen G. Kochan

UNIX® Text Processing
Dale Doughtery and Tim O'Reilly

Exploring the UNIX® System, Second Edition
Stephen G. Kochan and Patrick H. Wood

UNIX® Systems Administration
David Fiedler and Bruce H. Hunter

---

*For the retailer nearest you, or to order directly from the publisher,
call 800-257-5755. International orders telephone 609-461-6500.*

UNIX
SHELL PROGRAMMING
Revised Edition

STEPHEN G. KOCHAN AND PATRICK H. WOOD
Pipeline Associates, Inc.

HAYDEN BOOKS
A Division of Macmillan Computer Publishing
11711 North College, Carmel, Indiana 46032 USA

International Standard Book Number: 0-672-48448-X
Library of Congress Catalog Card Number: 89-63718

Acquisitions Editor: *Scott Arant*
Cover Art: *RTS Color Graphics*
Typesetting: *Pipeline Associates, Inc.*

This entire text was edited and processed under UNIX. The text was formatted using troff, with the assistance of tbl for the tables and MacDraw for the figures. The troff output was converted to PostScript using devps. The camera ready copy was printed on an Apple LaserWriter Plus, with no pasteup required.

Printed in the United States of America

Trademark Acknowledgements

All terms mentioned in this book that are known to be trademarks or service marks are listed below. SAMS cannot attest to the accuracy of this information. Use of a term in this book should not be regarded as affecting the validity of any trademark or service mark.

BSD is a trademark of University of California, Berkeley.
XENIX is a trademark of Microsoft Corporation.
DEC, VAX, and PDP are trademarks of Digital Equipment Corporation.
devps is a trademark of Pipeline Associates, Inc.
LaserWriter Plus is a trademark of Apple Computer, Inc.
MS-DOS and Xenix are trademarks of Microsoft Corporation.
PostScript is a registered trademark of Adobe Systems, Inc.
UNIX is a registered trademark of AT&T.

To my father

S.G.K.

To my father

P.H.W.

Hayden Books
UNIX
Library

The UNIX System Library is an integrated series of books covering basic to advanced topics related to the UNIX system. The books are written under the direction of Stephen G. Kochan and Patrick H. Wood, who worked for several years teaching introductory and advanced UNIX courses, and who themselves have written many books on the C programming language and the UNIX system.

The first title in the UNIX series is *Exploring the UNIX System*. The text introduces the new user to the UNIX system, covering things such as logging on, working with the file system, editing files with the `vi` editor, writing simple shell programs, and formatting documents. Also included in this text are descriptions of how to use electronic mail and networks and how to administrate a UNIX system.

UNIX Shell Programming uses a clear, step-by-step approach to teach all the features of the shell and shows the reader how to write programs using many actual examples. Also covered are tools used by many shell programmers, such as `grep`, `sed`, `tr`, `cut`, and `sort`, and a detailed discussion on how to write regular expressions. The newer Korn shell is also covered in detail in the book.

UNIX Text Processing gives a comprehensive treatment of the many tools that are available for formatting documents under UNIX. The book shows how `troff` can be used to format simple documents like letters and also how to exploit its capabilities to format larger documents like manuals and books. The text shows how to use the popular `mm` and `ms` macro packages and how to write custom macro packages.

UNIX System Administration is an essential guide to administration for anyone who owns or operates a UNIX system. The text describes how to set up file systems, make backups, configure a system, connect peripheral devices, install and administrate UUCP, work with the line printer spooler, and write shell programs to help make the administration process more manageable.

UNIX System Security is the only text devoted specifically to this important topic. Security for users, programmers, and administrators is covered in detail, as is network security. Source code listings for many useful security-related programs are given at the end of the book.

UNIX System Networking contains practical discussions of several important UNIX networking systems including UUCP, TCP/IP, NFS, RFS, Streams, and LAN Manager/X. Each chapter is written by a noted expert in the field of UNIX networking.

CONTENTS

♦   ♦   ♦   ♦   ♦   ♦   ♦   ♦

P R E F A C E

to the Revised Edition

Since the first edition of *UNIX Shell Programming* was released in 1985, the UNIX System has undergone many changes, some major and some minor. Luckily, most of these changes do not affect the typical shell programmer.

The first edition of this book focused on the System V, Release 2 shell. At that time, the Korn shell was a new emerging shell that was only beginning to gain popularity and support outside of AT&T Bell Labs.

The revised edition of this book focuses on the System V, Release 3 shell. Only minor differences exist between the Release 2 and Release 3 shell, the primary one being the addition of the `getopts` command.

We have devoted more space to the Korn shell in this edition. You will find that the Korn shell chapter has been expanded to reflect changes made to newer versions of this shell and also to provide more extensive coverage. In the previous edition, Appendix B just highlighted the differences between the Korn shell and the standard shell. In this edition, this appendix has been rewritten to provide a complete reference for the Korn shell.

Since the previous edition only gave a cursory introduction to the C shell, it was decided to drop that chapter completely in the revised edition. Those readers wishing a detailed coverage of the C shell should read *The UNIX C Shell Field Guide* (Anderson & Anderson, Prentice-Hall, 1986).

Introduction

It's no secret that the UNIX operating system is emerging as the standard operating system. For programmers who have been using UNIX for several years now, this comes as no surprise: the UNIX system provides an elegant and efficient environment for program development. After all, this is what Dennis Ritchie and Ken Thompson strived for when they developed UNIX at Bell Laboratories in the late 1960s.

One of the strongest features of the UNIX system is its wide collection of programs: over 200 basic commands are distributed with the standard operating system. These commands (also known as *tools*) do everything from counting the number of lines in a file, to sending electronic mail, to displaying a calendar for any desired year.

But the real strength of the UNIX system comes not entirely from this large collection of commands but from the elegance and ease with which these commands can be combined to perform far more sophisticated functions.

To further this end, and also to provide a consistent buffer between the user and the guts of the UNIX system (the *kernel*), the shell was developed. The shell is simply a program that reads in the commands you type and converts them into a form that is more readily understandable by the UNIX system. It also includes some fundamental programming constructs that let you make decisions, loop, and store values in variables.

The standard UNIX shell that is distributed by AT&T with the UNIX system evolved from a version originally written by Stephen Bourne at Bell Labs. New features have been added to the "Bourne" shell since then, some to improve its efficiency, and others to extend its capabilities. This shell, also known as the "standard" shell, is what we propose to teach you about in this book.

Because the shell offers an interpreted programming language, programs can be written, modified, and debugged quickly and easily. We turn to the shell as our first choice of programming language. Once you become adept at programming in the shell, you too may turn to it first.

This book assumes that you are familiar with the fundamentals of the UNIX system; that is, that you know how to log in, how to create files, edit them, remove them, and how to work with directories. But in case you haven't used the UNIX system for a while, we've included a quick review of the basics in Chapter 2. Besides the basic file commands, file name substitution, I/O redirection, and pipes are also reviewed in this chapter.

Chapter 3 reveals what the shell really is. You'll learn here about what happens every time you log into the system, how the shell program gets started, how it parses the command line, and how it executes other programs for you. One of the key points made in this chapter is that the shell is just a program; nothing more, nothing less.

Chapter 4 provides tutorials on tools that we find to be quite useful in writing shell programs. Covered in this chapter are cut, paste, sed, grep, sort, tr, and uniq. Admittedly, the selection is subjective, but it does set the stage for programs that we'll be developing throughout the remainder of the book. Also covered in this chapter is a detailed discussion of regular expressions, which are used by many UNIX commands like sed, grep, and ed.

Chapters 5 through 10 will teach you how to put the shell to work for writing programs. You'll learn here how to write your own commands, use variables, write programs that accept arguments, make decisions, use the shell's for, while, and until looping commands, and use the read command to read data from the terminal or from a file. A separate chapter, Chapter 6, is devoted entirely to a discussion on one of the most intriguing (and often confusing) aspects of the shell: the way it interprets quotes.

By this point in the book, all of the basic programming constructs in the shell will have been covered, and you should be able to write shell programs to solve your particular problems.

Chapter 11 covers a topic of great importance for a real understanding of the way the shell operates: the *environment*. You'll learn here about local and exported variables, subshells, special shell variables like HOME, PATH, and CDPATH, and how to set up your .profile file.

Chapters 12 and 13 tie up some loose ends, and Chapter 14 presents a final version of a phone-directory program called rolo that is developed throughout the book.

Chapter 15 discusses what seems destined to become the most popular shell: the Korn shell, also known as ksh. Since the Korn shell is upwards compatible with the standard Bourne shell, everything taught in the book up to this point applies equally for using ksh. The focus of this chapter is to present the unique features of the Korn shell.

The Appendixes summarize the features of the standard shell and the Korn shell.

The philosophy used in this book is to teach by example. Properly chosen examples do a far superior job at illustrating how a particular feature is used than ten times as many words. The old "A picture is worth..." adage seems to apply just as well to examples. You are encouraged to type in each example and test it on your system, for only by doing can you become adept at shell programming. You also should not be afraid to experiment. Try changing commands in the program examples to see the effect, or add different options or features to make the programs more useful or robust.

At the end of most chapters you will find exercises. These can be used as assignments in a classroom environment, or by yourself to test your progress.

This book teaches the standard shell as of UNIX System V, Release 3. Incompatibilities with earlier versions are noted in the text, and these tend to be rather minor.

Acknowledgments from the first edition of this book: We'd like to thank Tony Iannino and Dick Fritz for editing the manuscript. We'd also like to thank Juliann Colvin for performing her usual wonders copy editing this book. Finally, we'd like to thank Teri Zak, our acquisitions editor, and Maureen Connelly, our production editor. These two are not only the best at what they do, but they also make working with them a real pleasure.

For the revised edition of this book, we'd like to acknowledge the contributions made by Steven Levy and Ann Baker, and we'd like to also thank the following people from SAMS: Phil Kennedy, Wendy Ford, and Scott Arant.

A Quick Review of the Basics

T his chapter provides a review of the UNIX System, including the file system, basic commands, file name substitution, I/O redirection, and pipes.

◆ Some Basic Commands ◆

Displaying the Date and Time: The `date` Command

The `date` command tells the system to print the date and time:

```
$ date
Sat Oct 29 15:40:52 EDT 1983
$
```

date prints the day of the week, month, day, time (24 hour clock, eastern daylight time), and year. Throughout this book, whenever we use **boldface type like this**, it's to indicate what you, the user, types in. Normal face type like this is used to indicate what the UNIX system prints.

   Every UNIX command is ended with the pressing of the RETURN key. RETURN says that you are finished typing things in and are ready for the UNIX system to do its thing.

Finding Out Who's Logged In: The who Command

The `who` command can be used to get information about all users who are currently logged into the system:

```
$ who
pat          tty29    Oct 29 14:40
ruth         tty37    Oct 29 10:54
steve        tty25    Oct 29 15:52
$
```

Here there are three users logged in, pat, ruth, and steve. Along with each user id, is listed the *tty* number of that user and the day and time that user logged in. The tty number is a unique identification number the UNIX system gives to each terminal.

The who command also can be used to get information about yourself:

```
$ who am i
pat          tty29    Oct 29 14:40
$
```

who and who am i are actually the same command: who. In the latter case, the am and i are *arguments* to the who command.

Echoing Characters: The echo Command

The echo command prints (or *echoes*) at the terminal whatever else you happen to type on the line (there are some exceptions to this that you'll learn about later):

```
$ echo this is a test
this is a test
$ echo why not print out a longer line with echo?
why not print out a longer line with echo?
$ echo
                                    A blank line is displayed
$ echo one            two       three           four   five
one two three four five
$
```

You will notice from the last example that echo squeezes out extra blanks between words. That's because on a UNIX system, it's the words that are important; the blanks are merely there to separate the words. Generally, the UNIX system ignores extra blanks (you'll learn more about this in the next chapter).

♦ Working with Files ♦

The UNIX system recognizes only three basic types of files: *ordinary* files, *directory* files, and *special* files. An ordinary file is just that: any file on the system that contains data, text, program instructions, or just about anything else. Directories are described later in this chapter. As its name implies, a special file has a special meaning to the UNIX system, and is typically associated with some form of I/O.

A file name can be composed of just about any character directly available from the keyboard (and even some that aren't) provided the total number of characters contained in the name is not greater than 14. If more than 14 characters are specified, the UNIX system simply ignores the extra characters.

The UNIX system provides many tools that make working with files easy. Here we'll review many of the basic file manipulation commands.

Listing Files: The `ls` Command

To see what files you have stored in your directory, you can type the `ls` command:

```
$ ls
READ_ME
names
rje
$
```

This output indicates that three files called READ_ME, names, and rje are contained in the current directory.

Displaying the Contents of a File: The `cat` Command

You can examine the *contents* of a file by using the `cat` command. The argument to `cat` is the name of the file whose contents you wish to examine.

```
$ cat names
Susan
Jeff
Henry
Allan
Ken
$
```

Counting the Number of Words in a File: The `wc` Command

With the `wc` command, you can get a count of the total number of lines, words, and characters of information contained in a file. Once again, the name of the file is needed as the argument to this command:

```
$ wc names
        5       5        27 names
$
```

The wc command lists three numbers followed by the file name. The first number represents the number of lines contained in the file (5), the second the number of words contained in the file (in this case also 5), and the third the number of characters contained in the file (27).

Command Options

Most UNIX commands allow the specification of *options* at the time that a command is executed. These options generally follow the same format:

–letter

That is, a command option is a minus sign followed immediately by a single letter. For example, in order to count just the number of lines contained in a file, the option -l (that's the letter l) is given to the wc command:

```
$ wc -l names
        5 names
$
```

To count just the number of characters in a file, the -c option is specified:

```
$ wc -c names
        27 names
$
```

Finally, the -w option can be used to count the number of words contained in the file:

```
$ wc -w names
        5 names
$
```

Some commands require that the options be listed before the file name arguments. For example, sort names -r is acceptable whereas wc names -l is not. Let's generalize by saying that command options should *precede* file names on the command line.

Making a Copy of a File: The cp Command

In order to make a copy of a file, the cp command is used. The first argument to the command is the name of the file to be copied (known as the *source file*), and the second argument is the name of the file to place the copy into (known as the *destination file*). You can make a copy of the file names and call it saved_names as follows:

```
$ cp names saved_names
$
```

Execution of this command causes the file named names to be copied into a file named saved_names. As with many UNIX commands, the fact that a command prompt was displayed after the cp command was typed indicates that the command executed successfully.

Renaming a File: The mv Command

A file can be renamed with the mv command. The arguments to the mv command follow the same format as the cp command. The first argument is the name of the file to be renamed, and the second argument is the new name. So to change the name of the file saved_names to hold_it, for example, the following command would do the trick:

```
$ mv saved_names hold_it
$
```

When executing a mv or cp command, the UNIX system does not care whether the file specified as the second argument already exists. If it does, then the contents of the file will be lost.[†] So, for example, if a file called old_names exists, then executing the command

```
cp names old_names
```

would copy the file names to old_names, destroying the previous contents of old_names in the process. Similarly, the command

```
mv names old_names
```

would rename names to old_names, even if the file old_names existed prior to execution of the command.

---

† Assuming you have the proper permission to write to the file.

Removing a File: The rm Command

To remove a file from the system, you use the rm command. The argument to rm is simply the name of the file to be removed:

```
$ rm hold_it
$
```

You can remove more than one file at a time with the rm command by simply specifying all such files on the command line. For example, the following would remove the three files wb, collect, and mon:

```
$ rm wb collect mon
$
```

♦ Working with Directories ♦

Suppose you had a set of files consisting of various memos, proposals, and letters. Further suppose that you had a set of files that were computer programs. It would seem logical to group this first set of files into a directory called documents, for example, and the latter set of files into a directory called programs. Such a directory organization is illustrated in Fig. 2-1.

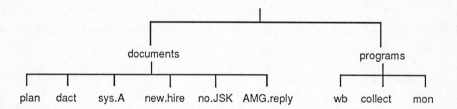

Fig. 2-1. Example directory structure

The file directory documents *contains* the files plan, dact, sys.A, new.hire, no.JSK, and AMG.reply. The directory programs contains the files wb, collect, and mon.

At some point you may decide to further categorize the files in a directory. This can be done by creating subdirectories and then placing each file into the appropriate subdirectory. For example, you might wish to create subdirectories called memos, proposals, and letters inside your documents directory, as shown in Fig. 2-2.

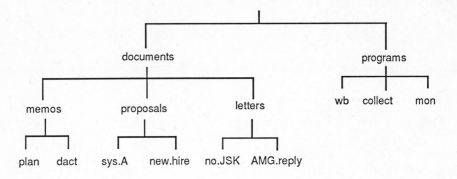

Fig. 2-2. Directories containing subdirectories

documents contains the subdirectories memos, proposals, and letters. Each of these directories in turn contains two files: memos contains plan and dact; proposals contains sys.A and new.hire; and letters contains no.JSK and AMG.reply.

While each file in a given directory must have a unique name, files contained in different directories do not. So, for example, you could have a file in your programs directory called dact, even though a file by that name also exists in the memos subdirectory.

The Home Directory and Path Names

The UNIX system always associates each user of the system with a particular directory. When you log into the system, you are placed automatically into a directory called your *home* directory.

Assume your home directory is called steve and that this directory is actually a subdirectory of a directory called usr. Therefore, if you had the directories documents and programs the overall directory structure would actually look something like the figure illustrated in Fig. 2-3. A special directory known as / (pronounced *slash*) is shown at the top of the directory tree. This directory is known as the *root*.

Whenever you are "inside" a particular directory (called your *current working* directory), the files contained within that directory are immediately accessible. If you wish to access a file from another directory, then you can either first issue a command to "change" to the appropriate directory and then access the particular file, or you can specify the particular file by its *path name*.

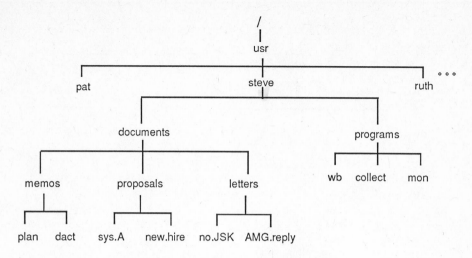

Fig. 2-3. Hierarchical directory structure

A path name enables you to uniquely identify a particular file to the UNIX system. In the specification of a path name, successive directories along the path are separated by the slash character /. A path name that *begins* with a slash character is known as a *full* path name, since it specifies a complete path from the root. So, for example, the path name /usr/steve identifies the directory steve contained under the directory usr. Similarly, the path name /usr/steve/documents references the directory documents as contained in the directory steve under usr. As a final example, the path name /usr/steve/documents/letters/AMG.reply identifies the file AMG.reply contained along the appropriate directory path.

In order to help reduce some of the typing that would otherwise be required, UNIX provides certain notational conveniences. Path names that do not begin with a slash character are known as *relative* path names. The path is relative to your current working directory. For example, if you just logged into the system and were placed into your home directory /usr/steve, then you could directly reference the directory documents simply by typing documents. Similarly, the relative path name programs/mon could be typed to access the file mon contained inside your programs directory.

By convention, the directory name .. always references the directory that is one level higher. For example, after logging in and being placed into your home directory /usr/steve, the path name .. would reference the directory usr. And if you had issued the appropriate command to change your working directory to documents/letters, then the path name .. would reference the documents directory, ../.. would reference the directory steve, and ../proposals/new.hire would reference the file new.hire contained in the proposals directory. Note that in this case, as in most cases, there is usually more than one way to specify a path to a particular file.

Another notational convention is the single period ., which always refers to the current directory.

Now it's time to examine commands designed for working with directories.

Displaying Your Working Directory: The pwd Command

The pwd command is used to help you "get your bearings" by telling you the name of your current working directory.

Recall the directory structure from Fig. 2-3. The directory that you are placed in upon logging into the system is called your home directory. You can assume from Fig. 2-3 that the home directory for the user steve is /usr/steve. Therefore, whenever steve logs into the system, he will *automatically* be placed inside this directory. To verify that this is the case, the pwd (print working directory) command can be issued:

```
$ pwd
/usr/steve
$
```

The output from the command verifies that steve's current working directory is /usr/steve.

Changing Directories: The cd Command

You can change your current working directory by using the cd command. This command takes as its argument the name of the directory you wish to change to.

Let's assume that you just logged into the system and were placed inside your home directory, /usr/steve. This is depicted by the => in Fig. 2-4.

You know that there are two directories directly "below" steve's home directory: documents and programs. In fact, this can be verified at the terminal by issuing the ls command:

```
$ ls
documents
programs
$
```

The ls command lists the two directories documents and programs the same way it listed other ordinary files in previous examples.

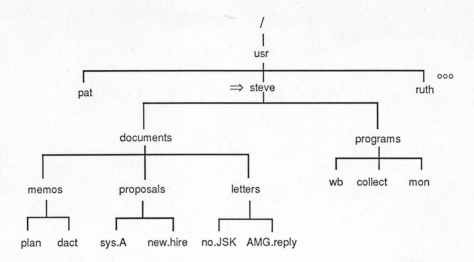

Fig. 2-4. Current working directory is steve

In order to change your current working directory, you issue the cd command, followed by the name of the directory to change to:

```
$ cd documents
$
```

After executing this command, you will be placed inside the documents directory, as depicted in Fig. 2-5.

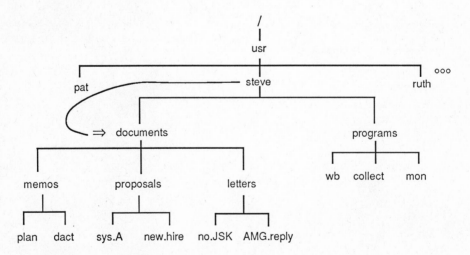

Fig. 2-5. cd documents

You can verify at the terminal that the working directory has been changed by issuing the `pwd` command:

```
$ pwd
/usr/steve/documents
$
```

The easiest way to get one level up in a directory is to issue the command

```
cd ..
```

since by convention `..` always refers to the directory one level up (known as the *parent* directory).

```
$ cd ..
$ pwd
/usr/steve
$
```

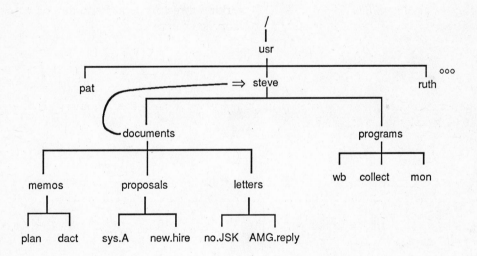

Fig. 2-6. `cd ..`

If you wanted to change to the `letters` directory, you could get there with a single `cd` command by specifying the relative path `documents/letters`:

```
$ cd documents/letters
$ pwd
/usr/steve/documents/letters
$
```

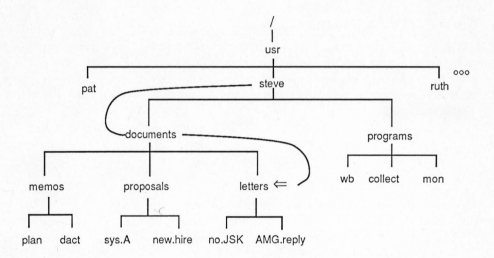

Fig. 2-7. `cd documents/letters`

You can get back up to the home directory with a single `cd` command as shown:

```
$ cd ../..
$ pwd
/usr/steve
$
```

Or you can get back to the home directory using a full path name instead of a relative one:

```
$ cd /usr/steve
$ pwd
/usr/steve
$
```

Finally, there is a third way to get back to the home directory that is also the easiest. Typing the command `cd` *without* an argument will *always* place you back into your home directory, no matter where you are in your directory path.

```
$ cd
$ pwd
/usr/steve
$
```

More on the `ls` Command

Whenever you type the command `ls`, it is the files contained in the current working directory that are listed. But you can also use `ls` to obtain a list of files in other directories by supplying an argument to the command. First let's get back to your home directory:

```
$ cd
$ pwd
/usr/steve
$
```

Now let's take a look at the files in the current working directory:

```
$ ls
documents
programs
$
```

If you supply the name of one of these directories to the `ls` command, then you can get a list of the contents of that directory. So, you can find out what's contained in the `documents` directory simply by typing the command `ls documents`:

```
$ ls documents
letters
memos
proposals
$
```

To take a look at the subdirectory `memos`, you follow a similar procedure:

```
$ ls documents/memos
dact
plan
$
```

If you specify a nondirectory file argument to the `ls` command, you simply get that file name echoed back at the terminal:

```
$ ls documents/memos/plan
documents/memos/plan
$
```

There is an option to the ls command that enables you to determine whether a particular file is a directory, among other things. The −1 option (the letter l) provides a more detailed description of the files in a directory. If you were currently in steve's home directory as indicated in Fig. 2-6, then the following would illustrate the effect of supplying the −1 option to the ls command:

```
$ ls -l
total 2
drwxr-xr-x   5 steve     DP3725      80 Jun 25 13:27 documents
drwxr-xr-x   2 steve     DP3725      96 Jun 25 13:31 programs
$
```

The first line of the display is a count of the total number of *blocks* (1,024 bytes as of UNIX System V) of storage that the listed files use. Each successive line displayed by the ls -l command contains detailed information about a file in the directory. The first character on each line tells whether the file is a directory. If the character is d, then it is a directory; if it is − then it is an ordinary file; finally, if it is b, c, or p, then it is a special file.

The next nine characters on the line tell how every user on the system can access the particular file. These *access modes* apply to the file's owner (the first three characters), other users in the same *group* as the file's owner (the next three characters), and finally to all other users on the system (the last three characters). They tell whether the user can read from the file, write to the file, or execute the contents of the file.

The ls -l command lists the *link* count (see later in this chapter), the owner of the file, the group owner of the file, how large the file is (i.e., how many characters are contained in it), and when the file was last modified. The information displayed last on the line is the file name itself.

```
$ ls -l programs
total 4
-rwxr-xr-x   1 steve     DP3725     358 Jun 25 13:31 collect
-rwxr-xr-x   1 steve     DP3725    1219 Jun 25 13:31 mon
-rwxr-xr-x   1 steve     DP3725      89 Jun 25 13:30 wb
$
```

The dash in the first column of each line indicates that the three files collect, mon, and wb are ordinary files and not directories.

Creating a Directory: The `mkdir` Command

To create a directory, the `mkdir` command must be used. The argument to this command is simply the name of the directory you want to make. As an example, assume that you are still working with the directory structure depicted in Fig. 2-7 and that you wish to create a new directory called `misc` *on the same level* as the directories `documents` and `programs`. Well, if you were currently in your home directory, then typing the command `mkdir misc` would achieve the desired effect:

```
$ mkdir misc
$
```

    Now if you execute an `ls` command, you should get the new directory listed:

```
$ ls
documents
misc
programs
$
```

The directory structure will now appear as shown in Fig. 2-8.

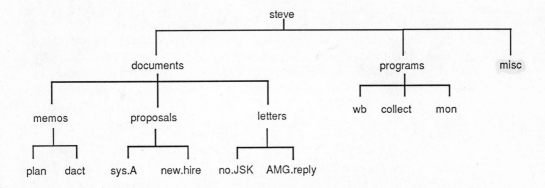

Fig. 2-8. Directory structure with newly created `misc` directory

Copying a File from One Directory to Another

The `cp` command can be used to make a copy of a file from one directory into another. For example, you can copy the file `wb` from the `programs` directory into a file called `wbx` in the `misc` directory as follows:

```
$ cp programs/wb misc/wbx
$
```

Since the two files are contained in different directories, it is not even necessary that they be given different names:

```
$ cp programs/wb misc/wb
$
```

When the destination file has the same name as the source file (in a different directory, of course), then it is necessary to specify only the destination directory as the second argument:

```
$ cp programs/wb misc
$
```

When this command gets executed, the UNIX system recognizes that the second argument is the name of a directory and copies the source file into that directory. The new file is given the same name as the source file. You can copy more than one file into a directory by listing the files to be copied before the name of the destination directory. If you were currently in the programs directory, then the command

```
$ cp wb collect mon ../misc
$
```

would copy the three files wb, collect, and mon into the misc directory, under the same names.

To copy a file from another directory into your current one and give it the same name, use the fact that the current directory can always be referenced as '.':

```
$ pwd
/usr/steve/misc
$ cp ../programs/collect .
$
```

The above command copies the file collect from the directory ../programs into the current directory (/usr/steve/misc).

Moving Files between Directories

You recall that the mv command can be used to rename a file. However, when the two arguments to this command reference different directories, then the file is actually moved from the first directory into the second directory. For example, first change from the home directory to the documents directory:

```
$ cd documents
$
```

Suppose now you decide that the file plan contained in the memos directory is really a proposal and not a memo. So you would like to move it from the memos directory into the proposals directory. The following would do the trick:

```
$ mv memos/plan proposals/plan
$
```

As with the cp command, if the source file and destination file have the same name, then only the name of the destination directory need be supplied.

```
$ mv memos/plan proposals
$
```

Also like the cp command, a group of files can be simultaneously moved into a directory by simply listing all files to be moved before the name of the destination directory:

```
$ pwd
/usr/steve/programs
$ mv wb collect mon ../misc
$
```

This would move the three files wb, collect, and mon into the directory misc.

You can also use the mv command to change the name of a directory. For example, the following will rename the directory programs to bin.

```
$ mv programs bin
$
```

Linking Files: The ln Command

In simplest terms, the ln command provides an easy way for you to give more than one name to a file. The general form of the command is

ln from to

This links the file *from* to the file *to*.

Recall the structure of steve's programs directory from Fig. 2-8. In that directory he has stored a program called wb. Suppose he decides that he'd also like to call the program writeback. The most obvious thing to do would be to simply create a copy of wb called `writeback`:

```
$ cp wb writeback
$
```

The drawback with this approach is that now twice as much disk space is being consumed by the program. Furthermore, if `steve` ever changes wb he may forget to make a new copy of `writeback`, resulting in two different copies of what he thinks is the same program.

By linking the file wb to the new name, these problems are avoided:

```
$ ln wb writeback
$
```

Now instead of two copies of the file existing, only one exists with two different names: wb and `writeback`. The two files have been logically linked by the UNIX system. As far as you're concerned, it appears as though you have two *different* files. Executing an `ls` command shows the two files separately:

```
$ ls
collect
mon
wb
writeback
$
```

Look what happens when you execute an `ls -l`:

```
$ ls -l
total 5
-rwxr-xr-x    1 steve    DP3725       358 Jun 25 13:31 collect
-rwxr-xr-x    1 steve    DP3725      1219 Jun 25 13:31 mon
-rwxr-xr-x    2 steve    DP3725        89 Jun 25 13:30 wb
-rwxr-xr-x    2 steve    DP3725        89 Jun 25 13:30 writeback
$
```

The number right before `steve` is 1 for `collect` and `mon` and 2 for wb and `writeback`. This number is the number of links to a file, normally 1 for non-linked, nondirectory files. Since wb and `writeback` are linked, this number is 2 for these files. This implies that you can link to a file more than once.

You can remove *either* of the two linked files at any time, and the other will *not* be removed:

```
$ rm writeback
$ ls -l
total 4
```

```
-rwxr-xr-x   1 steve    DP3725     358 Jun 25 13:31 collect
-rwxr-xr-x   1 steve    DP3725    1219 Jun 25 13:31 mon
-rwxr-xr-x   1 steve    DP3725      89 Jun 25 13:30 wb
$
```

Note that the number of links on wb went from 2 to 1 since one of its links was removed.

Most often, ln is used to link files between directories. For example, suppose pat wanted to have access to steve's wb program. Instead of making a copy for himself (subject to the same problems described above) or including steve's programs directory in his PATH (described in detail in a later chapter), he can simply link to the file from his own program directory; e.g.

```
$ pwd
/usr/pat/bin                        pat's program directory
$ ls -l
total 4
-rwxr-xr-x   1 pat      DP3822    1358 Jan 15 11:01 lcat
-rwxr-xr-x   1 pat      DP3822     504 Apr 21 18:30 xtr
$ ln /usr/steve/wb                  Link wb to pat's bin
$ ls -l
total 5
-rwxr-xr-x   1 pat      DP3822    1358 Jan 15 11:01 lcat
-rwxr-xr-x   2 steve    DP3725      89 Jun 25 13:30 wb
-rwxr-xr-x   1 pat      DP3822     504 Apr 21 18:30 xtr
$
```

Note that steve is still listed as the owner of wb, even though the listing came from pat's directory. This makes sense, since really only one copy of the file exists—and it's owned by steve.

The only stipulation on linking files is that the files to be linked together must reside on the same *file system*. If they don't, then you'll get an error from ln when you try to link them. (To determine the different files systems on your system, execute the df command. The first field on each line of output is the name of a file system.)

One last note before leaving this discussion: The ln command follows the same general format as cp and mv, meaning that you can link a bunch of files at once into a directory using the format

ln *files directory*

Removing a Directory: The rmdir Command

You can remove a directory with the rmdir command. The stipulation involved in removing a directory is that no files be contained in the directory. If there *are* files in the directory when `rmdir` is executed, then you will not be allowed to remove the directory. To remove the directory `misc` that you created earlier, the following could be used:

```
$ rmdir /usr/steve/misc
$
```

Once again, the above command will work only if no files are contained in the `misc` directory; otherwise, the following will happen:

```
$ rmdir /usr/steve/misc
rmdir: /usr/steve/misc not empty
$
```

If this happens and you still want to remove the `misc` directory, then you would first have to remove all of the files contained in that directory before reissuing the `rmdir` command.

As an alternate method for removing a directory and the files contained in it, you can use the `-r` option to the `rm` command. The format is simple:

$$\text{rm } -\text{r } \textit{dir}$$

where *dir* is the name of the directory that you want to remove. `rm` will remove the indicated directory and *all* files (including directories) in it.

◆ File Name Substitution ◆

The Asterisk

One very powerful feature of the UNIX system that is actually handled by the shell is *file name substitution*. Let's say your current directory has these files in it:

```
$ ls
chapt1
chapt2
chapt3
chapt4
$
```

Suppose you want to print their contents at the terminal. Well, you could take advantage of the fact that the `cat` command allows you to specify more than one file name at a time. When this is done, the contents of the files are displayed one after the other.

```
$ cat chapt1 chapt2 chapt3 chapt4
    . . .
$
```

But you can also type in:

```
$ cat *
    . . .
$
```

and get the same results. The shell automatically *substitutes* the names of all of the files in the current directory for the `*`. The same substitution occurs if you use `*` with the `echo` command:

```
$ echo *
chapt1 chapt2 chapt3 chapt4
$
```

Here the `*` is again replaced with the names of all the files contained in the current directory, and the `echo` command simply displays them at the terminal.

Any place that `*` appears on the command line, the shell performs its substitution:

```
$ echo * : *
chapt1 chapt2 chapt3 chapt4 : chapt1 chapt2 chapt3 chapt4
$
```

The `*` can also be used in combination with other characters to limit the file names that are substituted. For example, let's say that in your current directory you have not only `chapt1` through `chapt4` but also files `a`, `b`, and `c`:

```
$ ls
a
b
c
chapt1
chapt2
chapt3
chapt4
$
```

To display the contents of just the files beginning with `chapt`, you can type in:

```
$ cat chapt*
        .
        .
        .
$
```

The `chapt*` matches any file name that *begins* with `chapt`. All such file names matched are substituted on the command line.

The `*` is not limited to the end of a file name; it can be used at the beginning or in the middle as well:

```
$ echo *t1
chapt1
$ echo *t*
chapt1 chapt2 chapt3 chapt4
$ echo *x
*x
$
```

In the first `echo`, the `*t1` specifies all file names that end in the characters `t1`. In the second `echo`, the first `*` matches everything up to a `t` and the second everything after; thus, all file names containing a `t` are printed. Since there are no files ending with `x`, no substitution occurs in the last case. Therefore, the `echo` command simply displays `*x`.

Matching Single Characters

The asterisk (`*`) matches *zero* or more characters, meaning that `x*` will match the file `x` as well as `x1`, `x2`, `xabc`, etc. The question mark (`?`) matches exactly one character. So `cat ?` will print all files with one-character names, just as `cat x?` will print all files with two-character names beginning with `x`.

```
$ ls
a
aa
aax
alice
b
bb
c
cc
report1
report2
report3
$ echo ?
a b c
```

```
$ echo a?
aa
$ echo ??
aa bb cc
$ echo ??*
aa aax alice bb cc report1 report2 report3
$
```

In the last example, the `??` matches two characters, and the `*` matches zero or more up to the end. The net effect is to match all file names of two or more characters.

Another way to match a single character is to give a list of the characters to use in the match inside square brackets `[ ]`. For example, `[abc]` matches *one* letter `a`, `b`, or `c`. It's similar to the `?`, but it allows you to choose the characters that will be matched. The specification `[0-9]` matches the characters `0` *through* 9. The only restriction in specifying a *range* of characters is that the first character must be alphabetically less than the last character, so that `[z-f]` is not a valid range specification.

By mixing and matching ranges and characters in the list, you can perform some very complicated substitutions. For example, `[a-np-z]*` will match all files that start with the letters `a` through `n` *or* `p` through `z` (or more simply stated, any lowercase letter but `o`).

If the first character following the `[` is a `!`, then the sense of the match is inverted. That is, any character will be matched *except* those enclosed in the brackets. So

    `[!a-z]`

matches any character except a lowercase letter, and

    `*[!o]`

matches any file that doesn't end with the lowercase letter `o`.

Table 2-1 gives a few more examples of file name substitution.

TABLE 2-1. File name substitution examples

Command	Description
echo a*	Print the *names* of the files beginning with a
cat *.c	Print all files ending in .c
rm *.*	Remove all files containing a period
ls x*	List the names of all files beginning with x
rm *	Remove *all* files in the current directory (note: be careful when you use this)
echo a*b	Print the names of all files beginning with a and ending with b
cp ../programs/* .	Copy all files from ../programs into the current directory
ls [a-z]*[!0-9]	List files that begin with a lowercase letter and don't end with a digit.

♦ Standard Input/Output, and I/O Redirection ♦

Standard Input and Standard Output

Most UNIX system commands take input from your terminal and send the resulting output back to your terminal. A command normally reads its input from a place called *standard input,* which happens to be your terminal by default. Similarly, a command normally writes its output to *standard output*, which is also your terminal by default. This concept is depicted in Fig. 2-9.

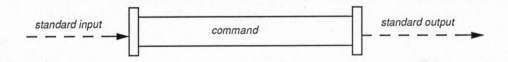

Fig. 2-9. Typical UNIX command

You will recall that executing the who command results in the display of the currently logged-in users. More formally, the who command writes a list of the logged-in users to standard output. This is depicted in Fig. 2-10.

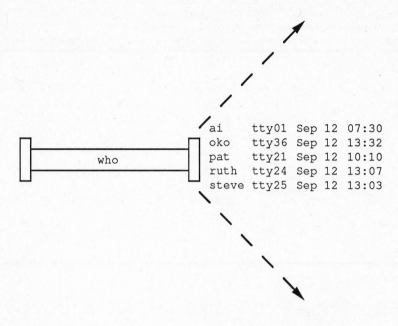

```
ai     tty01  Sep 12  07:30
oko    tty36  Sep 12  13:32
pat    tty21  Sep 12  10:10
ruth   tty24  Sep 12  13:07
steve  tty25  Sep 12  13:03
```

Fig. 2-10. who command

If a `sort` command is executed *without* a file name argument, then the command will take its input from standard input. As with standard output, this is your terminal by default.

When entering data to a command from the terminal, the `CTRL` and `D` keys (denoted *CTRL-d* in this text) must be simultaneously pressed after the last data item has been entered. This tells the command that you have finished entering data. As an example, let's use the `sort` command to sort the following four names: Tony, Barbara, Harry, Dick. Instead of first entering the names into a file, we'll enter them directly from the terminal:

```
$ sort
Tony
Barbara
Harry
Dick
CTRL-d
Barbara
Dick
Harry
Tony
$
```

Since no file name was specified to the sort command, the input was taken from standard input, the terminal. After the fourth name was typed in, the CTRL and D keys were pressed to signal the end of the data. At that point, the sort command sorted the four names and displayed the results on the standard output device, which is also the terminal. This is depicted in Fig. 2-11.

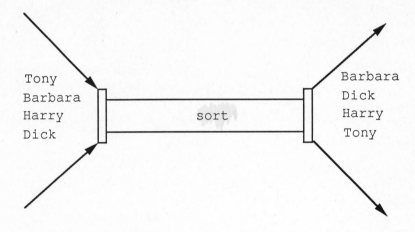

```
Tony                                                    Barbara
Barbara                                                 Dick
Harry                     sort                          Harry
Dick                                                    Tony
```

Fig. 2-11. sort command

The wc command is another example of a command that takes its input from standard input if no file name is specified on the command line. So the following shows an example of this command used to count the number of lines of text entered from the terminal:

```
$ wc -l
This is text that
is typed on the
standard input device.
CTRL-d
        3
$
```

You will note that the *CTRL-d* that is used to terminate the input is not counted as a separate line by the wc command. Furthermore, since no file name was specified to the wc command, only the count of the number of lines (3) is listed as the output of the command. (You will recall that this command normally prints the name of the file directly after the count.)

Output Redirection

The output from a command normally intended for standard output can be easily "diverted" to a file instead. This capability is known as *output redirection*.

If the notation > *file* is appended to *any* command that normally writes its output to standard output, then the output of that command will be written to *file* instead of your terminal:

```
$ who > users
$
```

This command line causes the who command to be executed and its output to be written into the file users. You will notice that no output appears at the terminal. This is because the output has been *redirected* from the default standard output device (the terminal) into the specified file:

```
$ cat users
oko     tty01   Sep 12 07:30
ai      tty15   Sep 12 13:32
ruth    tty21   Sep 12 10:10
pat     tty24   Sep 12 13:07
steve   tty25   Sep 12 13:03
$
```

If a command has its output redirected to a file and the file already contains some data, then that data will be lost. Consider this example:

```
$ echo line 1 > users
$ cat users
line 1
$ echo line 2 >> users
$ cat users
line 1
line 2
$
```

The second echo command uses a different type of output redirection indicated by the characters >>. This character pair causes the standard output from the command to be *appended* to the specified file. Therefore, the previous contents of the file are not lost and the new output simply gets added onto the end.

By using the redirection append characters >>, you can use cat to append the contents of one file onto the end of another:

```
$ cat file1
This is in file1.
$ cat file2
This is in file2.
$ cat file1 >> file2              Append file1 to file2
$ cat file2
This is in file2.
This is in file1.
$
```

Recall that specifying more than one file name to cat results in the display of the first file followed immediately by the second file, and so on:

```
$ cat file1
This is in file1.
$ cat file2
This is in file2.
$ cat file1 file2
This is in file1.
This is in file2.
$ cat file1 file2 > file3          Redirect it instead
$ cat file3
This is in file1.
This is in file2.
$
```

Now you can see where the cat command gets its name: when used with more than one file its effect is to *catenate* the files together.

Incidentally, the shell recognizes a special format of output redirection. If you type

> *file*

not preceded by a command, then the shell will create an empty (i.e., zero character length) *file* for you. If *file* previously exists, then its contents will be lost.

Input Redirection

Just as the output of a command can be redirected to a file, so can the input of a command be redirected from a file. And as the greater-than character > is used for output redirection, the less-than character < is used to redirect the input of a command. Of course, only commands that normally take their input from standard input can have their input redirected from a file in this manner.

In order to redirect the input of a command, you type the < character followed by the name of the file that the input is to be read from. So, for example, to count the number of lines in the file users, you know that you can execute the command `wc -l users`:

```
$ wc -l users
      2 users
$
```

Or, you can count the number of lines in the file by redirecting the input of the wc command from the terminal to the file `users`:

```
$ wc -l < users
      2
$
```

   You will note that there is a difference in the output produced by the two forms of the wc command. In the first case, the name of the file users is listed with the line count; in the second case, it is not. This points out the subtle distinction between the execution of the two commands. In the first case wc knows it is reading its input from the file users. In the second case, it only knows that it is reading its input from standard input. The shell redirects the input from the terminal to the file users (more about this in the next chapter). As far as wc is concerned, it doesn't know whether its input is coming from the terminal or from a file!

◆ Pipes ◆

As you will recall, the file users that was created previously contains a list of all the users currently logged into the system. Since you know that there will be one line in the file for each user logged into the system, you can easily determine the *number* of users logged in by simply counting the number of lines in the users file:

```
$ who > users
$ wc -l < users
      5
$
```

This output would indicate that there were currently five users logged in. Now you have a command sequence you can use whenever you want to know how many users are logged in.
   There is another approach to determine the number of logged-in users that bypasses the use of a file. The UNIX system allows you to effectively "connect" two commands together. This connection is known as a *pipe*, and it enables you to take the output from one command and feed it directly into the input of another command. A pipe is effected by the character |, which is placed

between the two commands. So to make a pipe between the who and wc -l commands, you simply type who | wc -l:

```
$ who | wc -l
        5
$
```

The pipe that is effected between these two commands is depicted in Fig. 2-12.

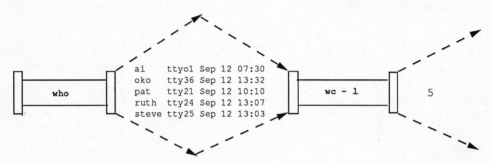

Fig. 2-12. Pipeline process: who | wc -l

When a pipe is set up between two commands, the standard output from the first command is connected directly to the standard input of the second command. You know that the who command writes its list of logged-in users to standard output. Furthermore, you know that if no file name argument is specified to the wc command then it takes its input from standard input. Therefore, the list of logged-in users that is output from the who command automatically becomes the input to the wc command. Note that you never see the output of the who command at the terminal, since it is *piped* directly into the wc command. This is depicted in Fig. 2-13.

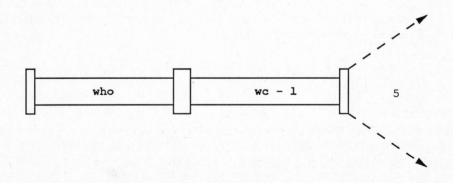

Fig. 2-13. Pipeline process

A pipe can be made between *any* two programs, provided the first program writes its output to standard output, and the second program reads its input from standard input.

As another example of a pipe, suppose you wanted to count the number of files contained in your directory. Knowledge of the fact that the `ls` command displays one line of output per file enables you to use the same type of approach as before:

```
$ ls | wc -l
       10
$
```

The output indicates that the current directory contains 10 files.

It is also possible to form a pipeline consisting of more than two programs, with the output of one program feeding into the input of the next.

Filters

The term *filter* is often used in UNIX terminology to refer to any program that can take input from standard input, perform some operation on that input, and write the results to standard output. More succinctly, a filter is any program that can be used between two other programs in a pipeline. So in the previous pipeline, `wc` is considered a filter. `ls` is not, since it does not read its input from standard input. As other examples, `cat` and `sort` are filters, while `who`, `date`, `cd`, `pwd`, `echo`, `rm`, `mv`, and `cp` are not.

◆ Standard Error ◆

In addition to standard input and standard output there is another place known as *standard error*. This is where most UNIX commands write their error messages. And as with the other two "standard" places, standard error is associated with your terminal by default. In most cases, you never know the difference between standard output and standard error:

```
$ ls n*                              List all files beginning with n
n* not found
$
```

Here the "not found" message is actually being written to standard error and not standard output by the `ls` command. You can verify that this message is not being written to standard output by redirecting the `ls` command's output:

```
$ ls n* > foo
n* not found
$
```

So you see you still get the message printed out at the terminal, even though you redirected standard output to the file foo.

The above example shows the raison d'être for standard error: so that error messages will still get displayed at the terminal even if standard output is redirected to a file or piped to another command.

You can also redirect standard error to a file by using the notation

command 2> *file*

No space is permitted between the 2 and the >. Any error messages normally intended for standard error will be diverted into the specified *file*, similar to the way standard output gets redirected.

```
$ ls n* 2> errors
$ cat errors
n* not found
$
```

♦ More on Commands ♦

Typing More Than One Command on a Line

You can type more than one command on a line provided you separate each command with a semicolon. For example, you can find out the current time and also your current working directory by typing in the date and pwd commands on the same line:

```
$ date; pwd
Wed Apr 25 20:14:32 EST 1985
/usr/pat/bin
$
```

You can string out as many commands as you like on the line, as long as each command is delimited by a semicolon.

Sending a Command to the Background

Normally, you type in a command and then wait for the results of the command to be displayed at the terminal. For all of the examples you have seen thus far, this waiting time is typically quite short—maybe a second or two. However, you may have to run commands that require many seconds or even minutes to execute. In those cases, you'll have to wait for the command to finish executing before you can proceed further *unless you execute the command in the background*.

If you type in a command followed by the ampersand character &, then that command will be sent to the background for execution. This means that the command will no longer tie up your terminal and you can then proceed with other work. The standard output from the command will still be directed to your terminal; however, in most cases the standard input will be dissociated from your terminal. If the command does try to read any input from standard input, it will be as if *CTRL-d* were typed.

```
$ sort data > out &          Send the sort to the background
1258                         Process id
$ date                       Your terminal is immediately available to do other work
Thu Apr 26 13:45:09 EST 1985
$
```

When a command is sent to the background, the UNIX system automatically displays a number, called the *process id* for that command. In the above example, 1258 was the process id assigned by the system. This number uniquely identifies the command that you sent to the background, and can be used to obtain status information about the command. This is done with the ps command.

The ps Command

The ps command gives you information about the processes that are running on the system. ps without any options prints the status of just your processes. If you type in ps at your terminal, you'll get a few lines back describing the processes you have running:

```
$ ps
   PID  TTY  TIME COMMAND
   195   01  0:21 sh          The shell
  1353   01  0:00 ps          This ps command
  1258   01  0:10 sort        The previous sort
$
```

The ps command prints out four columns of information: PID, the process id; TTY, the terminal number that the process was run from; TIME, the amount of computer time in minutes and seconds that process has used; and COMMAND, the name of the process. (The sh process in the above example is the shell that was started when you logged in, and it's used 21 seconds of computer time.) Until the command is finished, it shows up in the output of the ps command as a running process. Process number 1353 in the above example is the ps command that was typed in, and 1258 is the sort from above.

When used with the -f option, ps prints out more information about your processes, including the *parent* process id (PPID), the time the processes started (STIME), and the command arguments.

```
$ ps -f
     UID    PID  PPID  C    STIME TTY       TIME COMMAND
   steve    195    1   0 10:58:29 tty01     0:21 -sh
   steve   1360  195  43 13:54:48 tty01     0:01 ps -f
   steve   1258  195   0 13:45:04 tty01     3:17 sort data
$
```

◆ Command Summary ◆

The following table summarizes the commands reviewed in this chapter. In this table, *file* refers to a file, *file(s)* to one or more files, *dir* to a directory, and *dir(s)* to one or more directories.

TABLE 2-2. Command summary

Command	Description
cat *file(s)*	Display contents of *file(s)* or standard input if not supplied
cd *dir*	Change working directory to *dir*
cp *file$_1$ file$_2$*	Copy *file$_1$* to *file$_2$*
cp *file(s) dir*	Copy *file(s)* into *dir*
date	Display the date and time
echo *args*	Display *args*
ln *file$_1$ file$_2$*	Link *file$_1$* to *file$_2$*
ln *file(s) dir*	Link *file(s)* into *dir*
ls *file(s)*	List *file(s)*
ls *dir(s)*	List files in *dir(s)* or in current directory if *dir(s)* is not specified
mkdir *dir(s)*	Create directory *dir(s)*
mv *file$_1$ file$_2$*	Move *file$_1$* to *file$_2$* (simply rename it if both reference the same directory)
mv *file(s) dir*	Move *file(s)* into directory *dir*
ps	List information about active processes
pwd	Display current working directory path
rm *file(s)*	Remove *files(s)*
rmdir *dir(s)*	Remove empty directory *dir(s)*
sort *file(s)*	Sort lines of *file(s)* or standard input if not supplied
wc *file(s)*	Count the number of lines, words, and characters in *file(s)* or standard input if not supplied
who	Display who's logged in

◆ Exercises ◆

1. Given the following files in your current directory:

```
$ ls
feb86
jan12.89
jan19.89
jan26.89
jan5.89
jan85
jan86
jan87
jan88
mar88
memo1
memo10
memo2
memo2.sv
$
```

/USERS/BILL,

What would be the output from the following commands?

```
echo *          echo *[!0-9]
```
LIST files   *LIST Memo2.sv only*

```
echo m[a-df-z]*     echo [A-Z]*
```
mar88   *[A-Z]* No files with this start with this*

```
echo jan*           echo *.*
```
LIST all JAN —   *LIST files with . in them*

```
echo ?????          echo *89
```
LISTs all 5 char files   *all files ending in 89 No Space*

```
echo jan?? feb?? mar??   echo [fjm][ae][bnr]*
```
Jan85 Jan86 Jan87   *all feb jan + Mar files*
Jan88 feb86 MAR88.   *[fjm][ae][bnr]**

2. What is the effect of the following command sequences?

```
ls | wc -l        rm ???
```
14   *No 3 char files*

```
who | wc -l       mv progs/* /usr/steve/backup
```
1   *Can not access progs/**

```
ls *.c | wc -l    rm *.o
```
x.c Not found   *Can't access *.o*

```
who | sort        cd; pwd
```
same as who   *Home dir Print dir*

```
cp memo1 ..       plotdata 2>errors &
```
copies to   *Plotdata 2 Not found*
Dir ..
78

3

What is the Shell?

I n this chapter you'll learn what the shell is and what it does.

◆ The Kernel and the Utilities ◆

The "UNIX system" is itself logically divided into two pieces: the *kernel* and the *utilities* (see Fig. 3-1.)

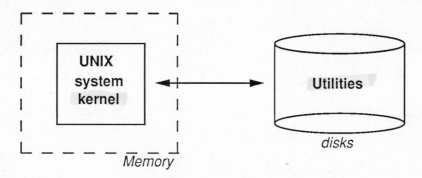

Fig. 3-1. The UNIX system

The kernel is the heart of the UNIX system and resides in the computer's memory from the time the computer is turned on and *booted* until the time it is shut down.

The utilities, on the other hand, reside on the computer's disk and are only brought into memory as requested. Virtually every command you know under the UNIX system is classified as a utility; therefore, the program resides on the disk and is brought into memory only when you request that the command be executed. So, for example, when you execute the `date` command, the UNIX system loads the program called `date` from the computer's disk into memory and initiates its execution.

The shell, too, is a utility program. It is loaded into memory for execution whenever you log into the system. In fact, it's worth learning the precise sequence of events that occurs when you do log into a system.

◆ Logging In ◆

A terminal is connected to a UNIX system through a direct wire, modem, or local area network. In the first case, as soon as you turn on the terminal (and hit the RETURN key a couple of times if necessary) you should get a `login:` message on your screen. In the last two cases, you must first dial the computer's number (or type in the name of the system) and get connected before the `login:` message appears.

For each terminal port on a system, a program called `getty` will be active. This is depicted in Fig. 3-2.

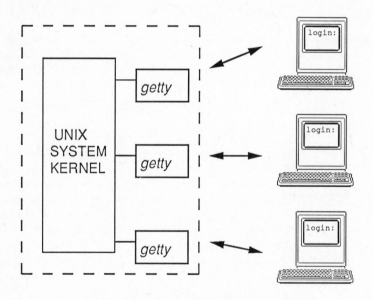

Fig. 3-2. The `getty` process

The UNIX system—more precisely a program called `init`—automatically starts up a `getty` program on each terminal port whenever the system is allowing users to log in. `getty` determines the baud rate, displays the message `login:`

at its assigned terminal, and then just waits for someone to type something in. As soon as someone types in some characters followed by RETURN, the getty program disappears; but before it goes away, it starts up a program called login to finish the process of logging in (see Fig. 3-3). It also gives login the characters you typed in at the terminal—characters that presumably represent your login name.

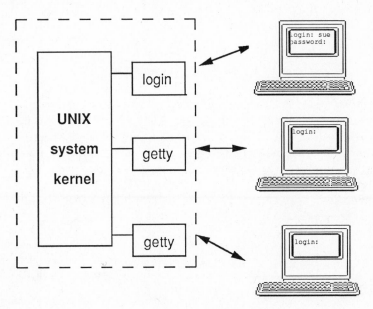

Fig. 3-3. login started on sue's terminal

When login begins execution, it displays the string Password: at the terminal and then waits for you to type your password. Once you have, login then proceeds to verify your login name and password against the corresponding entry in the file /etc/passwd. This file contains one line for each user of the system. That line specifies, among other things, the login name, password (in an encrypted form), home directory, and program to start up when that user logs in. The last bit of information (the program to start up) is stored after the *last* colon of each line. If nothing follows the last colon, then the *standard* shell /bin/sh is assumed by default. The three lines below show typical lines from /etc/passwd for three users of the system: sue, pat, and bob.

```
sue:fkrIboLrjdkK.:15:47::/usr/sue:
pat:MjvntQLddYop.:99:7::/usr/pat:/usr/lbin/ksh
bob:j9GTYQzHGwIG.:13:100::/usr/data:/usr/data/bin/data_entry
```

After login checks the password you typed in against the one stored in /etc/passwd, it then checks for the name of a program to execute. In most cases, this will be `/bin/sh`. In other cases, it may be a special custom-designed program. The main point here is that you can set up a login account to automatically run *any* program whatsoever whenever someone logs into it. The shell just happens to be the program most often selected.

So `login` will initiate execution of the standard shell on sue's terminal after validating her password (see Fig. 3-4).

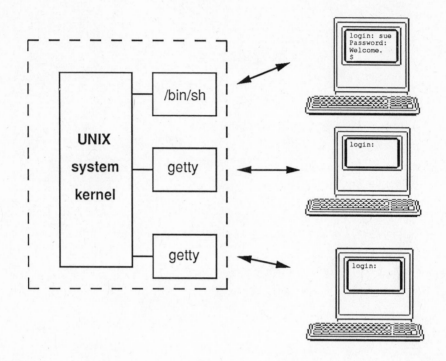

Fig. 3-4. login executes /bin/sh

According to the other entries from `/etc/passwd` shown previously, `pat` gets the program `ksh` stored in `/usr/lbin` (this is the *Korn* shell), and `bob` gets the program `data_entry` (see Fig. 3-5).

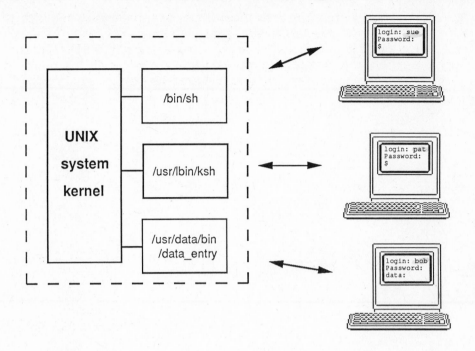

Fig. 3-5. Three users logged in

♦ Typing Commands to the Shell ♦

When the shell starts up, it displays a *command prompt*—typically a dollar sign $—at your terminal and then waits for you to type in a command (Fig. 3-6, Steps 1 & 2). Each time you type in a command and press the RETURN key (Step 3), the shell analyzes the line you typed and then proceeds to carry out your request (Step 4). If you ask it to execute a particular program, then the shell *searches* the disk until it finds the named program. Once found, the shell asks the kernel to initiate the program's execution and then the shell "goes to sleep" until the program has finished (Step 5). The kernel copies the specified program into memory and begins its execution. This copied program is called a *process*; in this way the distinction is made between a *program* that is kept in a file on the disk and a *process* that is in memory doing things.

  If the program writes output to standard output then it will appear at your terminal unless redirected or piped into another command. Similarly, if the program reads input from standard input, then it will wait for you to type in input unless redirected from a file or piped from another command (Step 6).

When the command has finished execution, control once again returns to the shell which awaits your next command (Steps 7 & 8).

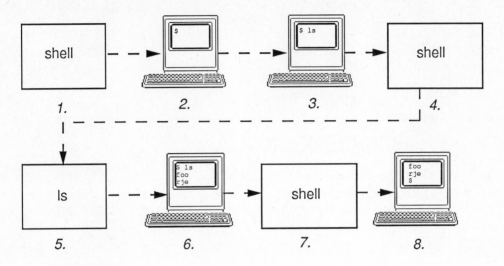

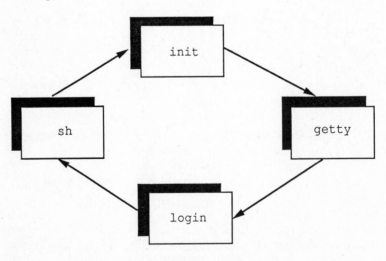

Fig. 3-6. Command cycle

Note that this cycle continues as long as you're logged in. When you log off the system, execution of the shell then terminates and the UNIX system starts up a new `getty` at the terminal that waits for someone else to log in. This cycle is illustrated in Fig. 3-7.

Fig. 3-7. Log-in cycle

It's important for you to recognize that the shell is just a program. It has *no* special privileges on the system, meaning that anyone with the capability and devotion can create their own shell program. This is in fact the reason why various flavors of the shell exist today, including the standard Bourne shell `sh`, developed by Stephen Bourne; the Korn shell `ksh` developed by David Korn; and the C shell `csh`, developed by Bill Joy. The chapters which follow describe the operation of the standard UNIX shell as of UNIX System V, Release 3. In later chapters you'll learn about the Korn shell and the C shell.

♦ The Shell's Responsibilities ♦

Now you know that the shell is the one that analyzes each line you type in and initiates execution of the selected program. But the shell also has other responsibilities as well. These are outlined in Fig. 3-8.

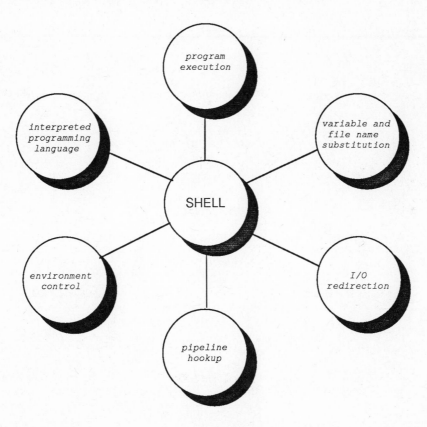

Fig. 3-8. The shell's responsibilities

Program Execution

The shell is responsible for the execution of all programs that you request from your terminal.

Each time you type in a line to the shell, the shell analyzes the line and then determines what to do. As far as the shell is concerned, each line follows the same basic format:

program-name arguments

The line that is typed to the shell is known more formally as the *command line*. The shell scans this command line and determines the name of the program to be executed and what arguments to pass to the program.

The shell uses special characters to determine where the program name starts and ends, and where each argument starts and ends. These characters are collectively called *whitespace* characters, and are the space character, the horizontal tab character, and the end-of-line character, known more formally as the *newline* character. Multiple occurrences of whitespace characters are simply ignored by the shell. When you type the command

```
mv rje/mazewars games
```

the shell scans the command line and takes everything from the start of the line to the first whitespace character as the name of the program to execute: mv. The set of characters up to the next whitespace character is the first argument to mv: rje/mazewars. The set of characters up to the next whitespace character (known as a *word* to the shell)—in this case the *newline*—is the second argument to mv: games. After analyzing the command line, the shell then proceeds to execute the mv command, giving it the two arguments rje/mazewars and games (see Fig. 3-9).

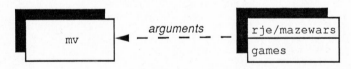

Fig. 3-9. Execution of mv with two arguments

As mentioned, multiple occurrences of whitespace characters are ignored by the shell. This means that when the shell processes this command line:

```
echo            when   do           we     eat?
```

it passes four arguments to the echo program: when, do, we, and eat? (see Fig. 3-10).

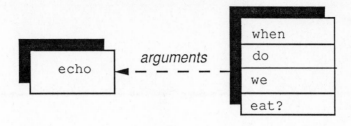

Fig. 3-10. Execution of echo with four arguments

Since echo takes it arguments and simply displays them at the terminal, separating each by a space character, the output from the following becomes easy to understand:

```
$ echo          when    do          we      eat?
when do we eat?
$
```

The fact of the matter is that the echo command *never sees those blank spaces;* they have been "gobbled up" by the shell. When we discuss quotes in Chapter 6, you'll see how you *can* include blank spaces in arguments to programs.

We mentioned earlier that the shell searches the disk until it finds the program you want to execute and then asks the UNIX kernel to initiate its execution. Well, this is true most of the time. However, there are some commands that the shell knows how to execute itself. These *built-in* commands include cd, pwd, and echo (the last two as of System V, Release 2). So before the shell goes searching the disk for a command, it first determines if it's a built-in command and if it is, it executes it directly.

Variable and File Name Substitution

Like any other programming language, the shell lets you assign values to *variables.* Whenever you specify one of these variables on the command line, preceded by a dollar sign, the shell substitutes the value that was assigned to the variable at that point. This topic is covered in complete detail in Chapter 5.

The shell also performs file name substitution on the command line. In fact, the shell scans the command line looking for file name substitution characters *, ?, or [...] *before* determining the name of the program to execute and its arguments. Suppose your current directory contains the files as shown:

```
$ ls
mrs.todd
prog1
shortcut
sweeney
$
```

Now let's use file name substitution for the echo command:

```
$ echo *                                    List all files
mrs.todd prog1 shortcut sweeney
$
```

How many arguments do you think were passed to the echo program, one or four? Well, since we said that the shell is the one that performs the file name substitution, the answer is four. When the shell analyzes the line

```
echo *
```

it recognizes the special character * and substitutes on the command line the names of all files in the current directory (it even alphabetizes them for you):

```
echo mrs.todd prog1 shortcut sweeney
```

Then the shell determines the arguments to be passed to the command. So echo never sees the asterisk. As far as it's concerned, four arguments were typed on the command line (see Fig. 3-11).

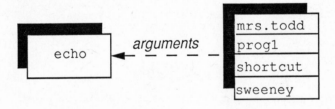

Fig. 3-11. Execution of echo

I/O Redirection

It is the shell's responsibility to take care of input and output redirection on the command line. It scans the command line for the occurrence of the special redirection characters <, >, or >> (also << as you'll learn about in a later chapter).

When you type the command

```
echo Remember to tape The Wonder Years > reminder
```

the shell recognizes the special output redirection character > and takes the next word on the command line as the name of the file that the output is to be redirected to. In this case the file is reminder. If reminder already exists and you have write access to it, then the previous contents are lost (if you don't have write access to it then the shell gives you an error message).

Before the shell starts execution of the desired program, it redirects the standard output of the program to the indicated file. As far as the program is concerned, it never knows its output is being redirected. It just goes about its merry way writing to standard output (which is normally your terminal, you'll recall), unaware that the shell has redirected it to a file.

Let's take another look at two nearly identical commands:

```
$ wc -l users
     5 users
$ wc -l < users
     5
$
```

In the first case, the shell analyzes the command line and determines the name of the program to execute is wc and it is to be passed two arguments: -l and users (see Fig. 3-12).

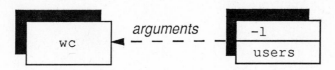

Fig. 3-12. Execution of wc -l users

When wc begins execution, it sees that it was passed two arguments. The first argument, -l, tells it to count the number of lines. The second argument specifies the name of the file whose lines are to be counted. So wc opens the file users, counts its lines, and then prints the count together with the file name at the terminal.

Operation of wc in the second case is slightly different. The shell spots the input redirection character < when it scans the command line. The word that follows on the command line is the name of the file input is to be redirected from. Having "gobbled up" the < users from the command line, the shell then starts execution of the wc program, redirecting its standard input from the file users and passing it the *single* argument -l (Fig. 3-13).

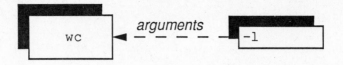

Fig. 3-13. Execution of wc -l < users

When wc begins execution this time, it sees that it was passed the single argument -l. Since no file name was specified, wc takes this as an indication that the number of lines appearing on standard input is to be counted. So wc counts the number of lines on standard input, unaware that it's actually counting the number of lines in the file users. The final tally is displayed at the terminal–without the name of a file since wc wasn't given one.

The difference in execution of the two commands is very important for you to understand. If you're still unclear on this point, please review the preceding section.

Pipeline Hookup

Just as the shell scans the command line looking for redirection characters, it also looks for the pipe character | (or ^ which is still recognized by the shell as an alternate pipe symbol for compatibility with earlier versions). For each such character that it finds, it connects the standard output from the command preceding the | to the standard input of the one following the |. It then initiates execution of both programs.

So when you type

```
who | wc -l
```

the shell finds the pipe symbol separating the commands who and wc. It connects the standard output of the former command to the standard input of the latter, and then initiates execution of both commands. When the who command executes, it makes a list of who's logged in and writes the results to standard output, unaware that this is not going to the terminal but to another command instead.

When the wc command executes, it recognizes that no file name was specified and counts the lines on standard input, unaware that standard input is not coming from the terminal but from the output of the who command.

Environment Control

The shell provides certain commands that let you customize your environment. Your environment includes your home directory, the characters that the shell displays to prompt you to type in a command, and a list of the directories to be searched whenever you request that a program be executed. You'll learn more about this in Chapter 11.

Interpreted Programming Language

The shell has its own built-in programming language. This language is interpreted, meaning that the shell analyzes each statement in the language one line at a time and then executes it. This differs from programming languages like C and FORTRAN, in which the programming statements are typically *compiled* into a machine-executable form before they are executed.

Programs developed in interpreted programming languages are typically easier to debug and modify than compiled ones. However, they usually take much longer to execute than their compiled equivalents.

The shell programming language provides features you'd find in most other programming languages; it has looping constructs, decision-making statements, and is procedure-oriented. However, the standard shell also lacks many features such as arrays, data typing, and built-in arithmetic operations. The Korn shell is much closer to a traditional structured programming language, providing some limited data types (including integers and arrays) and built-in integer arithmetic.

4

Tools of the Trade

This chapter provides detailed descriptions of some commonly used shell programming tools. Covered are `cut, paste, sed, tr, grep, uniq,` and `sort`. The more proficient you become at using these tools, the easier it'll be to write shell programs to solve your problems. In fact, that goes for all of the tools provided by the UNIX system.

◆ Regular Expressions ◆

Before getting into the tools, you should learn about something called *regular expressions*. Regular expressions are used by several different UNIX commands, including `ed, sed, awk, grep,` and, to a more limited extent, `vi`. They provide a convenient and consistent way of specifying *patterns* to be matched.

The shell recognizes a limited form of regular expressions when you use file name substitution. Recall that the asterisk `*` specifies zero or more characters to match, the question mark `?` specifies any single character, and the construct `[...]` specifies any character enclosed between the brackets.

The regular expressions recognized by the aforementioned programs are far more sophisticated than those recognized by the shell. Also be advised that the asterisk and the question mark are treated differently by these programs than by the shell.

Match Any Character: The period (.)

A period in a regular expression matches *any* single character, no matter what it is. So the regular expression

```
r.
```

specifies a pattern that will match an `r` followed by any single character.

The regular expression

```
.X.
```

will match an X that is surrounded by any two characters, not necessarily the same.

The ed command

```
/ ... /
```

will search forward in the file you are editing for the first line that contains any three characters surrounded by blanks:

```
$ ed intro
248
1,$p                            Print all the lines
The Unix operating system was pioneered by Ken
Thompson and Dennis Ritchie at Bell Laboratories
in the late 1960s.  One of the primary goals in
the design of the Unix system was to create an
environment that promoted efficient program
development.
/ ... /                         Look for three chars surrounded by blanks
The Unix operating system was pioneered by Ken
/                               Repeat last search
Thompson and Dennis Ritchie at Bell Laboratories
1,$s/p.o/XXX/g                  Change all p.os to XXX
1,$p                            Let's see what happened
The Unix operating system was XXXneered by Ken
ThomXXXn and Dennis Ritchie at Bell Laboratories
in the late 1960s.  One of the primary goals in
the design of the Unix system was to create an
environment that XXXmoted efficient XXXgram
development.
```

In the first search, ed started searching from the beginning of the file and found the characters " was " in the first line that matched the indicated pattern. Repeating the search (recall that the ed command / means to repeat the last search), resulted in the display of the second line of the file since " and " matched the pattern. The substitute command that followed specified that all occurrences of the character p, followed by any single character, followed by the character o were to be replaced by the characters XXX.

Matching the Beginning of the Line: ^

When the caret character ^ is used as the first character in a regular expression, it matches the beginning of the line. So the regular expression

```
^George
```

matches the characters `George` *only if they occur at the beginning of the line.*

```
$ ed intro
248
/^the/                          Find the line that starts with the
the design of the Unix system was to create an
1,$s/^/>>/                      Insert >> at the beginning of each line
1,$p
>>The Unix operating system was pioneered by Ken
>>Thompson and Dennis Ritchie at Bell Laboratories
>>in the late 1960s.  One of the primary goals in
>>the design of the Unix system was to create an
>>environment that promoted efficient program
>>development.
```

The last example shows how just the regular expression ^ can be used to match just the beginning of the line. Here it is used to insert the characters >> at the start of each line. A command such as

```
1,$s/^/     /
```

is commonly used to insert spaces at the start of each line (in this case five spaces would be inserted).

Matching the End of the Line: $

Just as the ^ is used to match the beginning of the line, so is the dollar sign $ used to match the end of the line. So the regular expression

```
contents$
```

will match the characters `contents` *only if they are the very last characters on the line.* What do you think would be matched by the regular expression

```
.$
```

Would this match a period character that ends a line? No. This matches any single character at the end of the line (including a period) recalling that the period matches any character. So how do you match a period? In general, if you want to match any of the characters that have a special meaning in forming regular expressions, you must precede the character by a backslash (\) to remove that special meaning. So the regular expression

```
\.$
```

matches any line that ends in a period, and the regular expression

```
^\.
```

matches any line that starts with one (good for searching for nroff commands in your text).

```
$ ed intro
248
/\.$/                               Search for a line that ends with a period
development.
1,$s/$/>>/                          Add >> to the end of each line
1,$p
The Unix operating system was pioneered by Ken>>
Thompson and Dennis Ritchie at Bell Laboratories>>
in the late 1960s.  One of the primary goals in>>
the design of the Unix system was to create an>>
environment that promoted efficient program>>
development.>>
1,$s/..$//                          Delete the last two characters from each line
1,$p
The Unix operating system was pioneered by Ken
Thompson and Dennis Ritchie at Bell Laboratories
in the late 1960s.  One of the primary goals in
the design of the Unix system was to create an
environment that promoted efficient program
development.
```

It's worth noting that the regular expression

```
^$
```

matches any line that contains *no* characters (such a line can be created in ed by simply hitting RETURN while in insert mode). This regular expression is to be distinguished from one such as

```
^ $
```

which matches any line that consists of a single space character.

Matching a Choice of Characters: The [...] Construct

Suppose you are editing a file and want to search for the first occurrence of the characters `the`. In `ed` this is easy: you simply type the command

```
/the/
```

This causes `ed` to search forward in its buffer until it finds a line containing the indicated string of characters. The first line that matches will be displayed by `ed`.

```
$ ed intro
248
/the/                                    Find line containing the
in the late 1960s.  One of the primary goals in
```

Notice that the first line of the file also contains the word `the`, except it starts a sentence and so begins with a capital T. You can tell `ed` to search for the first occurrence of the `the` *or* `The` by using a regular expression.

Just as in file name substitution, the characters `[` and `]` can be used in a regular expression to specify that one of the enclosed characters is to be matched. So, the regular expression

```
[tT]he
```

would match a lower or uppercase `t` followed immediately by the characters `he`:

```
$ ed intro
248
/[tT]he/                                 Look for the or The
The Unix operating system was pioneered by Ken
/                                        Continue the search
in the late 1960s.  One of the primary goals in
/                                        Once again
the design of the Unix system was to create an
1,$s/[aeiouAEIOU]//g                     Delete all vowels
1,$p
Th nx prtng systm ws pnrd by Kn
Thmpsn nd Dnns Rtch t Bll Lbrtrs
n th lt 1960s.  n f th prmry gls n
th dsgn f th nx systm ws t crt n
nvrnmnt tht prmtd ffcnt prgrm
dvlpmnt.
```

A range of characters can be specified inside the brackets. This can be done by separating the starting and ending characters of the range by a dash (–). So, to match any digit character 0 through 9, you could use the regular expression

```
[0123456789]
```

or, more succinctly, you could simply write

```
[0-9]
```

To match an uppercase letter, you write

```
[A-Z]
```

And to match an upper or lowercase letter, you write

```
[A-Za-z]
```

Here are some examples with ed:

```
$ ed intro
248
/[0-9]/                          Find a line containing a digit
in the late 1960s.  One of the primary goals in
/^[A-Z]/                         Find a line that starts with an uppercase letter
The Unix operating system was pioneered by Ken
/                                Again
Thompson and Dennis Ritchie at Bell Laboratories
1,$s/[A-Z]/*/g                   Change all uppercase letters to *s
1,$p
*he *nix operating system was pioneered by *en
*hompson and *ennis *itchie at *ell *aboratories
in the late 1960s.  *ne of the primary goals in
the design of the *nix system was to create an
environment that promoted efficient program
development.
```

As you'll learn shortly, the asterisk is a special character in regular expressions. However, you don't need to put a backslash before the asterisk in the replacement string of the substitute command. In general, regular expression characters like *, ., [...], $, and ^ are only meaningful in the search string and have no special meaning when they appear in the replacement string.

If a caret (^) appears as the first character after the left bracket, then the sense of the match is *inverted*[†]. For example, the regular expression

```
[^A-Z]
```

matches any character *except* an uppercase letter. Similarly,

```
[^A-Za-z]
```

matches any nonalphabetic character.

```
$ ed intro
248
1,$s/[^a-zA-Z]//g          Delete all nonalphabetic characters
1,$p
TheUnixoperatingsystemwaspioneeredbyKen
ThompsonandDennisRitchieatBellLaboratories
inthelates0neoftheprimarygoalsin
thedesignoftheUnixsystemwastocreatean
environmentthatpromotedefficientprogram
development
```

Matching Zero or More Characters: *

You know that the asterisk is used by the shell in file name substitution to match zero or more characters. In forming regular expressions, the asterisk is used to match zero or more occurrences of the *preceding* character in the regular expression (which may itself be another regular expression).

So, for example, the regular expression

```
X*
```

matches zero, one, two, three, ... capital X's. The expression

```
XX*
```

matches one or more capital X's, since the expression specifies a single X followed by zero or more X's. A similar type of pattern is frequently used to match the occurrence of one or more blank spaces.

---

† Recall that the shell uses the ! for this purpose.

```
$ ed lotsaspaces
85
1,$p
This        is    an example  of a
file    that contains      a   lot
of   blank spaces
1,$s/  */ /g                          Change multiple blanks to single blanks
1,$p
This is an example of a
file that contains a lot
of blank spaces
```

The ed command

```
1,$s/   */ /g
```

told ed to substitute all occurrences of a space followed by zero or more spaces with a single space.

The regular expression

```
.*
```

is often used to specify zero or more occurrences of *any* characters. Bear in mind that a regular expression matches the *longest* string of characters that match the pattern. Therefore, used by itself, this regular expression will always match the *entire* line of text.

As another example of the combination of . and *, the regular expression

```
e.*e
```

matches all the characters from the first e on a line to the last one.

```
$ ed intro
248
1,$s/e.*e/+++/
1,$p
Th+++n
Thompson and D+++s
in th+++ primary goals in
th+++ an
+++nt program
d+++nt.
```

Here's an interesting regular expression. What do you think it matches?

```
[A-Za-z][A-Za-z]*
```

That's right, this matches any alphabetic character followed by zero or more alphabetic characters. This is pretty close to a regular expression that will match words.

```
$ ed intro
248
1,$s/[A-Za-z][A-Za-z]*/X/g
1,$p
X X X X X X X
X X X X X X X
X X X 1960X.  X X X X X X
X X X X X X X X X X
X X X X X
X.
```

The only thing it didn't match in this example was 1960. We can change our regular expression to also consider a sequence of digits as a word:

```
$ ed intro
248
1,$s/[A-Za-z0-9][A-Za-z0-9]*/X/g
1,$p
X X X X X X X
X X X X X X X
X X X X.  X X X X X X
X X X X X X X X X X
X X X X X
X.
```

We could expand on this somewhat to consider hyphenated words and contracted words (e.g., don't), but we'll leave that as an exercise for you. As a point of note, if you want to match a dash character inside a bracketed choice of characters, you must put the dash immediately after the left bracket (and after the inversion character ^ if present) or immediately before the right bracket]. So the expression

```
[-0-9]
```

matches a single dash or digit character.

If you want to match a right bracket character, then it must appear after the opening left bracket (and after the ^ if present). So

```
[]a-z]
```

matches a right bracket or a lowercase letter.

Matching a Precise Number of Characters: \{ . . . \}

You saw in the examples above how you could use the asterisk to specify that *one* or more occurrences of the preceding regular expression are to be matched. For instance, the regular expression

    XX*

means match at least one consecutive X. Similarly,

    XXX*

means match at least *two* consecutive X's. There is a more general way to specify a precise number of characters to be matched: by using the construct

    \{*min*,*max*\}

where *min* specifies the minimum number of occurrences of the preceding regular expression to be matched, and *max* specifies the maximum. For example, the regular expression

    X\{1,10\}

matches from one to 10 consecutive X's. As stated before, whenever there is a choice, the largest pattern is matched; so if the input text contains eight consecutive X's at the beginning of the line, then that is how many will be matched by the above regular expression.

As another example, the regular expression

    [A-Za-z]\{4,7\}

matches a sequence of alphabetic letters from four to seven characters long.

```
$ ed intro
248
1,$s/[A-Za-z]\{4,7\}/X/g
1,$p
The X Xng X was Xed by Ken
Xn and X X at X XX
in the X 1960s.  One of the X X in
the X of the X X was to X an
XX X Xd Xnt X
XX.
```

There are a few special cases of this special construct worth noting. If only one number is enclosed between the braces, as in

```
\{10\}
```

then that number specifies that the preceding regular expression must be matched *exactly* that many times. So

```
[a-zA-Z]\{7\}
```

matches exactly seven alphabetic characters; and

```
.\{10\}
```

matches exactly 10 characters (no matter what they are):

```
$ ed intro
248
1,$s/^.\{10\}//                    Delete the first 10 chars from each line
1,$p
perating system was pioneered by Ken
nd Dennis Ritchie at Bell Laboratories
e 1960s.  One of the primary goals in
 of the Unix system was to create an
t that promoted efficient program
t.
1,$s/.\{5\}$//                     Delete the last 5 chars from each line
1,$p
perating system was pioneered b
nd Dennis Ritchie at Bell Laborat
e 1960s.  One of the primary goa
 of the Unix system was to crea
t that promoted efficient pr
t.
```

Note that the last line of the file didn't have five characters when the last substitute command was executed; therefore the match failed on that line and thus was left alone (recall that we specified that *exactly* five characters were to be deleted).

If a single number is enclosed in the braces, followed immediately by a comma, then *at least* that many occurrences of the previous regular expression must be matched. So

```
+\{5,\}
```

matches at least five consecutive plus signs. Once again, if more than five exist, then the largest number is matched.

```
$ ed intro
248
1,$s/[a-zA-Z]\{6,\}/X/g          Change words at least 6 letters long to X
1,$p
The Unix X X was X by Ken
X and X X at Bell X
in the late 1960s.  One of the X goals in
the X of the Unix X was to X an
X that X X X
X.
```

Saving Matched Characters: \ (. . . \)

It is possible to capture the characters that are matched within a regular expression by enclosing the characters inside backslashed parentheses. These captured characters are stored in "registers" numbered 1 through 9.

As an example, the regular expression

```
^\(.\)
```

will match the first character on the line, whatever it is, and store it into register 1. To retrieve the characters stored in a particular register, the construct \n is used, where n is from 1-9.

So the regular expression

```
^\(.\)\1
```

will match the first character on the line, and store it in register 1. Then the expression will match whatever is stored in register 1, as specified by the \1. The net effect of this regular expression is to match the first two characters on a line *if they are both the same character.* Go over this example if it doesn't seem clear.

The regular expression

```
^\(.\).*\1$
```

matches all lines in which the first character on the line (^.) is the same as the last character on the line (\1$). The .* matches all the characters in-between.

Successive occurrences of the \(...\) construct get assigned to successive registers. So when the following regular expression is used to match some text

```
^\(...\)\(...\)
```

the first three characters on the line will be stored into register 1, and the next three characters into register 2.

When using the substitute command in ed, a register can also be referenced as part of the replacement string.

```
$ ed phonebook
114
1,$p
Alice Chebba      596-2015
Barbara Swingle 598-9257
Liz Stachiw       775-2298
Susan Goldberg  338-7776
Tony Iannino     386-1295
1,$s/\(.*\)    \(.*\)/\2 \1/        Switch the two fields
1,$p
596-2015 Alice Chebba
598-9257 Barbara Swingle
775-2298 Liz Stachiw
338-7776 Susan Goldberg
386-1295 Tony Iannino
```

The names and the phone numbers are separated from each other in the phone-book file by a single tab character. The regular expression

```
\(.*\)        \(.*\)
```

says to match all of the characters up to the first tab (that's the character between the) and the \) and assign them to register 1, and to match all of the characters that follow the tab character and assign them to register 2. The replacement string

```
\2 \1
```

specifies the contents of register 2, followed by a space, followed by the contents of register 1.

So when ed applies the substitute command to the first line of the file:

```
Alice Chebba      596-2015
```

it matches everything up to the tab (Alice Chebba) and stores it into register 1, and everything after the tab (596-2015) and stores it into register 2. Then it substitutes the characters that were matched (the entire line) with the contents of register 2 (596-2015) followed by a space, followed by the contents of register 1 (Alice Chebba):

```
596-2015 Alice Chebba
```

As you can see, regular expressions are very powerful tools that enable you to match complex patterns. Table 4-1 summarizes the special characters recognized in regular expressions.

TABLE 4-1. Regular expression characters

Notation	Meaning	Example	Matches
.	*any* character	a..	a followed by any two characters
^	beginning of line	^wood	wood only if it appears at the beginning of the line
$	end of line	x$	x only if it is the last character on the line
		^INSERT$	a line containing just the characters INSERT
		^$	a line that contains *no* characters
*	zero or more occurrences of previous regular expression	x*	zero or more consecutive x's
		xx*	one or more consecutive x's
		.*	zero or more characters
		w.*s	w followed by zero or more characters followed by an s
[*chars*]	any character in *chars*	[tT]	lower or uppercase t
		[a-z]	lowercase letter
		[a-zA-Z]	lower or uppercase letter
[^*chars*]	any character *not* in *chars*	[^0-9]	any nonnumeric character
		[^a-zA-Z]	any nonalphabetic character
\{*min*,*max*\}	at least *min* and at most *max* occurrences of previous regular expressions	x\{1,5\}	at least 1 and at most 5 x's
		[0-9]\{3,9\}	anywhere from 3 to 9 successive digits.
		[0-9]\{3\}	exactly 3 digits
		[0-9]\{3,\}	at least 3 digits
\(...\)	store characters matched between parentheses in next register (1-9)	^\(.\)	first character on line and stores it in register 1
		^\(.\)\1	first and second characters on the line if they're the same

♦ cut ♦

This section will teach you about a very useful command known as `cut`. This command comes in handy when you need to extract (i.e., "cut out") various fields of data from a data file or the output of a command. The general format of the `cut` command is:

```
cut -cchars file
```

where *chars* specifies what characters you want to extract from *each* line of *file*. This can consist of a single number, as in `-c5` to extract character 5; a comma-separated list of numbers, as in `-c1,13,50` to extract characters 1, 13, and 50; or a dash-separated range of numbers, as in `-c20-50` to extract characters 20 through 50, inclusive. To extract characters to the end of the line, you can omit the second number of the range; so

```
cut -c5- data
```

will extract characters 5 through the end of the line from each line of `data` and write the results to standard output.

If *file* is not specified, `cut` reads its input from standard input, meaning that you can use `cut` as a filter in a pipeline.

Let's take another look at the output from the `who` command:

```
$ who
root       console Feb 24 08:54
steve      tty02   Feb 24 12:55
george     tty08   Feb 24 09:15
dawn       tty10   Feb 24 15:55
$
```

As shown, there are currently four people logged in. Suppose you just wanted to know the names of the logged-in users, and didn't care about what terminals they were on or when they logged in. You can use the `cut` command to cut out just the user names from the `who` command's output:

```
$ who | cut -c1-8          Extract the first 8 characters
root
steve
george
dawn
$
```

The `-c1-8` option to cut specifies that characters 1 through 8 are to be extracted from each line of input and written to standard output.

The following shows how you can tack a `sort` to the end of the above pipeline to get a sorted list of the logged-in users:

```
$ who | cut -c1-8 | sort
dawn
george
root
steve
$
```

If you wanted to see what terminals were currently being used, you could cut out just the tty numbers field from the who command's output:

```
$ who | cut -c10-16
console
tty02
tty08
tty10
$
```

How did you know that who displays the terminal identification in character positions 10 through 16? Simple! You executed the who command at your terminal and *counted* out the appropriate character positions.[†]
You can use cut to extract as many different characters from a line as you like. Here cut is used to display just the user name and login time of all logged-in users:

```
$ who | cut -c1-8,18-
root      Feb 24 08:54
steve     Feb 24 12:55
george    Feb 24 09:15
dawn      Feb 24 15:55
$
```

The option -c1-8,18- says "extract characters 1 through 8 (the user name) and also characters 18 through the end of the line (the login time)."[‡]

The -d and -f Options

The cut command as described above is very useful when you need to extract data from a file or command provided that file or command has a fixed format.

[†] On some versions of the UNIX system, this field starts in character position 12 and not 10.

[‡] Again, on some systems the login time field starts in column 25.

For example, you could use `cut` on the `who` command because you know that the user names are *always* displayed in character positions 1-8, the terminal in 10-16, and the login time in 18-29. Unfortunately, not all of your data will be so well organized! For instance, take a look at what the file `/etc/passwd` looks like:

```
$ cat /etc/passwd
root:TzDeRMProEU3M:0:0:The Super User:/:/usr/lbin/ksh
cron:NOLOGIN:1:1:Cron Daemon for periodic tasks:/:
bin:NOLOGIN:3:3:The owner of system files:/:
uucp:nc8k8XiSiLiZM:5:5::/usr/spool/uucp:/usr/lib/uucp/uucico
asg:NOLOGIN:6:6:The Owner of Assignable Devices:/:
steve:j9GTYQzHGwIG.:203:100::/usr/steve:/usr/lbin/ksh
other::4:4:Needed by secure program:/:
$
```

`/etc/passwd` is the master file that contains the user names and passwords (in an encrypted form[†]) of all users on your computer system. It also contains other information such as your user id number, your home directory, and the name of the program to start up when you log in. Anyway, getting back to the `cut` command, you can see that the data in this file does not align itself the same way `who`'s output does. So getting a list of all the possible users of your system can not be done using the `-c` option to `cut`.

One nice thing about the format of `/etc/passwd`, however, is that fields are delimited by a colon character. So while each field may not be the same length from one line to the next, you know that you can "count colons" to get the same field from each line.

The `-d` and `-f` options are used with `cut` when you have data that is delimited by a particular character. The format of the `cut` command in this case becomes

> `cut` `-d`*dchar* `-f`*fields*   *file*

where *dchar* is the character that delimits each field of the data, and *fields* specifies the fields to be extracted from *file*. Field numbers start at 1, and the same type of formats can be used to specify field numbers as was used to specify character positions before (e.g., `-f1,2,8`, `-f1-3`, `-f4-`).

So to extract the names of all users of your system from `/etc/passwd`, you could type the following:

[†] As of UNIX System V, Release 3.2, the encrypted passwords are kept in a special file called `/etc/shadow`. The password field in `/etc/passwd` still remains and contains an 'x'.

```
$ cut -d: -f1 /etc/passwd          Extract field 1
root
cron
bin
uucp
asg
steve
other
$
```

Given that the home directory of each user is in field 6, you can associate each user of the system with his or her home directory as shown:

```
$ cut -d: -f1,6 /etc/passwd          Extract fields 1 and 6
root:/
cron:/
bin:/
uucp:/usr/spool/uucp
asg:/
steve:/usr/steve
other:/
$
```

If the cut command is used to extract fields from a file and the -d option is not supplied, then cut uses the tab character as the default field delimiter.

The following depicts a common pitfall when using the cut command. Suppose you heve a file called phonebook that has the following contents:

```
$ cat phonebook
Alice Chebba      596-2015
Barbara Swingle 598-9257
Jeff Goldberg     295-3378
Liz Stachiw       775-2298
Susan Goldberg 338-7776
Tony Iannino      386-1295
$
```

If you just want to get the names of the people in your phone book, your first impulse would be to use cut as shown:

```
$ cut -c1-15 phonebook
Alice Chebba      59
Barbara Swingle
Jeff Goldberg     2
```

```
    Liz Stachiw      775
    Susan Goldberg
    Tony Iannino     38
    $
```

Not quite what you want! This happened because the name is separated from the phone number by a tab character and not blank spaces in the `phonebook` file. And as far as `cut` is concerned, tabs count as a single character when using the `-c` option. So `cut` extracts the first 15 characters from each line in the previous example, giving the results as shown.

Given that the fields are separated by tabs, you should use the `-f` option to cut instead:

```
$ cut -f1 phonebook
Alice Chebba
Barbara Swingle
Jeff Goldberg
Liz Stachiw
Susan Goldberg
Tony Iannino
$
```

Much better! Recall that you didn't have to specify the delimiter character with the `-d` option since `cut` assumes a tab character is the delimiter by default.

But how do you know in advance whether fields are delimited by blanks or tabs? Well, one way to find out is by trial and error as shown above. Another way is to type the command

```
sed -n l file
```

at your terminal. If the fields are separated by a tab character, then a greater-than sign (>) will be displayed instead of the tab:[†]

```
$ sed -n l phonebook
Alice Chebba>596-2015
Barbara Swingle>598-9257
Jeff Goldberg>295-3378
Liz Stachiw>775-2298
Susan Goldberg>338-7776
Tony Iannino>386-1295
$
```

---

† Actually, `sed` displays a dash (–), followed by a backspace character, followed by the greater-than character (>). If the output is directed to a printer that supports backspacing, then it will appear as ≯ on the printout.

The output verifies that each name is separated from each phone number by a tab character.   sed is covered in more detail shortly.

◆ **paste** ◆

The paste command is sort of the inverse of cut: instead of breaking lines apart, it puts them together. The general format of the paste command is:

paste *files*

where corresponding lines from each of the specified *files* are "pasted" together to form single lines which are then written to standard output. The dash character – can be used in *files* to specify that input is from standard input.
Suppose you have a set of names in a file called names:

```
$ cat names
Tubs
Emanuel
Lucy
Ralph
Fred
$
```

Suppose you also have a file called numbers that contains corresponding phone numbers for each name in names:

```
$ cat numbers
(307) 542-5356
(212) 954-3456
(212) MH6-9959
(212) BE0-7741
(212) HY3-0040
$
```

You can use paste to print the names and numbers side-by-side as shown:

```
$ paste names numbers          Paste them together
Tubs    (307) 542-5356
Emanuel (212) 954-3456
Lucy    (212) MH6-9959
Ralph   (212) BE0-7741
Fred    (212) HY3-0040
$
```

Each line from `names` is displayed with the corresponding line from `numbers`, separated by a tab.

The next example illustrates what happens when more than two files are specified.

```
$ cat addresses
55-23 Vine Street, Miami
39 University Place, New York
17 E. 25th Street, New York
38 Chauncey St., Bensonhurst
17 E. 25th Street, New York
$ paste names addresses numbers
Tubs     55-23 Vine Street, Miami          (307) 542-5356
Emanuel 39 University Place, New York      (212) 954-3456
Lucy     17 E. 25th Street, New York       (212) MH6-9959
Ralph    38 Chauncey St., Bensonhurst      (212) BE0-7741
Fred     17 E. 25th Street, New York       (212) HY3-0040
$
```

The –d Option

If you don't want the fields separated by tab characters, you can specify the –d option with the format

  –d*chars*

where *chars* is one or more characters that will be used to separate the lines that are pasted together. That is, the first character listed in *chars* will be used to separate lines from the first file that are pasted with lines from the second file; the second character listed in *chars* will be used to separate lines from the second file from lines from the third, and so on.

If there are more files than there are characters listed in *chars*, then `paste` "wraps around" the list of characters and starts again at the beginning.

In the simplest form of the –d option, specifying just a single delimiter character will cause that character to be used to separate *all* pasted fields.

```
$ paste -d'+' names addresses numbers
Tubs+55-23 Vine Street, Miami+(307) 542-5356
Emanuel+39 University Place, New York+(212) 954-3456
Lucy+17 E. 25th Street, New York+(212) MH6-9959
Ralph+38 Chauncey St., Bensonhurst+(212) BE0-7741
Fred+17 E. 25th Street, New York+(212) HY3-0040
```

It's always safest to enclose the delimiter characters in single quotes. The reason why will be explained shortly.

The −s Option

The −s option tells paste to paste together lines from the same file, not from alternate files. If just one file is specified, then the effect is to merge all of the lines from the file together, separated by tabs, or by the delimiter characters specified with the −d option.

```
$ paste -s names                Paste all lines from names
Tubs    Emanuel Lucy    Ralph   Fred
$ ls | paste -d' ' -s -          Paste ls's output, use space as delimiter
addresses intro lotsaspaces names numbers phonebook
$
```

In the last example, the output from ls is piped to paste, which merges the lines (−s option) from standard input (−), separating each field with a space (−d' ' option). Of course, you'll recall from Chapter 2 that the command

```
echo *
```

would have worked just as well (and is certainly more straightforward).

◆ sed ◆

sed is a program used for editing data. It stands for *stream editor*. Unlike ed, sed cannot be used interactively. However, its commands are very similar.
    The general form of the sed command is:

sed *command file*

where *command* is an ed-style command that is applied to *each* line of the specified *file*. If no file is specified, then standard input is assumed. As sed applies the indicated command to each line of the input, it writes the results to standard output.
    Recall the file intro from previous examples:

```
$ cat intro
The Unix operating system was pioneered by Ken
Thompson and Dennis Ritchie at Bell Laboratories
in the late 1960s.  One of the primary goals in
the design of the Unix system was to create an
environment that promoted efficient program
development.
$
```

Suppose you want to change all occurrences of "Unix" in the text to "UNIX." This can be easily done in sed as follows:

```
$ sed 's/Unix/UNIX/' intro          Substitute Unix with UNIX
The UNIX operating system was pioneered by Ken
Thompson and Dennis Ritchie at Bell Laboratories
in the late 1960s.  One of the primary goals in
the design of the UNIX system was to create an
environment that promoted efficient program
development.
$
```

For now, get into the habit of enclosing your sed command in a pair of single quotes. Later, you'll know when the quotes are necessary and when to use double quotes instead.

The sed command s/Unix/UNIX/ is applied to every line of intro. Whether or not the line gets changed by the command, it gets written to standard output all the same. Note that sed makes no changes to the original input file. In order to make the changes permanent, you must redirect the output from sed into a temporary file and then move the file back to the old one:

```
$ sed 's/Unix/UNIX/' intro > temp    Make the changes
$ mv temp intro                      And now make them permanent
$
```

You should always make sure that the correct changes were made to the file before you overwrite the original; a cat of temp could have been included between the two commands shown above to ensure that the sed succeeded as planned.

If your text included more than one occurrence of "Unix" on a line, then the above sed would have changed just the first occurrence on each line to "UNIX". By appending the *global* option g to the end of the s command, you can ensure that multiple occurrences of the string on a line will be changed. In this case, the sed command would read:

```
$ sed 's/Unix/UNIX/g' intro > temp
```

Suppose you wanted to extract just the user names from the output of who. Well, you already know how to do that with the cut command:

```
$ who | cut -c1-8
root
ruth
steve
pat
$
```

Alternatively, you can use sed to delete all of the characters from the first blank space (that marks the end of the user name) through the end of the line by using a regular expression in the edit command:

```
$ who | sed 's/ .*$//'
root
ruth
steve
pat
$
```

The sed command says to substitute a blank space followed by any characters up to the end of the line (.*$) with *nothing* (//); that is, delete the characters from the first blank to the end of the line from each line of the input.

The –n Option

We pointed out that sed always writes each line of input to standard output, whether or not it gets changed. Sometimes, however, you'll want to use sed just to extract some lines from a file. For such purposes, use the –n option. This option tells sed that you don't want it to print any lines unless explicitly told to do so. This is done with the p command. By specifying a line number or range of line numbers you can use sed to selectively print lines of text. So, for example, to print just the first 2 lines from a file, the following could be used:

```
$ sed -n '1,2p' intro              Just print the first 2 lines
The UNIX operating system was pioneered by Ken
Thompson and Dennis Ritchie at Bell Laboratories
$
```

If, instead of line numbers, you precede the p command with a string of characters enclosed in slashes, then sed will print just those lines from standard input that contain those characters. The following example shows how sed can be used to display just the lines that contain a particular string:

```
$ sed -n '/UNIX/p' intro            Just print lines containing UNIX
The UNIX operating system was pioneered by Ken
the design of the UNIX system was to create an
$
```

Deleting Lines

To delete entire lines of text, use the d command. By specifying a line number or range of numbers, you can delete specific lines from the input. In the following example, sed is used to delete the first two lines of text from intro.

```
$ sed '1,2d' intro              Delete lines 1 and 2
in the late 1960s.  One of the primary goals in
the design of the UNIX system was to create an
environment that promoted efficient program
development.
$
```

Remembering that by default sed writes all lines of the input to standard output, the remaining lines in text—that is, lines three through the end—simply get written to standard output.

By preceding the d command with a string of text, you can used sed to delete all lines that contain that text. In the following example, sed is used to delete all lines of text containing the word UNIX.

```
$ sed '/UNIX/d' intro           Delete all lines containing UNIX
Thompson and Dennis Ritchie at Bell Laboratories
in the late 1960s.  One of the primary goals in
environment that promoted efficient program
development.
$
```

The power and flexibility of sed goes far beyond what we've shown here. sed has facilities that enable you to loop, build text in a buffer, and combine many commands into a single editing script. Table 4-2 shows some more examples of sed commands.

TABLE 4-2. sed examples

sed *command*	Description
sed '5d'	Delete line 5
sed '/[Tt]est/d'	Delete all lines containing Test or test
sed -n '20,25p' text	Print only lines 20 through 25 from text
sed '1,10s/unix/UNIX/g' intro	Change unix to UNIX wherever it appears in the first 10 lines of intro
sed '/jan/s/-1/-5/'	Change the first -1 to -5 on all lines containing jan
sed 's/...//' data	Delete the first three characters from each line of data
sed 's/...$//' data	Delete the last 3 characters from each line of data
sed -n 'l' text	Print all lines from text, showing nonprinting characters as *nn* (where *nn* is the octal value of the character), and tab characters as >

♦ tr ♦

The tr filter is used to translate characters from standard input. The general form of the command is:

tr *from-chars to-chars*

where *from-chars* and *to-chars* are one or more single characters. Any character in *from-chars* encountered on the input will be translated into the corresponding character in *to-chars*. The result of the translation is written to standard output.

In its simplest form tr can be used to translate one character into another. Recall the file intro from earlier in this chapter:

```
$ cat intro
The UNIX operating system was pioneered by Ken
Thompson and Dennis Ritchie at Bell Laboratories
in the late 1960s.  One of the primary goals in
the design of the UNIX system was to create an
environment that promoted efficient program
development.
$
```

The following shows how `tr` can be used to translate all letter 'e's to 'x's:

```
$ tr e x < intro
Thx UNIX opxrating systxm was pionxxrxd by Kxn
Thompson and Dxnnis Ritchix at Bxll Laboratorixs
in thx latx 1960s.  Onx of thx primary goals in
thx dxsign of thx UNIX systxm was to crxatx an
xnvironmxnt that promotxd xfficixnt program
dxvxlopmxnt.
$
```

The input to `tr` must be redirected from the file `intro` since `tr` always expects its input to come from standard input. The results of the translation are written to standard output, leaving the original file untouched.

Showing a more practical example, recall the pipeline that you used to extract the user names and home directories of everyone on the system:

```
$ cut -d: -f1,6 /etc/passwd
root:/
cron:/
bin:/
uucp:/usr/spool/uucp
asg:/
steve:/usr/steve
other:/
$
```

You can translate the colons into tab characters to produce a more readable output simply by tacking an appropriate `tr` command to the end of the pipeline:

```
$ cut -d: -f1,6 /etc/passwd | tr : '	'
root    /
cron    /
bin     /
```

```
uucp      /usr/spool/uucp
asg       /
steve     /usr/steve
other     /
$
```

Enclosed between the single quotes is a tab character (even though you can't see it—just take our word for it). It must be enclosed in quotes to keep it from the shell and give `tr` a chance to see it.

The octal representation of a character can be given to `tr` in the format

\nnn

where *nnn* is the octal value of the character. For example, the octal value of the tab character is 11. If you are going to use this format, be sure to enclose the character in quotes. The `tr` command

```
tr : '\11'
```

will translate all colons to tabs, just as in the last example. Table 4-3 lists characters that you'll often want to specify in octal format.

TABLE 4-3. Octal values of some ASCII characters

Character	Octal value
Bell	7
Backspace	10
Tab	11
Newline	12
Linefeed	12
Formfeed	14
Carriage return	15
Escape	33

In the following example, `tr` takes the output from `date` and translates all spaces into newline characters. The net result is that each field of output from `date` appears on a different line.

```
$ date | tr ' ' '\12'            Translate spaces to newlines
Sun
Mar
10
```

```
19:13:46
EST
1985
$
```

tr can also take ranges of characters to translate. For example, the following shows how to translate all lowercase letters in intro to their uppercase equivalents:

```
$ tr '[a-z]' '[A-Z]' < intro
THE UNIX OPERATING SYSTEM WAS PIONEERED BY KEN
THOMPSON AND DENNIS RITCHIE AT BELL LABORATORIES
IN THE LATE 1960S.  ONE OF THE PRIMARY GOALS IN
THE DESIGN OF THE UNIX SYSTEM WAS TO CREATE AN
ENVIRONMENT THAT PROMOTED EFFICIENT PROGRAM
DEVELOPMENT.
$
```

The character ranges [a-z] and [A-Z] are enclosed in quotes to keep the shell from replacing the first range with all the files in your directory that are named a through z, and the second range with all the files in your directory that are named A through Z. (What do you think happens if no such files exist?)

By reversing the two arguments to tr, you can use it to translate all uppercase letters to lowercase:

```
$ tr '[A-Z]' '[a-z]' < intro
the unix operating system was pioneered by ken
thompson and dennis ritchie at bell laboratories
in the late 1960s.  one of the primary goals in
the design of the unix system was to create an
environment that promoted efficient program
development.
$
```

The -s Option

You can use the -s option to tr to "squeeze" out multiple occurrences of characters in *to-chars*. In other words, if more than one consecutive occurrence of a character specified in *to-chars* occurs after the translation is made, the characters will be replaced by a single character.

As an example, the following command translates all colons into tab characters, replacing multiple tabs with single tabs:

```
tr -s ':' '\11'
```

nsecutive colons on the input will be replaced by a *sin-
put.
ı file called `lotsaspaces` that has the contents as

```
                      ɘs
        an example    of a
        tains         a    lot
        ɘs.
```

ze out the multiple spaces by using the `-s` option and
ɘ character as the first and second argument.

```
$ tr -s ' ' ' ' < lotsaspaces
This is an example of a
file that contains a lot
of blank spaces.
$
```

The options to `tr` in effect say "translate space characters to space characters,
replacing multiple spaces in the output by a single space."

The -d Option

`tr` can also be used to delete single characters from a stream of input. The general format of `tr` in this case is

$$tr\ -d\quad \textit{from-chars}$$

where any single character listed in *from-chars* will be deleted from standard input. In the following example, `tr` is used to delete all blank spaces from the file `intro`:

```
$ tr -d ' ' < intro
TheUNIXoperatingsystemwaspioneeredbyKen
ThompsonandDennisRitchieatBellLaboratories
inthelate1960s.Oneoftheprimarygoalsin
thedesignoftheUNIXsystemwastocreatean
environmentthatpromotedefficientprogram
development.
$
```

Of course, you probably realize that you could have also used `sed` to achieve the same results:

```
$ sed 's/ //g' intro
TheUNIXoperatingsystemwaspioneeredbyKen
ThompsonandDennisRitchieatBellLaboratories
inthelate1960s.Oneoftheprimarygoalsin
thedesignoftheUNIXsystemwastocreatean
environmentthatpromotedefficientprogram
development.
$
```

This is not atypical for the UNIX system; there's almost always more than one approach to solving a particular problem. In the case we just saw, either approach is satisfactory (i.e., tr or sed); however, tr is probably a better choice in this case since it is a much smaller program and likely to execute a bit faster.

Table 4-4 summarizes how to use tr for translating and deleting characters. Bear in mind that tr works only on *single* characters. So if you need to translate anything longer than a single character (say all occurrences of Unix to UNIX, then you have to use a different program like sed instead.

TABLE 4-4. tr examples

tr *command*	*Description*
tr 'X' 'x'	Translate all capital X's to small x's.
tr '()' '{}'	Translate all open parens to open braces, all closed parens to closed braces
tr '[a-z]' '[A-Z]'	Translate all lowercase letters to uppercase
tr '[A-Z]' '[N-Z][A-M]'	Translate uppercase letters A-M to N-Z, and N-Z to A-M, respectively
tr ' ' ' '	Translate all tabs (character in first pair of quotes) to spaces
tr -s ' ' ' '	Translate multiple spaces to single spaces
tr -d '\14'	Delete all formfeed (octal 14) characters
tr -d '[0-9]'	Delete all digits

◆ grep ◆

grep allows you to search one or more files for particular character patterns. The general format of this command is:

grep *pattern files*

Every line of each file that contains *pattern* is displayed at the terminal. If more than one file is specified to grep, then each line is also immediately preceded by the name of the file, thus enabling you to identify the particular file that the pattern was found in.

Let's say you want to find every occurrence of the word shell in the file ed.cmd:

```
$ grep shell ed.cmd
files, and is independent of the shell.
to the shell, just type in a q.
$
```

This output indicates that two lines in the file ed.cmd contain the word shell.

If the pattern does not exist in the specified file(s), then the grep command simply displays nothing:

```
$ grep cracker ed.cmd
$
```

You saw in the section on sed how you could print all lines containing the string UNIX from the file intro with the command

```
sed -n '/UNIX/p' intro
```

But you could also use the following grep command to achieve the same result:

```
grep UNIX intro
```

Recall the phonebook file from before:

```
$ cat phone_book
Alice Chebba      596-2015
Barbara Swingle 598-9257
Jeff Goldberg   295-3378
Liz Stachiw     775-2298
Susan Goldberg  338-7776
Tony Iannino    386-1295
$
```

When you need to look up a particular phone number, the `grep` command comes in handy:

```
$ grep Susan phone_book
Susan Goldberg  338-7776
$
```

The `grep` command is useful when you have a lot of files and you want to find out which ones contain certain words or phrases. The following example shows how the `grep` command can be used to search for the word `shell` in *all* files in the current directory:

```
$ grep shell *
cmdfiles:shell that enables sophisticated
ed.cmd:files, and is independent of the shell.
ed.cmd:to the shell, just type in a q.
grep.cmd:occurrence of the word shell:
grep.cmd:$ grep shell *
grep.cmd:every use of the word shell.
$
```

As noted, when more than one file is specified to `grep`, each output line is preceded by the name of the file containing that line.

It's generally a good idea to enclose your `grep` pattern inside a pair of *single* quotes to "protect" it from the shell. For instance, if you want to find all the lines containing asterisks inside the file `stars`, then typing

```
grep * stars
```

will not work as expected because the shell will see the asterisk and will automatically substitute the names of all the files in your current directory!

```
$ ls
circles
polka.dots
squares
stars
stripes
$ grep * stars
$
```

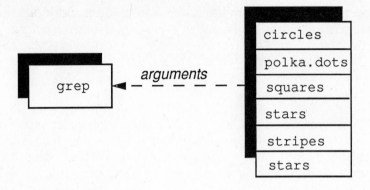

Fig. 4-1. grep * stars

In this case, the shell took the asterisk and substituted the list of files in your current directory. Then it started execution of grep, which took the first argument (circles) and tried to find it in the files specified by the remaining arguments (as shown in Fig. 4-1).

Enclosing the asterisk in quotes, however, removes its special meaning from the shell

```
$ grep '*' stars
The asterisk (*) is a special character that
**********
5 * 4 = 20
$
```

The quotes told the shell to leave the enclosed characters alone. It then started execution of grep, passing it the two arguments * (*without* the surrounding quotes; the shell removes them in the process) and stars (see Fig. 4-2).

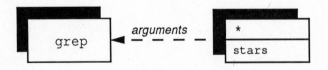

Fig. 4-2. grep '*' stars

There are characters other than * that otherwise have a special meaning and must be quoted when used in a pattern. The whole topic of how quotes are handled by the shell is a fascinating one; an entire chapter—Chapter 6— is devoted to it.

`grep` takes its input from standard input if no file name is specified. So you can use `grep` on the other side of a pipe to scan through the output of a command for something. For example, suppose you want to find out if the user `jim` is logged in. You can use `grep` to search through `who`'s output:

```
$ who | grep jim
jim          tty16          Feb 20 10:25
$
```

Note that by not specifying a file to search, `grep` automatically scans its standard input. Naturally, if the user `jim` were not logged in, then you simply get back a new prompt, because `grep` would not find `jim` in `who`'s output:

```
$ who | grep jim
$
```

Regular Expressions and `grep`

Let's take another look at the `intro` file:

```
$ cat intro
The UNIX operating system was pioneered by Ken
Thompson and Dennis Ritchie at Bell Laboratories
in the late 1960s.  One of the primary goals in
the design of the UNIX system was to create an
environment that promoted efficient program
development.
$
```

`grep` allows you to specify your pattern using regular expressions like in `ed`. Given this information, it means that you can specify the pattern

```
[tT]he
```

to have `grep` search for either a lower or uppercase `T` followed by the characters `he`.

So here's how to `grep` out all the lines containing the characters `the` or `The`:

```
$ grep '[tT]he' intro
The UNIX operating system was pioneered by Ken
in the late 1960s.  One of the primary goals in
the design of the UNIX system was to create an
$
```

It's worth noting that as of System V, Release 2 the `-i` option was added to `grep` to indicate that upper and lowercase letters are not to be distinguished in the matching process. That is, the command

```
grep -i 'the' intro
```

tells `grep` to ignore case when matching the pattern against the lines in `intro`. Therefore, lines containing `the` or `The` will be printed, as will lines containing `THE`, `THe`, `tHE`, and so on.

The following table shows other types of regular expressions that you can specify to `grep` and the types of patterns they'll match.

TABLE 4-5. Some grep examples

Command	Prints
grep '[A-Z]' list	lines from list containing a capital letter
grep '[0-9]' data	lines from data containing a number
grep '[A-Z]...[0-9]' list	lines from list containing five-character patterns that start with a capital letter and end with a digit
grep '\.pic$' filelist	lines from filelist that end in .pic

The −v Option

Sometimes you're interested not in finding the lines that contain a specified pattern, but those that *don't*. To do this with `grep` is simple: you simply use the −v option. In the next example, `grep` is used to find all of the lines in `intro` that don't contain the characters `UNIX`.

```
$ grep -v 'UNIX' intro          Print all lines that don't contain UNIX
Thompson and Dennis Ritchie at Bell Laboratories
in the late 1960s.  One of the primary goals in
environment that promoted efficient program
development.
$
```

The -l Option

At times you may not want to see the actual lines that match a pattern but may be only interested in knowing the names of the files that contain the pattern. For example, suppose you have a set of C programs in your current directory (these file names end with the characters .c) and you want to know which files use a variable called Move_history. The following example shows one way of finding the answer.

```
$ grep 'Move_history' *.c          Find Move_history in all C source files
exec.c:MOVE     Move_history[200] = {0};
exec.c:       cpymove(&Move_history[Number_half_moves -1],
exec.c:   undo_move(&Move_history[Number_half_moves-1]);
exec.c:   cpymove(&last_move,&Move_history[Number_half_moves-1]);
exec.c:   convert_move(&Move_history[Number_half_moves-1]),
exec.c:       convert_move(&Move_history[i-1]),
exec.c:   convert_move(&Move_history[Number_half_moves-1]),
makemove.c:IMPORT MOVE Move_history[];
makemove.c:     if ( Move_history[j].from != BOOK (i,j,from) OR
makemove.c:           Move_history[j].to   != BOOK (i,j,to) )
testch.c:GLOBAL MOVE Move_history[100] = {0};
testch.c:    Move_history[Number_half_moves-1].from = move.from;
testch.c:    Move_history[Number_half_moves-1].to = move.to;
$
```

Sifting through the above output, you discover that three files—exec.c, makemove.c, and testch.c—use the variable.

The -l option to grep gives you just a list of files that contain the specified pattern, not the matching lines from the files:

```
$ grep -l 'Move_history' *.c        List the files that contain Move_history
exec.c
makemove.c
testch.c
$
```

Since grep conveniently lists the files one per line, you can pipe the output from grep -l into wc to count the *number* of *files* that contain a particular pattern:

```
$ grep -l 'Move_history' *.c | wc -l
     3
$
```

So the above says that precisely three C program files reference the variable Move_history. (What are you counting if you use grep *without* the -l option?)

The –n Option

If the –n option is used with grep, then each line from the file that matches the specified pattern is preceded by its relative line number in the file. From previous examples we saw that the file testch.c was one of the three files that referenced the variable Move_history; the following shows how you can pinpoint the precise lines in the file that reference the variable:

```
$ grep -n 'Move_history' testch.c    Precede matches with line numbers
13:GLOBAL MOVE Move_history[100] = {0};
197:    Move_history[Number_half_moves-1].from = move.from;
198:    Move_history[Number_half_moves-1].to = move.to;
$
```

As you can see, Move_history is used on lines 13, 197, and 198 in testch.c.

♦ sort ♦

You're familiar with the basic operation of sort:

```
$ sort names
Crockett
Emanuel
Fred
Lucy
Ralph
Tubs
Tubs
$
```

By default, sort takes each line of the specified input file and sorts it into ascending order. Special characters are sorted according to the internal encoding of the characters. For example, on a machine that encodes characters in ASCII, the space character is represented internally as the number 32, and the double quote as the number 34. This means that the former would be sorted before the latter.

sort has many options that provide you with more flexibility in performing your sort. We'll just describe a few of the options here.

The –u Option

The –u option tells sort to eliminate duplicate lines from the output.

```
$ sort -u names
Crockett
Emanuel
Fred
Lucy
Ralph
Tubs
$
```

Here you see that the duplicate line that contained Tubs was eliminated from the output.

The -r Option

Use the -r option to *reverse* the order of the sort:

```
$ sort -r names                           Reverse sort
Tubs
Tubs
Ralph
Lucy
Fred
Emanuel
Crockett
$
```

The -o Option

By default sort writes the sorted data to standard output. To have it go into a file, you can use output redirection:

```
$ sort names > sorted_names
$
```

Alternatively, you can use the -o option to specify the output file. Simply list the name of the output file right after the -o:

```
$ sort names -o sorted_names
$
```

This sorts names and writes the results to sorted_names.

Frequently you want to sort the lines in a file and have the sorted data replace the original. Typing

```
$ sort names > names
$
```

won't work—it will end up wiping out the names file. However, with the -o option, it is okay to specify the same name for the output file as the input file:

```
$ sort names -o names
$ cat names
Crockett
Emanuel
Fred
Lucy
Ralph
Tubs
Tubs
$
```

The −n Option

Suppose you have a file containing pairs of (x, y) data points as shown:

```
$ cat data
5        27
2        12
3        33
23       2
-5       11
15       6
14       -9
$
```

Suppose you want to feed this data into a plotting program called plotdata, but that the program requires that the incoming data pairs be sorted in increasing value of x (the first value on each line).

The −n option to sort specifies that the first field on the line is to be considered a *number*, and the data is to be sorted arithmetically. Compare the output of sort used first without the −n option and then with it.

```
$ sort data
-5       11
14       -9
15       6
2        12
23       2
3        33
```

```
5          27
$ sort -n data                              Sort arithmetically
-5         11
2          12
3          33
5          27
14         -9
15         6
23         2
$
```

Skipping Fields

If you had to sort your data file by the *y* value; i.e., the second number in each line, then you could tell sort to skip past the first number on the line by using the option

```
+1n
```

instead of −n. The +1 says to skip the first field. Similarly, +5n would mean to skip the first five fields on each line and then sort the data numerically. Fields are delimited by space or tab characters by default. If a different delimiter is to be used, then the −t option must be used.

```
$ sort +1n data                             Skip the first field in the sort
14         -9
23         2
15         6
-5         11
2          12
5          27
3          33
$
```

The −t Option

As mentioned, if you skip over fields, then sort assumes that the fields being skipped are delimited by space or tab characters. The −t option says otherwise. In this case, the character that follows the −t is taken as the delimiter character.

Look at our sample password file again:

```
$ cat /etc/passwd
root:TzDefjvnrEU3M:0:0:The Super User:/:/usr/lbin/ksh
steve:odI.yN3WfkxEs,2.YA:203:100::/usr/steve:/usr/lbin/ksh
bin:NOLOGIN:3:3:The owner of system files:/:
cron:NOLOGIN:1:1:Cron Daemon for periodic tasks:/:
george:mFJ2zOFkkrnh6:75:75::/usr/george:/bin/rsh
pat:SZxihgtJkfkOI:300:300::/usr/pat:/usr/lbin/ksh
uucp:nc823ciSiLiZM:5:5::/usr/spool/uucppublic:/usr/lib/uucp/uucico
asg:NOLOGIN:6:6:The Owner of Assignable Devices:/:
sysinfo:NOLOGIN:10:10:Access to System Information:/:/bin/sh
mail:NOLOGIN:301:301::/usr/mail:
$
```

If you wanted to sort this file by user name (the first field on each line), you could just issue the command

```
sort /etc/passwd
```

To sort the file instead by the third colon-delimited field (which contains what is known as your *user id*), you would want an arithmetic sort, skipping the first two fields (+2n), specifying the colon character as the field delimiter (–t :):

```
$ sort +2n -t: /etc/passwd          Sort by user id
root:TzDefjvnrEU3M:0:0:The Super User:/:/usr/lbin/ksh
cron:NOLOGIN:1:1:Cron Daemon for periodic tasks:/:
bin:NOLOGIN:3:3:The owner of system files:/:
uucp:nc823ciSiLiZM:5:5::/usr/spool/uucppublic:/usr/lib/uucp/uucico
asg:NOLOGIN:6:6:The Owner of Assignable Devices:/:
sysinfo:NOLOGIN:10:10:Access to System Information:/:/bin/sh
george:mFJ2zOFkkrnh6:75:75::/usr/george:/bin/rsh
steve:odI.yN3WfkxEs,2.YA:203:100::/usr/steve:/usr/lbin/ksh
pat:SZxihgtJkfkOI:300:300::/usr/pat:/usr/lbin/ksh
mail:NOLOGIN:301:301::/usr/mail:
$
```

Here we've emboldened the third field of each line so that you can easily verify that the file was sorted correctly by user id.

Other Options

There are other options to sort that enable you to skip characters within a field, specify the field to *end* the sort on, merge sorted input files, and sort in "dictionary order" (only letters, numbers, and spaces are used for the comparison). For more details on these options look under sort in your *UNIX User's Manual*.

♦ uniq ♦

The uniq command is useful when you need to find duplicate lines in a file. The basic format of the command is:

uniq *in_file out_file*

In this format, uniq will copy *in_file* to *out_file*, removing any duplicate lines in the process. uniq's definition of duplicated lines are *consecutive-occurring* lines that match exactly.

If *out_file* is not specified, then the results will be written to standard output. If *in_file* is also not specified, then uniq acts as a filter, and reads its input from standard input.

Here's some examples to see how uniq works. Suppose you have a file called names with contents as shown:

```
$ cat names
Crockett
Tubs
Emanuel
Lucy
Ralph
Fred
Tubs
$
```

You can see that the name Tubs appears twice in the file. You can use uniq to "remove" such duplicate entries:

```
$ uniq names                         Print unique lines
Crockett
Tubs
Emanuel
Lucy
Ralph
Fred
Tubs
$
```

Tubs still appeared twice in the output because the multiple occurrences were not consecutive in the file, and thus uniq's definition of duplicate was not satisfied. To remedy this situation, sort is often used to get the duplicate lines adjacent to each other. The result of the sort is then run through uniq:

```
$ sort names | uniq
Crockett
Emanuel
Fred
Lucy
Ralph
Tubs
$
```

So the `sort` moved the two `Tubs` lines together, and then `uniq` filtered out the duplicate line (recall that `sort` with the `-u` option performs precisely this function).

The -d Option

Frequently, you'll be interested in finding the duplicate entries in a file. The `-d` option to `uniq` should be used for such purposes: it tells `uniq` to write only the duplicated lines to *out_file* (or standard output). Such lines are written just once, no matter how many consecutive occurrences there are.

```
$ sort names | uniq -d            List duplicate lines
Tubs
$
```

As a more practical example, let's return to our `/etc/passwd` file. This file contains information about each user on the system. It's conceivable that over the course of adding and removing users from this file that perhaps the same user name has been inadvertently entered more than once. You can easily find such duplicate entries by first sorting `/etc/passwd` and piping the results into `uniq -d` as done previously:

```
$ sort /etc/passwd | uniq -d      Find duplicate entries in /etc/passwd
$
```

So there are no duplicate entries. But I think what you really want to find is duplicate entries for the same user name. This means that you want to just look at the first field from each line of `/etc/passwd` (recall that the leading characters of each line of `/etc/passwd` up to the colon are the user name). This can't be done directly through an option to `uniq`, but can be accomplished indirectly by using `cut` to extract the user name from each line of the password file before sending it to `uniq`.

```
$ sort /etc/passwd | cut -f1 -d: | uniq -d   Find duplicates
cem
harry
$
```

So there are multiple entries in /etc/passwd for cem and harry. If you wanted more information on the particular entries, you could grep them from /etc/passwd:

```
$ grep -n 'cem' /etc/passwd
20:cem:jT6yCioowC9VM,M.p9:91:91::/usr/cem:
166:cem:1f9kfiQOwC5VN,M.r0:91:91::/usr/cem:
$ grep -n 'harry' /etc/passwd
29:harry:AO8rlTalqSojQ,M.q9:103:103:Harry Johnson:/usr/harry:
79:harry:eU5tB3RNisOPA,M.o9:90:90:Harry Johnson:/usr/harry:
$
```

The -n option was used to find out where the duplicate entries occur. In the case of cem, there's two entries on lines 20 and 166; in harry's case, the two entries are on lines 29 and 79.

If you now wanted to remove the second cem entry, you could use sed:

```
$ sed '166d' /etc/passwd > /tmp/passwd    Remove duplicate
$ mv /tmp/passwd /etc/passwd
mv: /etc/passwd: 444 modey
mv: cannot unlink /etc/passwd
$
```

Naturally, /etc/passwd is one of the most important files on a UNIX system. As such, only the *super-user* is allowed to write to the file. That's why the mv command failed.

Other Options

The -c option to uniq behaves like uniq with no options (i.e., duplicate lines are removed), except each output line gets preceded by a count of the number of times the line occured in the input.

```
$ sort names | uniq -c          Count line occurrences
    1 Crockett
    1 Emanuel
    1 Fred
    1 Lucy
    1 Ralph
    2 Tubs
$
```

Two other options that won't be described enable you to tell uniq to ignore leading characters/fields on a line. For more information, consult your *UNIX User's Manual.*

We would be remiss if we neglected to mention the program awk that can be quite useful when writing shell programs. However, to do justice to this program would require more space than we can provide in this text. The reader is referred to the document *Awk - A Pattern Scanning and Processing Language*, by Aho, et al., in the *UNIX Programmer's Manual, Volume II* for a description of this program. Kernighan and Pike's *The UNIX Programming Environment* (Prentice-Hall, 1984) also contains a detailed discussion of awk.

♦ Exercises ♦

1. What will be matched by the following regular expressions?

```
x*                       [0-9]\{3\}

xx*                      [0-9]\{3,5\}

x\{1,5\}                 [0-9]\{1,3\},[0-9]\{3\}

x\{5,\}                  ^\...

x\{10\}                  [A-Za-z_][A-Za-z_0-9]*

[0-9]                    \([A-Za-z0-9]\{1,\}\)\1

[0-9]*                   ^Begin$

[0-9][0-9][0-9]          ^\(.\).*\1$
```

2. What will be the effect of the following commands?

```
who | grep 'mary'

who | grep '^mary '

grep '[Uu]nix' ch?/*

ls -l | sort +4n

sed '/^$/d' text > text.out

sed 's/\([Uu]nix\)/\1(TM)/g' text > text.out

date | cut -c12-16

date | cut -c5-11,25- | sed 's/\([0-9]\{1,2\}\)/\1,/'
```

3. Write the commands to:

    a. Find all logged-in users with user names of at least four characters.

    b. Find all users on your system whose user ids are greater than 99.   *None only*

    c. Find the number of users on your system whose user ids are greater than 99.

    d. List all the files in your directory in decreasing order of file size.

[handwritten notes:]

a
who | grep `^[a-z A-z] \{4,\}` cut -c -8

cut -d: -f₁₁₃ /etc/Pswd | grep
[a-9]\{3, \}

#! /bin/sh

And Away We Go

Based upon the discussions in Chapter 3, you should realize that whenever you type something like

```
who | wc -l
```

that you are actually programming in the shell! That's because the shell's the one that's interpreting the command line, recognizing the pipe symbol, connecting the output of the first command to the input of the second, and initiating execution of both commands.

In this chapter, you'll learn how to write your own commands and how to use shell *variables*.

◆ Command Files ◆

A shell program can be typed directly at the terminal, as in

```
$ who | wc -l
```

or it can be first typed into a file and then the file can be executed by the shell. For example, suppose you needed to find out the number of logged-in users several times throughout the day. Well, it's not unreasonable to type the above pipeline in each time you wanted the information, but for the sake of example, let's type this pipeline into a file. We'll call the file nu (for *nu*mber of *u*sers) and its contents will be just the pipeline shown above:

```
$ cat nu
who | wc -l
$
```

To execute the commands contained inside the file nu, all you now have to do is
type nu as the command name to the shell:

```
$ nu
sh: nu: cannot execute
$
```

Oops! We forgot to mention one thing. Before you can execute a program this
way, you must change the file's permissions and make it *executable*. This is done
with the change mode command chmod. To add execute permission to the file
nu, you simply type

```
chmod +x file(s)
```

The +x says make the *file(s)* that follow executable. The shell requires that a file
be *both* readable and executable by you before you can execute it.

```
$ ls -l nu
-rw-rw-r--   1 steve   steve      12 Jul 10 11:42 nu
$ chmod +x nu                       Make it executable
$ ls -l nu
-rwxrwxr-x   1 steve   steve      12 Jul 10 11:42 nu
$
```

Now that you've made it executable, try it again:

```
$ nu
        8
$
```

This time it worked.

You can put any commands at all inside a file, make the file executable,
and then execute its contents simply by typing its name to the shell. It's that simple and that powerful.

The standard shell mechanisms like I/O redirection and pipes can be used
on your own programs as well:

```
$ nu > tally
$ cat tally
        8
$
```

Suppose you're working on a proposal called sys.caps and that the following command sequence is needed every time you want to generate a new
copy of the proposal:

```
tbl sys.caps | nroff -mm -Tlp | lp
```

Once again, you can save yourself some typing by simply placing this command sequence into a file—let's call it run—making it executable, and then just typing the name run whenever you wanted to get a new copy of the proposal:

```
$ cat run
tbl sys.caps | nroff -mm -Tlp | lp
$ chmod +x run
$ run
request id is laser1-15 (standard input)
$
```

(The request id message is issued by the lp command.) For the next example, let's suppose you wanted to write a shell program called stats that printed the date and time, the number of users logged in, and your current working directory. You know that the three command sequences you need to use to get this information are date, who | wc -l, and pwd:

```
$ cat stats
date
who | wc -l
pwd
$ chmod +x stats
$ stats                          Try it out
Wed Jul 10 11:55:50 EDT 1985
      13
/usr/steve/documents/proposals
$
```

You can add some echo commands to stats to make the output a bit more informative:

```
$ cat stats
echo The current date and time is:
date
echo
echo The number of users on the system is:
who | wc -l
echo
echo Your current working directory is:
pwd
$ stats                          Execute it
```

```
The current date and time is:
Wed Jul 10 12:00:27 EDT 1985

The number of users on the system is:
     13

Your current working directory is:
/usr/steve/documents/proposals
$
```

Recall that echo without any arguments simply skips a line in the display. Shortly you'll see how to have the message and the data displayed on the same line, like this:

```
The current date and time is: Wed Jul 10 12:00:27 EDT 1985
```

Comments

The shell programming language would not be complete without a *comment* statement. A comment is a way for you to insert remarks or comments inside the program that otherwise have no effect on its execution.

Whenever the shell encounters the special character # at the start of a word, it takes whatever characters follow the # to the end of the line as comments and simply ignores them. If the # starts the line, then the entire line is treated as a comment by the shell. Here are examples of valid comments:

```
# Here is an entire commentary line

who | wc -l         # count the number of users

#
#   Test to see if the correct arguments were supplied
#
```

Note that the # is usually your default erase character. If so, to enter the character into an editor like ed or vi, you'll have to "escape" it by preceding it with a \. Alternatively, you can change your erase character to something else with the stty command.

Comments are useful for documenting commands or sequences of commands whose purposes may not be obvious, or are sufficiently complex so that if you were to look at the program again in a week you might forget why they're there or what they do. Judicious use of comments can help make shell programs easier to debug and to maintain—both by you and by someone else who may have to support your programs.

Let's go back to the `stats` program and insert some comments.

```
$ cat stats
#
# stats -- prints: date, number of users logged on,
#          and current working directory
#

echo The current date and time is:
date

echo
echo The number of users on the system is:
who | wc -l

echo
echo Your current working directory is:
pwd
$
```

The extra blank lines cost little in terms of program space yet add much in terms of program readability. They're simply ignored by the shell.

◆ Variables ◆

Like virtually all programming languages, the shell allows you to store values into *variables*. A shell variable begins with an alphabetic or underscore (_) character, and is followed by zero or more alphanumeric or underscore characters.

To store a value inside a shell variable, you simply write the name of the variable, followed immediately by the equals sign =, followed immediately by the value you want to store in the variable:

variable=value

For example, to assign the value 1 to the shell variable `count`, you simply write

```
count=1
```

and to assign the value /usr/steve/bin to the shell variable `my_bin`, you simply write

```
my_bin=/usr/steve/bin
```

A few important points here. First, spaces are not permitted on either side of the equals sign. Keep that in mind, especially if you're in the good programming habit of inserting spaces around operators. In the shell language, you can't put those spaces in.

Second, unlike most other programming languages, the shell has no concept whatsoever of *data types*. Whenever you assign a value to a shell variable, no matter what it is, the shell simply interprets that value as a string of characters. So when you assigned 1 to the variable count previously, the shell simply stored the *character* 1 inside the variable count, making no observation whatsoever that an integer value was being stored in the variable.

If you're used to programming in a language like C or Pascal, where all variables must be *declared*, then you're in for another readjustment. Since the shell has no concept of data types, variables are not declared before they're used; they're simply assigned values when you want to use them.

Since the shell is an interpretive language, you can assign values to variables directly at your terminal:

```
$ count=1                        Assign character 1 to count
$ my_bin=/usr/steve/bin          Assign /usr/steve/bin to my_bin
$
```

So now that you know how to assign values to variables, what good is it? Glad you asked.

Displaying the Values of Variables

The echo command is used to display the value that is stored inside a shell variable. In order to do this, you simply write

```
echo $variable
```

The $ character is a special character to the shell. If a valid variable name follows the $, then the shell takes this as an indication that the value stored inside that variable is to be substituted at that point. So, when you type

```
echo $count
```

the shell replaces $count with the value that is stored there; then it executes the echo command:

```
$ echo $count
1
$
```

Remember, the shell performs variable substitution *before* it executes the command (see Fig. 5-1).

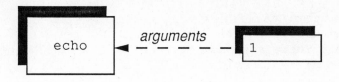

Fig. 5-1. `echo $count`

You can have the value of more than one variable substituted at a time:

```
$ echo $my_bin
/usr/steve/bin
$ echo $my_bin $count
/usr/steve/bin 1
$
```

In the second example, the shell substituted the value of `my_bin` and `count` and then executed the `echo` command (see Fig. 5-2).

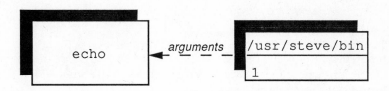

Fig. 5-2. `echo $my_bin $count`

The values of variables can be used anywhere on the command line, as the next examples illustrate.

```
$ ls $my_bin
mon
nu
testx
$ pwd                              Where are we?
/usr/steve/documents/memos
$ cd $my_bin                       Change to my bin directory
$ pwd
```

```
/usr/steve/bin
$ number=99
$ echo There are $number bottles of beer on the wall
There are 99 bottles of beer on the wall
$
```

Here are some more examples:

```
$ command=sort
$ $command names
Crockett
Emanuel
Fred
Lucy
Ralph
Tubs
Tubs
$ command=wc
$ option=-l
$ file=names
$ $command $option $file
      7 names
$
```

So you see, even the name of a command can be stored inside a variable. Since the shell performs its substitution before determining the name of the program to execute and its arguments, it scans the line

```
$command $option $file
```

and turns it into

```
wc -l names
```

Then it executes wc, passing the two arguments -l and names.
      Variables can even be assigned to other variables, as shown in the next example:

```
$ value1=10
$ value2=value1
$ echo $value2
value1                          Didn't do that right
$ value2=$value1
$ echo $value2
10                              That's better
$
```

Remember that a dollar sign must always be placed before the variable name whenever you want to use the value stored in that variable.

The Null Value

What do you think happens when try to display the value of a variable that you never assigned a value to? Try it and see:

```
$ echo $nosuch                    Never assigned it a value

$
```

You don't get an error message. Did the `echo` command display anything at all? Let's see if we can more precisely determine that:

```
$ echo :$nosuch:                  Surround its value with colons
::
$
```

So you see *no* characters were substituted by the shell for the value of `nosuch`.

A variable that contains no value is said to contain the *null* value. It is the default case for variables that you never store values in. When the shell performs its variable substitution, any values that are null are *completely* removed from the command line, without a trace:

```
$ wc  $nosuch -l $nosuch $nosuch names
       7 names
$
```

The shell scanned the command line substituting the null value for the variable `nosuch`. After the scan was completed, the line effectively looked like this:

```
wc -l names
```

which explains why it worked.

Sometimes you may want to explicitly set a variable null in a program. This can be done by simply assigning no value to the variable, as in

```
dataflag=
```

Alternatively, you can list two adjacent pairs of quotes after the =. So

```
dataflag=""
```

and

```
dataflag=''
```

both have the same effect of assigning the null value to `dataflag`.
    Be advised that the assignment

```
dataflag=" "
```

is *not* equivalent to the three previous ones, as it assigns a single space character
to `dataflag`; that's quite different from assigning *no* characters to it.

File Name Substitution and Variables

Here's a puzzle for you: If you type

```
x=*
```

will the shell store the character `*` into the variable `x`, or will it store the names
of all of the files in your current directory into the variable `x`? Let's try it out
and see:

```
$ ls                          What files do we have?
addresses
intro
lotsaspaces
names
nu
numbers
phonebook
stat
$ x=*
$ echo $x
addresses intro lotsaspaces names nu numbers phonebook stat
$
```

There's a lot to be learned from this small example. Was the list of files stored
into the variable x when

```
x=*
```

was executed, or did the shell do the substitution when

```
echo $x
```

was executed?

The answer is that the shell does not perform file name substitution when assigning values to variables. Therefore,

```
x=*
```

assigns the single character * to x. This means that the shell did the file name substitution when executing the echo command. In fact, the precise sequence of steps that occurred when

```
echo $x
```

was executed was as follows:

1. The shell scanned the line, substituting * as the value of x.

2. The shell then rescanned the line, encountered the * and then substituted the names of all files in the current directory.

3. The shell then initiated execution of echo, passing it the file list as arguments (see Fig 5-3).

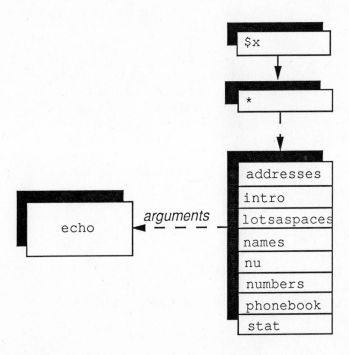

Fig. 5-3. echo $x

This order of evaluation is very important. Remember, first the shell does variable substitution, then file name substitution, then it parses the line into arguments.

The ${*variable*} Construct

Suppose you have the name of a file stored in the variable `filename`. If you wanted to rename that file so that the new name was the same as the old, except with an X added to the end, then your first impulse would be to type

```
mv $filename $filenameX
```

When the shell scans this command line it substitutes the value of the variable `filename` *and also the value of the variable* `filenameX`. The shell thinks `filenameX` is the full name of the variable since it's composed entirely of valid variable name characters. In order to avoid this problem, you can delimit the end of the variable name by enclosing the entire name (but not the leading dollar sign) in a pair of curly braces, as in

```
${filename}X
```

This removes the ambiguity, and the `mv` command will then work as desired:

```
mv $filename ${filename}X
```

Remember that the braces are only necessary if the last character of the variable name is followed by an alphanumeric character or an underscore.

That concludes our introduction to writing commands and using variables. The next chapter goes into detail on the quoting mechanisms in the shell.

◆ **Exercises** ◆

1. Which of the following are valid variable names?

```
XxXxXx
12345                    _
file.name               HOMEDIR
file_name               _date
file1                   x0-9
                        $limit
```

2. Suppose your HOME directory is /usr/steve and that you have subdirectories as shown in the following figure:

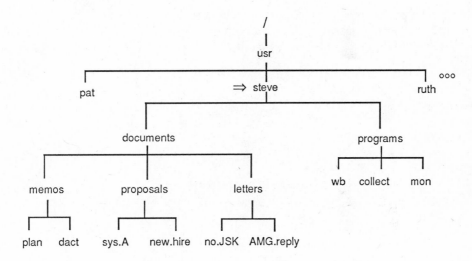

Assuming you just logged onto the system and executed the following commands:

```
$ docs=/usr/steve/documents
$ let=$docs/letters
$ prop=$docs/proposals
$
```

write the commands in terms of these variables to

   a. List the contents of the documents directory.
   b. Copy all files from the letters directory to the proposals directory.

    c. Move all files whose names contain a capital letter from the `letters` directory to the current directory.

    d. Count the number of files in the `memos` directory.

What would be the effect of the following commands?

    a. `ls $let/..`
    b. `cat $prop/sys.A >> $let/no.JSK`
    c. `echo $let/*`
    d. `cp $let/no.JSK $progs`
    e. `cd $prop`

3. Write a program called `nf` to display the number of files in your current directory. Type in the program and test it out.

4. Write a program called `whos` to display a sorted list of the logged in users. Just display the user names and no other information. Type in the program and test it out.

♦   ♦   ♦   ♦   ♦   ♦

6

Can I Quote You on That?

This chapter will teach you about one of the most unique features of the shell programming language: the way it interprets quote characters. Basically, there are four different types of quote characters that the shell recognizes:

1. The single quote character `'`

2. The double quote character `"`

3. The backslash character `\`

4. The back quote character `` ` ``

The first two and the last characters must occur in pairs, whereas the third is unary in nature.   Each of these quotes has a distinct meaning to the shell. We'll cover them in separate sections of this chapter.

♦ The Single Quote ♦

There are several reasons for needing to use quotes in the shell. One of these is to keep characters that are otherwise separated by whitespace characters together. Let's look at an example. Here's a file called phonebook that contains names and phone numbers:

```
$ cat phonebook
Alice Chebba      596-2015
Barbara Swingle 598-9257
Liz Stachiw       775-2298
Susan Goldberg 338-7776
Susan Topple      243-4932
Tony Iannino      386-1295
$
```

To look someone up in our phonebook file—which has been kept small here for the sake of example—you use `grep`:

```
$ grep Alice phonebook
Alice Chebba      596-2015
$
```

Look what happens when you look up `Susan`:

```
$ grep Susan phonebook
Susan Goldberg 338-7776
Susan Topple      243-4932
$
```

There are two lines that contain `Susan`, thus explaining the two lines of output. One way to overcome this problem would be to further qualify the name. For example, you could specify the last name as well:

```
$ grep Susan Goldberg phonebook
grep: can't open Goldberg
Susan Goldberg 338-7776
Susan Topple      243-4932
$
```

Recalling that the shell uses one or more whitespace characters to separate the arguments on the line, the above command line results in `grep` being passed three arguments: `Susan`, `Goldberg`, and `phonebook` (see Fig. 6-1).

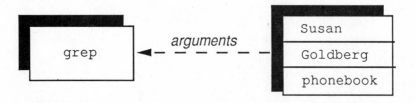

Fig. 6-1. `grep Susan Goldberg phonebook`

When `grep` is executed, it takes the first argument as the pattern, and the remaining arguments as the names of the files to search for the pattern. In this case, `grep` thinks it's supposed to look for `Susan` in the files `Goldberg` and `phonebook`. So it tries to open the file `Goldberg`, can't find it, and issues the error message

```
grep: can't open Goldberg
```

Then it goes to the next file, `phonebook`, opens it, searches for the pattern `Susan` and prints the two matching lines.

The problem boils down to trying to pass whitespace characters as arguments to programs. This can be done by enclosing the entire argument inside a pair of single quotes, as in

```
grep 'Susan Goldberg' phonebook
```

When the shell sees the first single quote, *it ignores any otherwise special characters that follow until it sees the closing quote.*

```
$ grep 'Susan Goldberg' phonebook
Susan Goldberg   338-7776
$
```

In this case, the shell encountered the first `'`, and ignored any special characters until it found the close `'`. So the space between `Susan` and `Goldberg`, which would have normally delimited the two arguments, was ignored by the shell. The shell therefore divided the command line into *two* arguments, the first `Susan Goldberg` (which includes the space character) and the second `phonebook`. It then executed `grep`, passing it these two arguments (see Fig. 6-2).

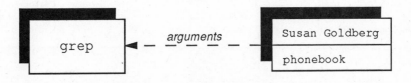

Fig. 6-2. `grep 'Susan Goldberg' phonebook`

`grep` then took the first argument, `Susan Goldberg`, and looked for it in the file specified by the second argument, `phonebook`. Note that the shell *removes* the quotes from the command line and does not pass them to the program.

No matter how many space characters are enclosed between quotes, they are preserved by the shell.

```
$ echo   one           two        three    four
one two three four
$ echo 'one            two        three    four'
one            two        three    four
$
```

In the first case, the shell removes the extra whitespace characters from the line and passes echo the four arguments one, two, three, and four (see Fig. 6-3).

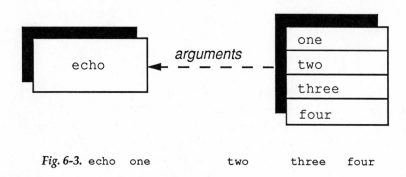

Fig. 6-3. echo   one   two   three   four

In the second case, the space characters are preserved, and the shell treats the entire string of characters enclosed between the quotes as a single argument when executing echo (see Fig. 6-4).

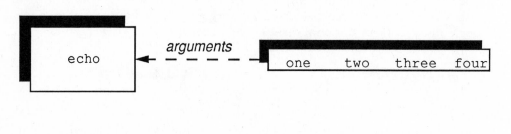

Fig. 6-4. echo   'one   two   three   four'

As we mentioned, all special characters are ignored by the shell if they appear inside single quotes. That explains the output from the following.

```
$ file=/usr/steve/bin/prog1
$ echo $file
/usr/steve/bin/prog1
$ echo '$file'
$file                              $ not interpreted
```

```
$ echo *
addresses intro lotsaspaces names nu numbers phonebook stat
$ echo '*'
*
$ echo '< > | ; ( ) { } >> " ` &'
< > | ; ( ) { } >> " ` &
$
```

Even embedded newline characters will be ignored by the shell if they're enclosed in quotes:

```
$ echo 'How are you today,
> John'
How are you today,
John
$
```

After typing the first line, the shell saw that the quote wasn't matched, so it waited for you to type in the closing quote. As an indication that the shell was waiting for you to finish typing in a command, it changed your prompt character from $ to > . This is known as your *secondary* prompt character, and is displayed by the shell whenever it's waiting for you to finish typing a command.

Quotes are also needed when assigning values containing whitespace or special characters to shell variables.

```
$ message='I must say, this sure is fun'
$ echo $message
I must say, this sure is fun
$ text='* means all files in the directory'
$ echo $text
names nu numbers phonebook stat means all files in the directory
$
```

The quotes were needed in the assignments made to the variables message and text because of the embedded spaces. In the last example you are reminded that the shell still does file name substitution after variable name substitution, meaning that the * was replaced by the names of the all files in the current directory before the echo was executed. There is a way to overcome this annoyance, and it's through the use of double quotes.

♦ The Double Quote ♦

Double quotes work similarly to single quotes, except they're not quite as restrictive. Whereas the latter type tells the shell to ignore *all* enclosed characters, the former type says to ignore *most*. In particular, the following three characters are not ignored inside double quotes:

1. Dollar signs

2. Back quotes

3. Backslashes

The fact that dollar signs are not ignored means that variable name substitution is done by the shell inside double quotes.

```
$ x=*
$ echo $x
addresses intro lotsaspaces names nu numbers phonebook stat
$ echo '$x'
$x
$ echo "$x"
*
$
```

Here you see the major differences between no quotes, single quotes, and double quotes. In the first case, the shell saw the asterisk and substituted all the file names from the current directory. In the second case, the shell left the characters enclosed within the single quotes alone, which resulted in the display of $x. In the final case, the double quotes indicated to the shell that variable name substitution was still to be performed inside the quotes. So the shell substituted * for $x. Since file name substitution is *not* done inside double quotes, * was then passed to echo as the value to be displayed.

So if you want to have the value of a variable substituted, but don't want the shell to treat the substituted characters specially, then you must enclose the variable inside double quotes.

Here's another example illustrating the difference between double quotes and no quotes:

```
$ address="39 East 12th Street
> New York, N. Y. 10003"
$ echo $address
39 East 12th Street New York, N. Y. 10003
$ echo "$address"
```

```
39 East 12th Street
New York, N. Y. 10003
$
```

It makes no difference whether the value assigned to address was enclosed in single quotes or double quotes. The shell displays the secondary command prompt in either case to tell you it's waiting for the corresponding closed quote.

After assigning the two-line address to address, the value of the variable is displayed by echo. Notice that the address is displayed on a single line. The reason is the same as what caused

```
echo one            two          three     four
```

to be displayed as

```
one two three four
```

Recalling that the shell removes spaces, tabs, and newlines (i.e., whitespace characters) from the command line and then cuts it up into arguments, in the case of

```
echo $address
```

the shell simply removed the embedded newline character, treating it as it would a space or tab: as an argument delimiter. Then it passed the *nine* arguments to echo to be displayed. echo never got a chance to see that newline; the shell got to it first (see Fig. 6-5).

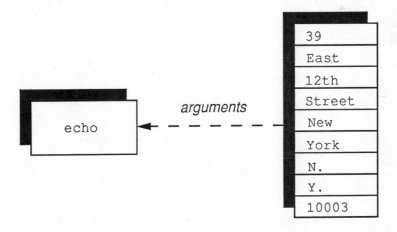

Fig. 6-5. echo $address

When the command

```
echo "$address"
```

is used instead, the shell substitutes the value of `address` as before, except the double quotes tell it to leave any embedded whitespace characters alone. So in this case the shell passes a single argument to `echo`—an argument that contains an embedded newline. `echo` simply displays its single argument at the terminal. Figure 6-6 illustrates this. The newline character is depicted by the characters \n.

Fig. 6-6. `echo  "$address"`

Double quotes can be used to hide single quotes from the shell, and vice versa.

```
$ x="'Hello,' he said"
$ echo $x
'Hello,' he said
$ article='"Keeping the Logins from Lagging," Bell Labs Record'
$ echo $article
"Keeping the Logins from Lagging," Bell Labs Record
$
```

♦ The Backslash ♦

Basically, the backslash is equivalent to placing single quotes around a single character, with a few minor exceptions. The backslash quotes the single character that immediately follows it. The general format is:

\c

where *c* is the character you want to quote. Any special meaning normally attached to that character is removed. Here is an example:

```
$ echo >
```

```
syntax error: `newline or ;' unexpected
$ echo \>
>
$
```

In the first case, the shell saw the > and thought you wanted to redirect echo's output to a file. So it expected a file name to follow. Since it didn't, it issued the error message. In the next case, the backslash removed the special meaning of the >, so it was passed along to echo to be displayed.

```
$ x=*
$ echo \$x
$x
$
```

In this case, the shell ignored the $ that followed the backslash; and as a result, variable substitution was not performed.

Since a backslash removes the special meaning of the character that follows, can you guess what happens if that character is another backslash? Right, it serves to remove the special meaning of the backslash:

```
$ echo \\
\
$
```

Naturally, you could have also written

```
$ echo '\'
\
$
```

Using the Backslash for Continuing Lines

As mentioned at the start of this section, \c is basically equivalent to 'c'. One exception to this rule is when the backslash is used as the very last character on the line:

```
$ lines=one'
> 'two                          Single quotes tell shell to ignore newline
$ echo "$lines"
one
two
```

```
$ lines=one\                        Try it with a \ instead
> two
$ echo "$lines"
onetwo
$
```

The shell treats a backslash at the end of the line as a line continuation. It *removes* the newline character that follows, and also does not treat the newline as an argument delimiter (it's as if it wasn't even typed). This construct is most often used for typing long commands over multiple lines.

The Backslash Inside Double Quotes

We noted earlier that the backslash is one of the three characters interpreted by the shell inside double quotes. This means that you can use the backslash inside these quotes to remove the meaning of characters that otherwise *would* be interpreted inside double quotes (i.e., other backslashes, dollar signs, back quotes, newlines, and other double quotes). If the backslash precedes any other character inside double quotes, then the backslash is ignored by the shell and passed on to the program:

```
$ echo "\$x"
$x
$ echo "\ is the backslash character"
\ is the backslash character
$ x=5
$ echo "The value of x is \"$x\""
The value of x is "5"
$
```

In the first example, the backslash preceded the dollar sign, interpreted by the shell inside double quotes. So the shell ignored the dollar sign, removed the backslash, and executed echo. In the second example, the backslash preceded a space, *not* interpreted by the shell inside double quotes. So the shell ignored the backslash, and passed it on to the echo command. The last example shows the backslash used to enclose double quotes inside a double-quoted string.

As an exercise in the use of quotes, let's say you wanted to display the following line at the terminal:

```
<<< echo $x >>> displays the value of x, which is $x
```

The intention here is to substitute the value of x in the second instance of $x, but not in the first. Let's first assign a value to x:

```
$ x=1
$
```

Now try displaying the line without using any quotes:

```
$ echo <<< echo $x >>> displays the value of x, which is $x
syntax error: `<' unexpected
$
```

The < signals input redirection to the shell, this the reason for the error message.

If you put the entire message inside single quotes, then the value of x won't be substituted at the end. If you enclose the entire string in double quotes, then both occurrences of $x will be substituted. Here are two different ways to do the quoting properly (and realize that there are usually several different ways to quote a string of characters to get the results you want):

```
$ echo "<<< echo \$x >>> displays the value of x, which is $x"
<<< echo $x >>> displays the value of x, which is 1
$ echo '<<< echo $x >>> displays the value of x, which is' $x
<<< echo $x >>> displays the value of x, which is 1
$
```

In the first case, everything was enclosed in double quotes, and the backslash used to prevent the shell from performing variable substitution in the first instance of $x. In the second case, everything up to the last $x was enclosed in single quotes. If the variable x might have contained some file name substitution or whitespace characters, then a safer way of writing the echo would have been

```
echo '<<< echo $x >>> displays the value of x, which is' "$x"
```

♦ The Back Quote ♦

The back quote is unlike any of the previously encountered types of quotes. Its purpose is not to protect characters from the shell but to tell the shell to execute the enclosed command and to insert the standard output from the command at that point on the command line. The general format for using back quotes is

`command`

where command is the name of the command to be executed and whose output is to be inserted at that point. This construct also goes under the name of command substitution.

Here is an example:

```
$ echo The date and time is: `date`
The date and time is: Tue Jul 16 09:14:22 EDT 1985
$
```

When the shell does its initial scan of the command line, it notices the back quote and expects the name of a command to follow. In this case, the shell finds that the date command is to be executed. So it executes date, and replaces the `date` on the command line with the output from the date. After that, it divides the command line into arguments in the normal manner and then initiates execution of the echo command.

```
$ echo Your current working directory is `pwd`
Your current working directory is /usr/steve/shell/ch6
$
```

Here the shell executed pwd, inserted its output on the command line, and then executed the echo.

You are not restricted to executing a single command in the back quotes: several commands can be executed if separated by semicolons. Also, pipelines can be used. Here's a modified version of the nu program that displays the number of logged-on users:

```
$ cat nu
echo There are `who | wc -l` users logged on
$ nu                                    Execute it
There are 13 users logged on
$
```

Since single quotes protect everything, the following output should be clear:

```
$ echo ' `who | wc -l` tells how many users are logged in'
`who | wc -l` tells how many users are logged in
$
```

But back quotes *are* interpreted inside double quotes:

```
$ echo "You have `ls | wc -l` files in your directory"
You have       7 files in your directory
$
```

(What causes those leading spaces before the 7?) Remember that the shell is responsible for executing the command enclosed between the quotes. The only thing the echo command sees is the output that has been inserted by the shell.

Suppose you're writing a shell program and want to assign the current date and time to a variable called now, perhaps to display it later at the top of a report, or log it into a file. The problem here is that you somehow would like to take the output from date and assign it to the variable. The back quote mechanism can be used for this.

```
$ now=`date`                      Execute date and store the output in now
$ echo $now                       See what got assigned
Tue Jul 16 09:34:40 EDT 1985
$
```

When you write

```
now=`date`
```

the shell realizes that the entire output from date is to be assigned to now. Therefore, you don't need to enclose `date` inside double quotes.

Even commands that produce more than a single line of output can be stored inside a variable:

```
$ filelist=`ls`
$ echo $filelist
addresses intro lotsaspaces names nu numbers phonebook stat
$
```

What happened here? You ended up with a horizontal listing of the files even though the newlines from ls were stored inside the filelist variable (take our word for it). The newlines got eaten up when the value of filelist was substituted by the shell in processing the echo command line. Double quotes around the variable will preserve the newlines:

```
$ echo "$filelist"
addresses
intro
lotsaspaces
names
nu
numbers
phonebook
stat
$
```

To store the contents of a file into a variable, you can use cat:

```
$ namelist=`cat names`
$ echo "$names"
Crockett
Emanuel
Fred
Lucy
Ralph
Tubs
Tubs
$
```

If you wanted to mail the contents of the file memo to all of the people listed in the names file (who we'll assume here are users on your system), then you can do the following:

```
$ mail `cat names` < memo
$
```

Here the shell executes the cat and inserts the output on the command line so it looks like this:

```
mail Crockett Emanuel Fred Lucy Ralph Tubs Tubs < memo
```

Then it executes mail, redirecting its standard input from the file memo, and passing it the names of seven users who are to receive the mail.

You'll notice that Tubs will receive the same mail twice, since he's listed twice in the names file. You can remove any duplicate entries from the file by using sort with the -u option (remove duplicate lines) instead of the cat to ensure that each person only receives mail once:

```
$ mail `sort -u names` < memo
$
```

It's worth noting that the shell does file name substitution *after* it substitutes the output from back-quoted commands. Enclosing the commands inside double quotes will prevent the shell from doing the file name substitution on this output if desired.

The back-quoting mechanism is often used to change the value stored in a shell variable. For example, if the shell variable name contains someone's name, and you wanted to convert every character in that variable to uppercase, you could use echo to get the variable to tr's input, perform the translation, and then assign the result back to the variable:

```
$ name="Ralph Kramden"
$ name=`echo $name | tr '[a-z]' '[A-Z]'`   Translate to uppercase
$ echo $name
```

```
RALPH KRAMDEN
$
```

The technique of using echo in a pipeline to write data to the standard input of the following command is a very simple yet powerful technique; it's used quite often in shell programs.

The next example shows how cut is used to extract the first character from the value stored in a variable called filename:

```
$ filename=/usr/steve/memos
$ firstchar=`echo $filename | cut -c1`
$ echo $firstchar
/
$
```

sed is also often used to "edit" the value stored in a variable. Here it is used to extract the last character from the variable file:

```
$ file=exec.o
$ lastchar=`echo $file | sed 's/.*\(.\)$/\1/'`
$ echo $lastchar
o
$
```

The sed command says to replace all of the characters on the line with the last one. The result of the sed is stored in the variable lastchar. The single quotes around the sed command are important, as they prevent the shell from messing around with the backslashes (would double quotes also have worked?).

Arithmetic on Shell Variables

You'll remember that we said that the shell has no notion of data types: any value that is assigned to a variable is just considered a string of characters. The shell also has no concept of performing arithmetic on values stored inside variables, as the following seems to indicate:

```
$ i=1
$ i=$i+1                         What's being assigned here?
$ echo $i                        Relieve the suspense
1+1
$
```

When you execute

```
i=$i+1
```

the shell just performs a literal substitution of the value of i (which is 1) and tacks on the characters +1, thus explaining the results.

A UNIX program called expr evaluates an expression given to it on the command line:

```
$ expr 1 + 2
3
$
```

Each operator and operand given to expr must be a separate argument, thus explaining the output from the following:

```
$ expr 1+2
1+2
$
```

The usual arithmetic operators are recognized by expr: + for addition, − for subtraction, / for division, * for multiplication, and % for modulus (remainder).

```
$ expr 10 + 20 / 2
20
$
```

Multiplication, division, and modulus have higher precedence than addition and subtraction. Thus, in the above example the division was performed before the addition.

```
$ expr 17 * 6
expr: syntax error
$
```

What happened here? The answer: the shell saw the * and substituted the names of all of the files in your directory! It has to be quoted to keep it from the shell:

```
$ expr "17 * 6"
17 * 6
$
```

That's not the way to do it. Remember that expr must see each operator and operand as a separate argument; the above sends the whole expression in as a single argument.

```
$ expr 17 \* 6
102
$
```

Naturally, one or more of the arguments to expr can be the value stored inside a shell variable, since the shell takes care of the substitution first anyway:

```
$ i=1
$ expr $i + 1
2
$
```

Bingo! We've just hit on the method for performing arithmetic on shell variables: do the same type of thing as shown above only use the back-quoting mechanism to assign the output from expr back to the variable:

```
$ i=1
$ i=`expr $i + 1`             Add 1 to i
$ echo $i
2
$
```

Note that expr only evaluates integer arithmetic expressions. You can use awk or bc if you need to do floating point calculations. Also note that expr has other operators. One of the most frequently used ones is the : operator, which is used to match characters in the first operand against a regular expression given as the second operand. By default it returns the number of characters matched.

The expr command

```
expr "$file" : ".*"
```

returns the number of characters stored in the variable file, since the regular expression .* matches all of the characters in the string. For more details on expr, consult your *UNIX User's Manual*.

Table A-4 in Appendix A summarizes the way quotes are handled by the shell.

◆ Exercises ◆

1. Given the following assignments:

```
$ x=*
$ y=?
$ z='one
> two
> three'
$ now=`date`
$ symbol='>'
$
```

and these files in your current directory:

```
$ echo *
names test1 u vv zebra
$
```

What will the output be from the following commands?

echo *** error ***	echo 'Is 5 * 4 > 18 ?'
echo $x	echo What is your name?
echo $y	echo Would you like to play a game?
echo "$y"	echo ***
echo $z | wc -l	echo \$$symbol
echo "$z" | wc -l	echo $\$symbol
echo '$z' | wc -l	echo "\"
echo _$now_	echo "\\"
echo hello $symbol out	echo \\
echo "\""	echo I don't understand

2. Write the commands to remove all of the space characters stored in the shell variable text. Be sure to assign the result back to text. First use tr to do it and then do the same thing with sed.

3. Write the commands to count the number of characters stored in the shell variable `text`. Then write the commands to count all of the alphabetic characters (hint: use `sed` and `wc`). What happens to special character sequences like \n if they're stored inside `text`?

4. Write the commands to assign the unique lines in the file `names` to the shell variable `namelist`.

C H A P T E R

♦ · ♦ · ♦ · ♦ · ♦ · ♦

7

Passing Arguments

Shell programs become far more useful once you learn how to process arguments passed to them. In this chapter, you'll learn how to write shell programs that take arguments typed on the command line. Remember the program run that you wrote in Chapter 5 to run the file sys.caps through tbl, nroff, and lp?

```
$ cat run
tbl sys.caps | nroff -mm -Tlp | lp
$
```

Suppose you needed to run other files besides sys.caps through this same command sequence? Well, you could make a separate version of run for each such file; or, you could modify the run program so that you could specify the name of the file to be run on the command line. That is, you could change run so that you could type

```
run new.hire
```

for example, to specify that the file new.hire is to be run through this command sequence, or

```
run sys.caps
```

to specify the file sys.caps.

Whenever you execute a shell program, the shell automatically stores the first argument in the special shell variable 1, the second argument in the variable 2, and so on. These special variables—more formally known as *positional parameters*—are assigned after the shell has done its normal command line processing (i.e., I/O redirection, variable substitution, file name substitution, etc.)

To modify the run program to accept the name of the file as an argument, all you do to the program is change the reference to the file sys.caps so that it instead references the first argument typed on the command line:

```
$ cat run
tbl $1 | nroff -mm -Tlp | lp
$
$ run new.hire                          Execute it with new.hire as the argument
request id is laser1-24 (standard input)
$
```

Each time you execute the run program, whatever word follows on the command line will be stored inside the first positional parameter by the shell. In the example, new.hire will be stored in this parameter. Substitution of positional parameters is identical to substitution of other types of variables, so when the shell sees

```
tbl $1
```

it replaces the $1 with the first argument supplied to the program: new.hire.

As another example, the following program, called ison, will let you know if a specified user is logged on.

```
$ cat ison
who | grep $1
$ who                                   See who's on
root       console Jul  7 08:37
barney     tty03   Jul  8 12:28
fred       tty04   Jul  8 13:40
joanne     tty07   Jul  8 09:35
tony       tty19   Jul  8 08:30
lulu       tty23   Jul  8 09:55
$ ison tony
tony       tty19   Jul  8 08:30
$ ison pat
$                                       Not logged on
```

The $# Variable

Whenever you execute a shell program, the special shell variable $# gets set to the number of arguments that were typed on the command line. As you'll see in the next chapter, this variable can be tested by the program to determine if the correct number of arguments were typed by the user.

The next program called args was written just to get you more familiar with the way arguments are passed to shell programs. Study the output from each example and make sure you understand it.

```
$ cat args                        Look at the program
echo $# arguments passed
echo arg 1 = :$1:   arg 2 = :$2:   arg 3 = :$3:
$ args a b c                      Execute it
3 arguments passed
arg 1 = :a:   arg 2 = :b:   arg 3 = :c:
$ args a b                        Try it with two arguments
2 arguments passed
arg 1 = :a: arg 2 = :b:   arg 3 = ::          Unassigned args are null
$ args                            Try it with no arguments
0 arguments passed
arg 1 = ::   arg 2 = ::   arg 3 = ::
$ args "a b c"                    Try quotes
1 arguments passed
arg 1 = :a b c:   arg 2 = ::   arg 3 = ::
$ ls x*                          See what files start with x
xact
xtra
$ args x*                        Try file name substitution
2 arguments passed
arg 1 = :xact:   arg 2 = :xtra:   arg 3 = ::
$ my_bin=/usr/steve/bin
$ args $my_bin                   And variable substitution
1 arguments passed
arg 1 = :/usr/steve/bin:   arg 2 = ::   arg 3 = ::
$ args `cat names`               Pass the contents of names
7 arguments passed
arg 1 = :Crockett:   arg 2 = :Emanuel:   arg3 = :Fred:
$
```

As you can see, the shell does its normal command line processing even when it's executing your shell programs. This means that you can take advantage of the normal niceties like file name substitution and variable substitution when specifying arguments to your programs.

The $* Variable

The special variable $* references *all* of the arguments passed to the program. This is often useful in programs that take an indeterminate or *variable* number of arguments. You'll see some more practical examples later. Here's a program that illustrates its use:

```
$ cat args2
echo $# arguments passed
echo they are :$*:
```

```
$ args2 a b c
3 arguments passed
they are :a b c:
$ args2 one              two
2 arguments passed
they are :one two:
$ args2
0 arguments passed
they are ::
$ args2 *
8 arguments passed
they are :args args2 names nu phonebook stat xact xtra:
$
```

A Program to Look Someone up in the Phone Book

Here's the phonebook file from previous examples:

```
$ cat phonebook
Alice Chebba      596-2015
Barbara Swingle 598-9257
Liz Stachiw       775-2298
Susan Goldberg  338-7776
Susan Topple    243-4932
Tony Iannino    386-1295
$
```

You know how to look someone up in the file by using grep:

```
$ grep Cheb phonebook
Alice Chebba      596-2015
$
```

And you know that if you want to look someone up by the full name, then you'd better put quotes around it to keep the argument together:

```
$ grep "Susan T" phonebook
Susan Topple    243-4932
$
```

It would be nice to write a shell program that you could use to look someone up. Let's call the program lu and have it take as its argument the name of the person to look up:

```
$ cat lu
#
# Look someone up in the phone book
#

grep $1 phonebook
$
```

Here's a sample use of lu:

```
$ lu Alice
Alice Chebba      596-2015
$ lu Susan
Susan Goldberg   338-7776
Susan Topple     243-4932
$ lu "Susan T"
grep: can't open T
phonebook:Susan Goldberg   338-7776
phonebook:Susan Topple     243-4932
$
```

In the last example, you were careful to enclose Susan T in double quotes, so what happened? Look again at the grep that is executed in the lu program:

```
grep $1 phonebook
```

Even though enclosing Susan T inside double quotes does result in its getting passed to lu as a single argument, when the shell substitutes this value for $1 on grep's command line, it then will pass it as *two* arguments to grep (remember we had this same sort of discussion when we talked about variable substitution—first the shell substitutes the value of the variable, then it divides the line into arguments).

You can alleviate this problem by enclosing $1 inside double quotes (why not single?) in the lu program:

```
$ cat lu
#
# Look someone up in the phone book -- version 2
#

grep "$1" phonebook
$
```

Now let's try it again.

```
$ lu Tony
Tony Iannino      386-1295            This still works
$ lu "Susan T"                        Now try this again
Susan Topple      243-4932
$
```

A Program to Add Someone to the Phone Book

Let's continue with the development of programs that work with the phone-book file. You'll probably want to add someone to the file, particularly since our phonebook file is so small. You can write a program called add that takes two arguments: the name of the person to be added and the number. Then you can simply write the name and number, separated from each other by a tab character, onto the end of the phonebook file:

```
$ cat add
#
# Add someone to the phone book
#

echo "$1        $2" >> phonebook
$
```

Although you can't tell, there's a tab character that separates the $1 from the $2 in the above echo command. This tab must be quoted in order to make it to echo without getting gobbled up by the shell.

Let's try out the program:

```
$ add 'Stromboli Pizza' 543-9478
$ lu Pizza                            See if we can find the new entry
Stromboli Pizza 543-9478              So far, so good
$ cat phonebook                       See what happened
Alice Chebba      596-2015
Barbara Swingle 598-9257
Liz Stachiw       775-2298
Susan Goldberg    338-7776
Susan Topple      243-4932
Tony Iannino      386-1295
Stromboli Pizza 543-9478
$
```

Stromboli Pizza was quoted so that the shell passed it along to add as a single argument (what would have happened if it wasn't quoted?). After add finished executing, lu was run to see if it could find the new entry, and it did. The cat command was executed to see what the modified phonebook file looked like. The new entry was added to the end, as was intended. Unfortunately, the new file is no longer sorted. This won't affect the operation of the lu program, but you can add a sort to the add program to keep the file sorted after new entries are added:

```
$ cat add
#
# Add someone to the phonebook file -- version 2
#

echo "$1        $2" >> phonebook
sort -o phonebook phonebook
$
```

Recall that the −o option to sort specifies where the sorted output is to be written, and that this can be the same as the input file.

```
$ add 'Billy Bach' 331-7618
$ cat phonebook
Alice Chebba    596-2015
Barbara Swingle 598-9257
Billy Bach      331-7618
Liz Stachiw     775-2298
Stromboli Pizza 543-9478
Susan Goldberg  338-7776
Susan Topple    243-4932
Tony Iannino    386-1295
$
```

So each time a new entry is added, the phonebook file will get resorted.

A Program to Remove Someone from the Phone Book

No set of programs that enabled you to look someone up or add someone to the phone book would be complete without a program to remove someone from the phone book. We'll call the program rem and have it take as its argument the name of the person to be removed. What should the strategy be for developing the program? Essentially, you want to remove the line from the file that contains the specified name. The −v option to grep can be used here, as it prints lines from a file that *don't* match a pattern.

```
$ cat rem
#
# Remove someone from the phone book
#
```

```
grep -v "$1" phonebook > /tmp/phonebook
mv /tmp/phonebook phonebook
$
```

The grep writes all lines that don't match into the file /tmp/phonebook[†]. After the grep is done, the old phonebook file is replaced by the new one from /tmp.

$ **rem 'Stromboli Pizza'**		*Remove this entry*
$ **cat phonebook**		
Alice Chebba	596-2015	
Barbara Swingle	598-9257	
Billy Bach	331-7618	
Liz Stachiw	775-2298	
Susan Goldberg	338-7776	
Susan Topple	243-4932	
Tony Iannino	386-1295	
$ **rem Susan**		
$ **cat phonebook**		
Alice Chebba	596-2015	
Barbara Swingle	598-9257	
Billy Bach	331-7618	
Liz Stachiw	775-2298	
Tony Iannino	386-1295	
$		

The first case, where Stromboli Pizza was removed, worked fine. In the second case, however, both Susan entries were removed since they both matched the pattern. You can use the add program to add them back to the phone book:

```
$ add 'Susan Goldberg' 338-7776
$ add 'Susan Topple' 243-4932
$
```

In the next chapter you'll learn how you can determine if more than one matching entry is found and take some other action if that's the case. For example, you might want to alert the user that more than one match has been found and further qualification of the name is required.

Incidentally, before leaving this program, you should note that sed could have also been used to delete the matching entry. In such a case, the grep could be replaced with

---

[†] /tmp is a directory on all UNIX systems that anyone can write to. It's used by programs to create "temporary" files. The next time the system gets rebooted, all the files in /tmp are automatically removed.

```
sed "/$1/d" phonebook > /tmp/phonebook
```

to achieve the same result. The double quotes are needed around the sed command to ensure that the value of $1 is substituted, while at the same time ensuring that the shell doesn't see a command line like

```
sed /Stromboli Pizza/d phonebook > /tmp/phonebook
```

and pass three arguments to sed instead of two.

♦ The `shift` Command ♦

If you supply more than nine arguments to a program, you should be aware that there is no way to explicitly reference arguments 10 and up. This is because the shell only accepts a single digit following the dollar sign. So if you try to access the 10th argument directly by writing

```
$10
```

the shell will actually substitute the value of $1 followed by a 0.

There is a way to get at those extra arguments. The shift command allows you to effectively *left shift* your positional parameters. If you execute the command

```
shift
```

then whatever was previously stored inside $2 will be assigned to $1, whatever was previously stored in $3 will be assigned to $2, and so on. The old value of $1 will be irretrievably lost.

When this command is executed, $# (the number of arguments variable) is also automatically decremented by one.

```
$ cat tshift                    Program to test the shift
echo $# $*
shift
echo $# $*
shift
echo $# S*
shift
echo $# $*
shift
echo $# S*
shift
echo $# $*
```

```
$ tshift a b c d e
5 a b c d e
4 b c d e
3 c d e
2 d e
1 e
0
$
```

If you try to shift when there are no variables to shift (i.e., when $# already equals zero), then you'll get the following error message from the shell:

```
prog: cannot shift
```

where *prog* is the name of the program that executed the offending shift.

You can shift more than one "place" at once by writing a *count* immediately after shift[†], as in

```
shift 3
```

This command has the same effect as performing three separate shifts:

```
shift
shift
shift
```

So if you have a program that needs to explicitly access the tenth positional parameter, the easiest way to do it would be to execute a shift and then access the value as $9. Naturally, you should first save the value of $1 if you'll need it later in the program:

```
arg1=$1
shift
arg10=$9
```

Remember that after executing the above commands, $1 will now actually reference the old $2, and so on.

The shift command is very useful when processing a variable number of arguments. You'll see it put to use when you learn about loops in Chapter 9.

---

† The shift count option was added to the shift command as of UNIX System V.

♦ Exercises ♦

1. If you're running UNIX System V, Release 2 or later, modify `lu` so that it ignores case when doing the lookup.

2. What happens if you forget to supply an argument to the `lu` program? What happens if the argument is null (as in, `lu ""`)?

3. The program `ison` from this chapter has a shortcoming as shown in the following example:

   ```
   $ ison ed
   fred      tty03    Sep  4 14:53
   $
   ```

   The output indicates that `fred` is logged on, while we were checking to see if `ed` were logged on.

   Modify `ison` to correct this problem.

4. Write a program called `twice` that takes a single integer argument and doubles its value:

   ```
   $ twice 15
   30
   $ twice 0
   0
   $
   ```

   What happens if a noninteger value is typed? What if the argument is omitted?

5. Write a program called `home` that takes the name of a user as its single argument and prints that user's home directory. So

   ```
   home steve
   ```

   would print

   ```
   /usr/steve
   ```

   if /usr/steve is steve's home directory. (Hint: recall that the home directory is the sixth field stored in the file `/etc/passwd`.)

6. Write a program called `suffix` that renames a file by adding the characters given as the second argument to the end of the name of the file given as the first argument. So

Suffiy   memol   hp

```
suffix memo1 .sv
```

should rename `memo1` to `memo1.sv`.

7. Write a program called `unsuffix` that removes the characters given as the second argument from the end of the name of the file given as the first argument. So

```
unsuffix memo1.sv .sv
```

should rename `memo1.sv` to `memo1`. Be sure that the characters are removed from the end, so

```
unsuffix test1test test
```

should result in `test1test` being renamed to `test1`. (Hint: use `sed` and the back quoting mechanism.)

Rmove

Org 2

8

Decisions, Decisions

This chapter introduces a statement that is present in almost all programming languages: `if`. It enables you to test a condition and then change the flow of program execution based upon the result of the test.

The general format of the `if` command is:

```
if command_t
then
        command
        command
        . . .
fi
```

where *command_t* is executed and its *exit status* is tested. If the exit status is zero, then the commands that follow between the `then` and the `fi` are executed; otherwise they are skipped.

♦ Exit Status ♦

Whenever any program completes execution under the UNIX system, it returns an exit status back to the system. This status is a number that usually indicates whether the program successfully ran or not. By convention, an exit status of zero is used to indicate that a program succeeded, and nonzero to indicate that it failed. Failures can be caused by invalid arguments passed to the program, or by an error condition that is detected by the program. For example, the `cp` command returns a nonzero exit status if the copy fails for some reason (e.g., if it can't create the destination file), or if the arguments aren't correctly specified (e.g., wrong number of arguments, or more than two arguments and the last one isn't a directory). In the case of `grep`, an exit status of zero (success) is returned if it finds the specified pattern in at least one of the files; a nonzero value is returned if it can't find the pattern or if an error occurs (the arguments aren't correctly specified or it can't open one of the files).

In a pipeline, the exit status is that of the last command in the pipe. So in

```
who | grep fred
```

the exit status of the grep is used by the shell as the exit status for the pipeline. In this case, an exit status of zero means that fred was found in who's output (i.e., fred was logged on at the time that this command was executed).

The $? Variable

The shell variable $? is automatically set by the shell to the exit status of the last command executed. Naturally, you can use echo to display its value at the terminal.

```
$ cp phonebook phone2
$ echo $?
0                                    Copy "succeeded"
$ cp nosuch backup
cp: cannot access nosuch
$ echo $?
2                                    Copy "failed"
$ who                                See who's logged on
root       console Jul  8 10:06
wilma      tty03   Jul  8 12:36
barney     tty04   Jul  8 14:57
betty      tty15   Jul  8 15:03
$ who | grep barney
barney     tty04   Jul  8 14:57
$ echo $?                            Print exit status of last command (grep)
0                                    grep "succeeded"
$ who | grep fred
$ echo $?
1                                    grep "failed"
$ echo $?
0                                    Exit status of last echo
$
```

Let's now write a shell program called on that tells us whether or not a specified user is logged onto the system. The name of the user to check will be passed to the program on the command line. If the user is logged on, then we'll print a message to that effect; otherwise we'll say nothing. Here then is the program:

```
$ cat on
#
# determine if someone is logged on
#

user="$1"

if who | grep "$user"
then
        echo "$user is logged on"
fi
$
```

This first argument typed on the command line is stored in the shell variable user. Then the if command executes the pipeline

```
who | grep "$user"
```

and tests the exit status returned by grep. If the exit status is zero, then grep found user in who's output. In that case, the echo command that follows is executed. If the exit status is nonzero, then the specified user is not logged on, and the echo command is skipped. The echo command is indented from the left margin for aesthetic reasons only (tab characters are usually used for such purposes as it's easier to type a tab character than an equivalent number of spaces). In this case, just a single command is enclosed between the then and fi. When more commands are included, and when the nesting gets deeper, indentation can have a dramatic effect on the program's readability. Later examples will help illustrate this point.

Here's some sample uses of on:

```
$ who
root        console  Jul  8 10:37
barney      tty03    Jul  8 12:38
fred        tty04    Jul  8 13:40
joanne      tty07    Jul  8 09:35
tony        tty19    Jul  8 08:30
lulu        tty23    Jul  8 09:55
$ on tony                              We know he's on
tony        tty19    Jul  8 08:30      Where did this come from?
tony is logged on
$ on steve                             We know he's not on
$ on ann                               Try this one
joanne      tty07    Jul  8 09:35
ann is logged on
$
```

We seem to have uncovered a couple of problems with the program. When the specified user is logged on, then the corresponding line from who's output is also displayed. This may not be such a bad thing, but the program requirements only called for a message to be displayed and nothing else.

This line is displayed because not only does grep return an exit status in the pipeline

```
who | grep "$user"
```

but it also goes about its normal function of writing any matching lines to standard output, even though we're really not interested in that. We can dispose of grep's output by redirecting it to the system's "garbage can," /dev/null. This is a special file on the system that anyone can read from (and get an immediate end of file) or write to. When you write to it, the bits go to that great bit bucket in the sky!

```
who | grep "$user" > /dev/null
```

The second problem with on appears when the program is executed with the argument ann. Even though ann is not logged on, grep matched the characters ann for the user joanne. What you need here is a more restrictive pattern specification, which you learned how to do in Chapter 4 where we talked about regular expressions. Since who lists each user name in column one of each output line, we can anchor the pattern to match the beginning of the line by preceding the pattern with the character ^:

```
who | grep "^$user" > /dev/null
```

But that's not enough. grep will still match a line like

```
bobby    tty07    Jul  8 09:35
```

if you ask it to search for the pattern bob. What you need to do is also anchor the pattern on the right. Realizing that who ends each user name with one or more spaces, the pattern

```
"^$user "
```

will now only match lines for the specified user.

Let's try the new and improved version of on:

```
$ cat on
#
# determine if someone is logged on -- version 2
#
```

```
user="$1"

if who | grep "^$user " > /dev/null
then
        echo "$user is logged on"
fi
$ who                           Who's on now?
root      console Jul  8 10:37
barney    tty03   Jul  8 12:38
fred      tty04   Jul  8 13:40
joanne    tty07   Jul  8 09:35
tony      tty19   Jul  8 08:30
lulu      tty23   Jul  8 09:55
$ on lulu
lulu is logged on
$ on ann                        Try this again
$ on                            What happens if we don't give any arguments?
$
```

If no arguments are specified, then user will be null. grep will then look through who's output for lines that start with a blank (why?). It won't find any, and so just a command prompt will be returned. In the next section you'll see how you can test to see whether the correct number of arguments have been supplied to a program, and take some action if not.

♦ The test Command ♦

A command called test is most often used for testing one or more conditions in an if command. This command is a shell built-in as of UNIX System V. Its general format is

```
test    expression
```

where *expression* represents the condition you're testing. test evaluates *expression*, and if the result is *true*, it returns an exit status of zero; otherwise the result is *false*, and it returns a nonzero exit status.

String Operators

As an example of the use of test, the following command will return a zero exit status if the shell variable name contains the characters julio:

```
test "$name" = julio
```

The = operator is used to test if two values are identical. In this case, we're testing to see if the *contents* of the shell variable name is identical to the characters julio. If it is, then test returns an exit status of zero; nonzero otherwise.

Note that test must see all operands ($name and julio) and operators (=) as separate arguments, meaning that they must be delimited by one or more whitespace characters.

Getting back to the if command, to echo the message "Would you like to play a game?" if name contains the characters julio, you would write your if command like this:

```
if test "$name" = julio
then
        echo "Would you like to play a game?"
fi
```

(Why is it better to play it safe and enclose the message that is displayed by echo inside quotes?) When the if command gets executed, the command that follows the if is executed and its exit status is tested. The test command is passed the three arguments $name (with its value substituted, of course), =, and julio. test then tests to see if the first argument is identical to the third argument and returns a zero exit status if it is and a nonzero exit status if it is not.

The exit status that is returned by test is then tested. If it's zero, then the commands between then and fi are executed; in this case the single echo command is executed. If the exit status is nonzero then the echo command is skipped.

It's good programming practice to enclose shell variables that are arguments to test inside a pair of *double* quotes (to allow variable substitution). This ensures that test sees the argument in the case where its value is null. For example, consider the following example

```
$ name=                              Set name null
$ test $name = julio
sh: test: argument expected
$
```

Because name was null, only two arguments were passed to test: = and julio, since the shell substituted the value of name *before* parsing the command line into arguments. In fact, after $name was substituted by the shell, it was as if you typed the following:

```
test = julio
```

When test executed, it only saw two arguments (see Fig. 8-1) and therefore issued the error message.

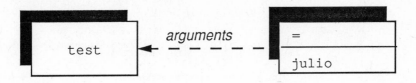

Fig. 8-1. `test $name = julio` with name null

By placing double quotes around the variable, you ensure that `test` sees the argument, since quotes act as a "placeholder" when the argument is null.

```
$ test "$name" = julio
$ echo $?                          Print the exit status
1
$
```

Even if `name` is null, the shell will still pass three arguments to `test`, the first one null (see Fig. 8-2).

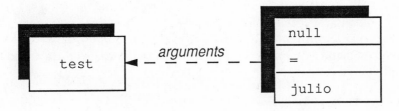

Fig. 8-2. `test "$name" = julio` with name null

There are other operators that can be used to test character strings. These operators are summarized in Table 8-1.

TABLE 8-1. test string operators

Operator	Returns TRUE (exit status of 0) if
$string_1 = string_2$	$string_1$ is identical to $string_2$
$string_1 != string_2$	$string_1$ is *not* identical to $string_2$
$string$	$string$ is not null
-n $string$	$string$ is not null (and $string$ must be seen by test)
-z $string$	$string$ is null (and $string$ must be seen by test)

You've seen how the = operator is used. The != operator is similar, only it tests two strings for inequality. That is, the exit status from test is zero if the two strings are not equal, and nonzero if they are.

Let's look at three very similar examples.

```
$ day="monday"
$ test "$day" = monday
$ echo $?
0                                    True
$
```

The test command returns an exit status of 0 since the value of day is equal to the characters monday. Now look at the following:

```
$ day="monday "
$ test "$day" = monday
$ echo $?
1                                    False
$
```

Here we assigned the characters monday—*including the space character that immediately followed*—to day. Therefore, when the above test was made, test returned false since the characters "monday " were not identical to the characters "monday".

If you wanted these two values to be considered equal, then omitting the double quotes would have caused the shell to "eat up" the trailing space character and test would have never seen it:

```
$ day="monday "
$ test $day = monday
$ echo $?
0                                    True
$
```

Although this seems to violate our rule about always quoting shell variables that are arguments to `test`, it's okay to omit the quotes if you're sure that the variable is not null (and not composed entirely of whitespace characters).

You can test to see if a shell variable has a null value with the third operator listed in Table 8-1:

```
test "$day"
```

This will return true if `day` is not null and false if it is. Quotes are not necessary here since `test` doesn't care if it sees an argument in this case. Nevertheless you are better off using them here as well since if the variable consists entirely of whitespace characters, then the shell will get rid of the argument if not enclosed in quotes.

```
$ blanks="     "
$ test $blanks          Is it not null?
$ echo $?
1                       False—it's null
$ test "$blanks"        And now?
$ echo $?
0                       True—it's not null
$
```

In the first case, `test` was not passed *any* arguments since the shell ate up the four spaces in `blanks`. In the second case, `test` got one argument consisting of four space characters; obviously not null.

In case we seem to be belaboring the point about blanks and quotes, realize that this is a sticky area that is a frequent source of shell programming errors. It's good to really understand the principles here to save yourself a lot of programming headaches in the future.

There is another way to test to see if a string is null or not, and that's with either of the last two operators listed in the table. The -n operator returns an exit status of zero if the argument that follows is not null. Think of this operator as testing for nonzero length.

The -z operator tests the argument that follows to see if it is null, and returns an exit status of zero if it is. Think of this operator as testing to see if the following argument has zero length.

So the command

```
test -n "$day"
```

will return an exit status of 0 if day contains at least one character. The command

```
test -z "$dataflag"
```

will return an exit status of 0 if `dataflag` doesn't contain any characters.

Be forewarned that both of the above operators expect an argument to follow; therefore get into the habit of enclosing that argument inside double quotes.

```
$ nullvar=
$ nonnullvar=abc
$ test -n "$nullvar"                Does nullvar have nonzero length?
$ echo $?
1                                   No
$ test -n "$nonnullvar"             And what about nonnullvar?
$ echo $?
0                                   Yes
$ test -z "$nullvar"                Does nullvar have zero length?
$ echo $?
0                                   Yes
$ test -z "$nonnullvar"             And nonnullvar?
$ echo $?
1                                   No
$
```

You should note that `test` can be quite picky about its arguments. For example, if the shell variable `symbol` contains an equal sign, look at what happens if you try to test it for zero length:

```
$ echo $symbol
=
$ test -z "$symbol"
sh: test: argument expected
$
```

The `=` operator has higher precedence than the `-z` operator, so `test` expects an argument to follow. To avoid this sort of problem, you can write your command as

```
test X"$symbol" = X
```

which will be true if `symbol` is null, and false if it's not. The `X` in front of `symbol` prevents `test` from interpreting the characters stored in `symbol` as an operator.

An Alternate Format for `test`

The `test` command is used so often by shell programmers that an alternate format of the command is recognized. This format improves the readability of the command, especially when used in `if` commands.

You'll recall that the general format of the `test` command is

    test   *expression*

This can also be expressed in the alternate format as

    [*expression*]

The `[` is actually the name of the command (who said anything about command names having to be alphanumeric characters?). It still initiates execution of the same `test` command, only in this format, `test` expects to see a closing `]` at the end of the expression. Naturally, spaces must appear after the `[` and before the `]`.

You can rewrite the `test` command shown in a previous example with this alternate format as shown:

```
$ [ -z "$nonnullvar" ]
$ echo $?
1
$
```

When used in an `if` command, this alternate format looks like this:

```
if [ "$name" = julio ]
then
        echo "Would you like to play a game?"
fi
```

Which format of the `if` command you use is up to you; we prefer the `[...]` format, so that's what we'll use throughout the remainder of the book.

Integer Operators

`test` has an assortment of operators for performing integer comparisons. These operators are summarized in Table 8-2.

TABLE 8-2. test integer operators

Operator	Returns TRUE (exit status of 0) if
int_1 -eq int_2	int_1 is equal to int_2
int_1 -ge int_2	int_1 is greater than or equal to int_2
int_1 -gt int_2	int_1 is greater than int_2
int_1 -le int_2	int_1 is less than or equal to int_2
int_1 -lt int_2	int_1 is less than int_2
int_1 -ne int_2	int_1 is not equal to int_2

For example, the operator -eq tests to see if two integers are equal. So if you had a shell variable called count and you wanted to test to see if its value was equal to zero, you would write

```
[ "$count" -eq 0 ]
```

Other integer operators behave similarly, so

```
[ "$choice" -lt 5 ]
```

tests to see if the variable choice is less than 5; the command

```
[ "$index" -ne "$max" ]
```

tests to see if the value of index is not equal to the value of max; and, finally

```
[ "$#" -ne 0 ]
```

tests to see if the number of arguments passed to the command is not equal to zero.

Remember that the shell makes no distinction about the type of value stored in a variable; as far as it's concerned, it's just a bunch of characters. It is the test operator that interprets the value as an integer when an integer operator is used, and not the shell.

Let's reinforce the difference between test's string and integer operators by taking a look at a few examples.

```
$ x1="005"
$ x2="  10"
$ [ "$x1" = 5 ]                    String comparison
$ echo $?
1                                  False
$ [ "$x1" -eq 5 ]                  Integer comparison
$ echo $?
0                                  True
$ [ "$x2" = 10 ]                   String comparison
$ echo $?
1                                  False
$ [ "$x2" -eq 10 ]                 Integer comparison
$ echo $?
0                                  True
$
```

The first test

```
[ "$x1" = 5 ]
```

uses the string comparison operator = to test if the two strings are identical. They're not, since the first string is composed of the three characters 005 and the second the single character 5.

In the second test, the integer comparison operator -eq is used. Treating the two values as integers, 005 is equal to 5, as verified by the exit status returned by test.

The third and fourth tests are similar, only in this case you can see how even a leading space stored in the variable x2 can influence a test made with a string operator versus one made with an integer operator.

File Operators

Virtually every shell program deals with one or more files. For this reason, a wide assortment of operators are provided by test to enable you to ask various questions about files. Each of these operators is *unary* in nature, meaning they expect a single argument to follow. In all cases, this argument is the name of a file (and that includes a directory file, of course).

The commonly used file operators are listed in Table 8-3.

TABLE 8-3. Commonly used test file operators

Operator	Returns TRUE (exit status of 0) if
-d *file*	*file* is a directory
-f *file*	*file* is an ordinary file
-r *file*	*file* is readable by the process
-s *file*	*file* has nonzero length
-w *file*	*file* is writable by the process
-x *file*	*file* is executable

The command

```
[ -f /usr/steve/phonebook ]
```

will test to see if the file /usr/steve/phonebook exists and is an ordinary file (that is, is not a directory and not a special file).
The command

```
[ -r /usr/steve/phonebook ]
```

will test to see if the indicated file exists and is also readable by you.
The command

```
[ -s /usr/steve/phonebook ]
```

will test to see if the indicated file contains at least one byte of information in it. This is useful, for example, if you create an error log file in your program and you want to test to see if anything was written to it:

```
if [ -s $ERRFILE ]
then
        echo "Errors found:"
        cat $ERRFILE
fi
```

There are a few more test operators which, when combined with the previously described operators, enable you to make more complex types of tests.

The Logical Negation Operator !

The unary logical negation operator ! can be placed in front of any other test expression to *negate* the result of the evaluation of that expression. For example,

```
[ ! -r /usr/steve/phonebook ]
```

will return a zero exit status (true) if /usr/steve/phonebook is *not* readable; and

```
[ ! -f "$mailfile" ]
```

will return true if the file specified by $mailfile does *not* exist or is not an ordinary file. Finally,

```
[ ! "$x1" = "$x2" ]
```

will return true if $x1 is not identical to $x2, and is obviously equivalent to

```
[ "$x1" != "$x2" ]
```


The Logical AND Operator −a

The operator −a performs a logical *AND* of two expressions and will return true only if the two joined expressions are both true. So

```
[ -f "$mailfile"  -a  -r "$mailfile" ]
```

will return true if the file specified by $mailfile is an ordinary file and is readable by you. An extra space was place around the −a operator to aid in the expression's readability, and obviously has no effect on its execution.

The command

```
[ "$count" -ge 0  -a  "$count" -lt 10 ]
```

will be true if the variable count contains an integer value that is greater than or equal to zero but less than 10. The −a operator has lower *precedence* than the integer comparison operators (and the string and file operators, for that matter), meaning that the above expression gets evaluated as

```
("$count" -ge 0) -a ("$count" -lt 10)
```

as you would expect.

Parentheses

Incidentally, you *can* use parentheses in a `test` expression to alter the order of evaluation; just make sure that the parentheses are quoted since they have a special meaning to the shell. So to translate the above into a `test` command, you would write

```
[ \( "$count" -ge 0 \) -a \( "$count" -lt 10 \) ]
```

As is typical, spaces must surround the parentheses, since `test` expects to see them as separate arguments.

The Logical OR Operator -o

The `-o` operator is similar to the `-a` operator, only it forms a logical *OR* of two expressions. That is, evaluation of the expression will be true if *either* the first expression is true or the second expression is true.

```
[ -n "$mailopt"  -o  -r $HOME/mailfile ]
```

This command will be true if the variable `mailopt` is not null *or* if the file `$HOME/mailfile` is readable by you.

The `-o` operator has lower precedence than the `-a` operator, meaning that the expression

```
"$a" -eq 0  -o  "$b" -eq 2  -a "$c" -eq 10
```

gets evaluated by `test` as

```
"$a" -eq 0  -o  ("$b" -eq 2  -a "$c" -eq 10)
```

Naturally, you can use parentheses to change this order if necessary:

```
\( "$a" -eq 0  -o  "$b" -eq 2  \) -a "$c" -eq 10
```

You will see many uses of the `test` command throughout the book. Table A-9 in Appendix A summarizes all of the `test` operators that are available.

◆ The `else` Construct ◆

A construct known as the `else` can be added to the `if` command, with the general format as shown:

```
if command_t
then
        command
        command
        . . .
else
        command
        command
        . . .
fi
```

Execution of this form of the command starts as before; *command_t* is executed and its exit status tested. If it's zero, then the commands that follow between the then and the else are executed, and the commands between the else and fi are skipped. Otherwise, the exit status is nonzero and the commands between the then and else are skipped and the commands between the else and fi are executed. In either case, only one set of commands gets executed: the first set if the exit status is zero, and the second set if it's nonzero.

Let's now write a modified version of on. Instead of printing nothing if the requested user is not logged on, we'll have the program print a message to that effect. Here is version 3 of the program.

```
$ cat on
#
# determine if someone is logged on   -- version 3
#

user="$1"

if who | grep "^$user " > /dev/null
then
        echo "$user is logged on"
else
        echo "$user is not logged on"
fi
$
```

If the user specified as the first argument to on is logged on, then the grep will succeed and the message $user is logged on will be displayed; otherwise the message $user is not logged on will be displayed.

```
$ who                                          Who's on?
root        console  Jul  8 10:37
barney      tty03    Jul  8 12:38
fred        tty04    Jul  8 13:40
joanne      tty07    Jul  8 09:35
tony        tty19    Jul  8 08:30
lulu        tty23    Jul  8 09:55
$ on pat
pat is not logged on
$ on tony
tony is logged on
$
```

Another nice touch when writing shell programs is to check to make sure that the correct number of arguments is passed to the program. If an incorrect number is supplied, then an error message to that effect can be displayed, together with information on the proper usage of the program.

```
$ cat on
#
# determine if someone is logged on  -- version 4
#


#
# see if the correct number of arguments were supplied
#

if [ "$#" -ne 1 ]
then
        echo "Incorrect number of arguments"
        echo "Usage:  on  user"
else
        user="$1"

        if who | grep "^$user " > /dev/null
        then
                echo "$user is logged on"
        else
                echo "$user is not logged on"
        fi
fi
$
```

Compare this program with the previous version and note the changes that were made. An additional `if` command was added to test to see if the correct number of arguments were supplied. If `$#` is not equal to 1, then the program prints two messages; otherwise the commands after the else clause are executed. These commands are the same as appeared in the last version of on: they assign $1 to user and then see if user is logged on, printing a message in either case. Note that two fis are required, since there are two if commands used.

The indentation that is used goes a long way towards aiding the program's readability. Make sure you get into the habit of setting and following indentation rules in your programs.

```
$ on                                    No arguments
Incorrect number of arguments
Usage:  on  user
$ on priscilla                          One argument
priscilla is not logged on
$ on jo anne                            Two arguments
Incorrect number of arguments
Usage:  on  user
$
```

◆ The exit Command ◆

A built-in shell command called exit enables you to immediately terminate execution of your shell program. The general format of this command is

```
exit n
```

where *n* is the exit status that you want returned. If none is specified, then the exit status used is that of the last command executed before the exit.

Be advised that executing the exit command directly from your terminal will log you off the system, since it will have the effect of terminating execution of your login shell.

A Second Look at the rem Program

exit is frequently used as a convenient way to terminate execution of a shell program. For example, let's take another look at the rem program, which removes an entry from the phonebook file:

```
$ cat rem
#
# Remove someone from the phone book
#

grep -v "$1" phonebook > /tmp/phonebook
mv /tmp/phonebook phonebook
$
```

This program has the potential to do unintended things to the phonebook file. For example, suppose you type in

```
rem Susan Topple
```

Here the shell will pass two arguments to rem. The rem program will end up removing all Susan entries, as specified by $1.

It's always best to take precautions with a potentially destructive program like rem and to be certain as possible that the action intended by the user is consistent with the action that the program is taking.

One of the first checks that can be made in rem is for the correct number of arguments, as was done before with the on program. This time, we'll use the exit command to terminate the program if the correct number of arguments aren't supplied:

```
$ cat rem
#
# Remove someone from the phone book -- version 2
#

if [ "$#" -ne 1 ]
then
        echo "Incorrect number of arguments."
        echo "Usage: rem name"
        exit 1
fi

grep -v "$1" phonebook > /tmp/phonebook
mv /tmp/phonebook phonebook
$ rem Susan Goldberg            Try it out
Incorrect number of arguments.
Usage: rem name
$
```

The `exit` command returns an exit status of 1, to signal "failure," in case some other program wants to check it. How could you have written the above program with an `if-else` instead of using the `exit` (hint: look at the last version of `on`)?

Whether you use the `exit` or an `if-else` is up to you. Sometimes the `exit` is a more convenient way to get out of the program quickly, particularly if it's done early in the program.

◆ The `elif` Construct ◆

As your programs become more complex, you may find yourself needing to write nested `if` statements of the form:

```
if command₁
then
        command
        command
        . . .
else
        if command₂
        then
                command
                command
                . . .
        else
                . . .
                        if commandₙ
                        then
                                command
                                command
                                . . .
                        else
                                command
                                command
                                . . .
                        fi
                . . .
        fi
fi
```

This type of command sequence is useful when you need to make more than just a two way decision as afforded by the `if-else` construct. In this case, a multi-way decision is made, with the last `else` clause executed if none of the preceding conditions is satisfied.

As an example, suppose you wanted to write a program called greet-ings that would print a friendly "Good morning," "Good afternoon," or "Good evening" whenever you logged onto the system. For purposes of the example, consider any time from midnight to noon to be the morning, noon to 6 pm the afternoon, and 6 pm to midnight the evening.

In order to write this program, you have to find out what time it is.   date serves just fine for this purpose. Take another look at the output from this command:

```
$ date
Fri Jul 19 10:16:07 EDT 1985
$
```

The format of date's output is fixed, a fact that you can use to your advantage when writing greetings since this means that the time will always appear in character positions 12 through 19. Actually, for this program, you really only need the hour that is displayed in positions 12 and 13. So to get the hour from date you can write

```
$ date | cut -c12-13
10
$
```

Now the task of writing the greetings program is straightforward:

```
$ cat greetings
#
# Program to print a greeting
#

hour=`date | cut -c12-13`

if [ "$hour" -ge 0  -a  "$hour" -le 11 ]
then
        echo "Good morning"
else
        if [ "$hour" -ge 12  -a  "$hour" -le 17 ]
        then
                echo "Good afternoon"
        else
                echo "Good evening"
        fi
fi
$
```

If `hour` is greater than or equal to 0 (midnight) and less than or equal to 11 (up to 11:59:59) then "Good morning" is displayed; otherwise, if `hour` is greater than or equal to 12 (noon) and less than or equal to 17 (up to 5:59:59 pm) then "Good afternoon" is displayed; otherwise, neither of the preceding two conditions were satisfied so "Good evening" is displayed.

```
$ greetings
Good morning
$
```

As noted, the nested `if` command sequence used in `greetings` is so common that a special `elif` construct is available to more easily express this sequence. The general format of this construct is:

```
if command₁
then
            command
            command
            . . .
elif command₂
then
            command
            command
            . . .

. . .
elif commandₙ
then
            command
            command
            . . .
else
            command
            command
            . . .
fi
```

$command_1$, $command_2$, ... $command_n$ are executed in turn and their exit statuses tested. As soon as one returns an exit status of zero, the commands listed after the `then` that follows are executed up to another `elif`, `else`, or `fi`. If none of the commands returns a zero exit status, then the commands listed after the optional `else` are executed.

You could rewrite the `greetings` program using this new format as shown:

```
$ cat greetings
#
# Program to print a greeting -- version 2
#

hour=`date | cut -c12-13`

if [ "$hour" -ge 0  -a  "$hour" -le 11 ]
then
        echo "Good morning"
elif [ "$hour" -ge 12  -a  "$hour" -le 17 ]
then
        echo "Good afternoon"
else
        echo "Good evening"
fi
$
```

This version is easier to read, and it doesn't have the tendency to disappear off the right margin due to excessive indentation. Incidentally, you should note that date provides a wide assortment of options. One of these, %H, can be used to get the hour directly from date:

```
$ date +%H
10
$
```

As an exercise, you should change greetings to make use of this fact.

Yet Another Version of rem

Another way to add some robustness to the rem program would be to check the *number* of entries that matched before doing the removal. If there's more than one match, then you could issue a message to the effect and then terminate execution of the program. But how do you determine the number of matching entries? One approach is to do a normal grep on the phonebook file and then count the number of matches that come out with wc. If the number of matches is greater than one, then the appropriate message can be issued.

```
$ cat rem
#
# Remove someone from the phone book -- version 3
#

if [ "$#" -ne 1 ]
then
        echo "Incorrect number of arguments."
        echo "Usage: rem name"
        exit 1
fi

name=$1

#
# Find number of matching entries
#

matches=`grep "$name" phonebook | wc -l`

#
# If more than one match, issue message, else remove it
#

if [ "$matches" -gt 1 ]
then
        echo "More than one match; please qualify further"
elif [ "$matches" -eq 1 ]
then
        grep -v "$name" phonebook > /tmp/phonebook
        mv /tmp/phonebook phonebook
else
        echo "I couldn't find $name in the phone book"
fi
$
```

The positional parameter $1 is assigned to the variable name after the number of arguments check is performed to add readability to the program. Subsequently using $name is a lot clearer than using $1.

The if...elif...else command first checks to see if the number of matches is greater than one. If it is, then the "More than one match" message is printed. If it's not, then a test is made to see if the number of matches is equal to one. If it is, then the entry is removed from the phone book. If it's not, then the number of matches must be zero, in which case a message is displayed to alert the user of this fact.

Note that the `grep` command is used twice in this program: first to determine the number of matches, and then with the `-v` option to remove the single matching entry.

Here's some sample runs of the third version of `rem`:

```
$ rem
Incorrect number of arguments.
Usage: rem name
$ rem Susan
More than one match; please further qualify
$ rem 'Susan Topple'
$ rem 'Susan Topple'
I couldn't find Susan Topple in the phone book  She's history
$
```

Now you have a fairly robust `rem` program: it checks for the correct number of arguments, printing the proper usage if the correct number isn't supplied; it also checks to make sure precisely one entry is removed from the `phonebook` file.

◆ The case Command ◆

The `case` command allows you to compare a single value against other values and to execute one or more commands when a match is found. The general format of this command is

```
case value in
      pat₁ )    command
                command

                . . .

                command; ;
      pat₂ )    command
                command

                . . .

                command; ;

      . . .
      patₙ )    command
                command

                . . .

                command; ;
esac
```

The word *value* is successively compared against the values pat_1, pat_2, ..., pat_n, until a match is found. When a match is found, the commands listed after the matching value, up to the double semicolons, are executed. Once the double semicolons are reached, execution of the case is terminated. If a match is not found, then none of the commands listed in the case are executed.

As an example of the use of the case, the following program called number takes a single digit and translates it to its English equivalent:

```
$ cat number
#
# Translate a digit to English
#

if [ "$#" -ne 1 ]
then
        echo "Usage:  number  digit"
        exit 1
fi

case "$1"
in
        0)  echo zero;;
        1)  echo one;;
        2)  echo two;;
        3)  echo three;;
        4)  echo four;;
        5)  echo five;;
        6)  echo six;;
        7)  echo seven;;
        8)  echo eight;;
        9)  echo nine;;
esac
$
```

Now to test it:

```
$ number 0
zero
$ number 3
three
$ number                          Try no arguments
Usage:  number  digit
$ number 17                       Try a two-digit number
$
```

The last case shows what happens when you type in more than one digit: $1 doesn't match any of the values listed in the case, so none of the echo commands is executed.

Special Pattern Matching Characters

The shell lets you use the same special characters for specifying the patterns in a case as you can with file name substitution. That is, ? can be used to specify any single character; * can be used to specify zero or more occurrences of any character; and [...] can be used to specify any single character enclosed between the brackets.

Since the pattern * matches *anything* (just as when it's used for file name substitution it matches all of the files in your directory), it's frequently used at the very end of the case as the "catchall" value. That is, if none of the previous values in the case match, then this one's guaranteed to match. Here's a second version of the number program that has such a catchall case.

```
$ cat number
#
# Translate a digit to English -- version 2
#

if [ "$#" -ne 1 ]
then
        echo "Usage:  number  digit"
        exit 1
fi

case "$1"
in
        0)  echo zero;;
        1)  echo one;;
        2)  echo two;;
        3)  echo three;;
        4)  echo four;;
        5)  echo five;;
        6)  echo six;;
        7)  echo seven;;
        8)  echo eight;;
        9)  echo nine;;
        *)  echo "Bad argument; please specify a single digit";;
esac
$ number 9
nine
$ number 99
Bad argument; please specify a single digit
$
```

Here's another program called ctype that prints the type of the single character given as an argument. Character types recognized are digits, uppercase letters, lowercase letters, and special characters (anything not in the first three categories). As an added check, the program makes sure that just a single character is given as the argument.

```
$ cat ctype
#
# Classify character given as argument
#

if [ $# -ne 1 ]
then
        echo Usage: ctype  char
        exit 1
fi


#
# Ensure that only one character was typed
#

char="$1"
numchars=`echo "$char" | wc -c`

if [ "$numchars" -ne 1 ]
then
        echo Please type a single character
        exit 1
fi


#
# Now classify it
#

case "$char"
in
        [0-9] )    echo digit;;
        [a-z] )    echo lowercase letter;;
        [A-Z] )    echo uppercase letter;;
        *     )    echo special character;;
esac
$
```

Some sample runs:

```
$ ctype a
Please type a single character
$ ctype 7
Please type a single character
$
```

The −x Option for Debugging Programs

Something seems to be amiss. The counting portion of our program doesn't seem to be working properly. This seems like a good point to introduce the shell's −x option. You can trace the execution of any program by typing in sh −x followed by the name of the program and its arguments. This starts up a new shell to execute the indicated program with the −x option enabled. In this mode, commands are printed at the terminal as they are executed, preceded by a plus sign (variable assignments aren't preceded by a plus sign). Let's try it out.

```
$ sh -x ctype a                      Trace execution
+ [ 1 -ne 1 ]                        $# equals 1
char=a                               Assignment of $1 to char
+ echo a
+ wc -c
numchars=        2                   wc returned 2???
+ [        2 -ne 1 ]                 That's why this test succeeded
+ echo Please type a single character
Please type a single character
+ exit 1
$
```

The trace output indicates that wc returned 2 when

```
echo "$char" | wc -c
```

was executed. But why? There seemed to be only one character in wc's input. The truth of the matter is that two characters were actually given to wc: the single character a and the "invisible" newline character that echo automatically prints at the end of each line. So the program really should be testing for the number of characters equal to two: the character typed plus the newline added by echo.

Go back to the ctype program and replace the if command that reads

```
if [ "$numchars" -ne 1 ]
then
        echo Please type a single character
        exit 1
fi
```

with

```
if [ "$numchars" -ne 2 ]
then
        echo Please type a single character
        exit 1
fi
```

and try it again.

```
$ ctype a
lowercase letter
$ ctype abc
Please type a single character
$ ctype 9
digit
$ ctype K
uppercase letter
$ ctype :
special character
$ ctype
Usage: ctype  char
$
```

Now it seems to work just fine.

Later you'll learn how you can turn this trace feature on and off at will from *inside* your program.

Before leaving the ctype program, here's a version that avoids the use of wc and handles everything with the case:

```
$ cat ctype
#
# Classify character given as argument -- version 2
#

if [ $# -ne 1 ]
then
        echo Usage: ctype  char
        exit  1
fi

#
# Now classify char, making sure only one was typed
#

char=$1

case "$char"
in
        [0-9] )    echo digit;;
        [a-z] )    echo lowercase letter;;
        [A-Z] )    echo uppercase letter;;
        ?     )    echo special character;;
        *     )    echo Please type a single character;;
esac
$
```

The ? matches any single character. If this pattern is matched, then the character is a special character. If this pattern isn't matched, then more than one character was typed, so the catchall case is executed to print the message.

```
$ ctype u
lowercase letter
$ ctype '>'
special character
$ ctype xx
Please type a single character
$
```

Back to the `case`

The symbol | has the effect of a logical OR when used between two patterns. That is, the pattern

$$pat_1 \mid pat_2$$

specifies that either pat_1 or pat_2 is to be matched. For example,

```
-l | -list
```

will match either the value -l or -list; and

```
dmd | 5620 | tty5620
```

will match either dmd or 5620 or tty5620.

The greetings program that you saw earlier in this chapter can be rewritten to use a case statement instead of the if-elif. Here is such a version of the program. This time, advantage was taken of the fact that date with the +%H option writes a two-digit hour to standard output.

```
$ cat greetings
#
# Program to print a greeting -- case version
#

hour=`date +%H`


case "$hour"
in
        0? | 1[01] )    echo "Good morning";;
        1[2-7]     )    echo "Good afternoon";;
        *          )    echo "Good evening";;
esac
$
```

The two-digit hour obtained from date is assigned to the shell variable hour. Then the case statement is executed. The value of hour is compared against the first pattern:

```
0? | 1[01]
```

which matches any value that starts with a zero followed by any character (midnight through 9 am), or any value that starts with a one and is followed by a zero or one (10 or 11 am).

The second pattern

```
1[2-7]
```

matches a value that starts with a one and is followed by any one of the digits two through seven (noon through 5 pm).

The last case, the catchall, matches anything else (6 pm through 11 pm).

```
$ date
Fri Jul 19 15:07:48 EDT 1985
$ greetings
Good afternoon
$
```

◆ The Null Command : ◆

This seems about as good a time as any to talk about the shell's built-in *null* command. The format of this command is simply

```
:
```

and the purpose of it is—you guessed it—to do nothing. So what is it good for? Well, in most cases it's used to satisfy the requirement that a command appear, particularly in if commands. Suppose you want to check to make sure that the value stored in the variable system exists in the file /usr/steve/mail/systems, and if it doesn't you want to issue an error message and exit from the program. So you start by writing something like

```
if grep "^$system " /usr/steve/mail/systems > /dev/null
then
```

but you don't know what to write after the then, since you want to test for the nonexistence of the system in the file and don't want to do anything special if the grep succeeds. Unfortunately, the shell requires that you write a command after the then. Here's where the null command comes to the rescue:

```
if grep "^$system " /usr/steve/mail/systems > /dev/null
then
        :
else
        echo "$system is not a valid system"
        exit 1
fi
```

So if the system is valid, nothing is done. If it's not valid, the error message is issued and the program exited.

Remember this simple command when these types of situations arise.

◆ The && and || Constructs ◆

The shell has two special constructs that enable you to execute a command based upon whether the preceding command succeeds or fails. In case you think this sounds similar to the `if` command, well it is. It's sort of a shorthand form of the `if`.

If you write

$command_1$ && $command_2$

anywhere where the shell expects to see a command, then $command_1$ will be executed, and if it returns an exit status of zero, then $command_2$ will be executed. If $command_1$ returns an exit status of nonzero, then $command_2$ gets skipped.

For example, if you write

```
sort bigdata > /tmp/sortout  &&  mv /tmp/sortout bigdata
```

then the `mv` command will be executed only if the `sort` is successful. Note that this is equivalent to writing

```
if sort bigdata > /tmp/sortout
then
        mv /tmp/sortout bigdata
fi
```

The command

```
[ -z "$EDITOR" ]  &&  EDITOR=/bin/ed
```

tests the value of the variable `EDITOR`. If it's null, then `/bin/ed` is assigned to it.

The `||` construct works similarly, only the second command gets executed only if the exit status of the first is nonzero. So if you write

```
grep "$name" phonebook  ||  echo "Couldn't find $name"
```

then the `echo` command will get executed only if the `grep` fails (i.e., if it couldn't find `$name` in `phonebook`, or if it couldn't open the file `phonebook`). In this case, the equivalent `if` command would look like

```
if grep "$name" phonebook
then
        :
else
        echo "Couldn't find $name"
fi
```

You can write a pipeline on either the left or right-hand sides of these constructs. On the left, the exit status tested is that of the last command in the pipeline; thus

```
who | grep "^$name " > /dev/null ||  echo "$name's not logged on"
```

will cause execution of the echo if the grep fails.

The && and || can also be combined on the same command line:

```
who | grep "^$name " > /dev/null  &&  echo "$name is logged on" \
    ||  echo "$name's not logged on"
```

(Recall that when \ is used at the end of the line it signals line continuation to the shell.) The first echo gets executed if the grep succeeds, the second if it fails.

These constructs are also often used in if commands:

```
if validsys "$sys"  &&  timeok
then
        sendmail "$sys!$user" < $message
fi
```

If validsys returns an exit status of zero, then timeok is executed. The exit status from this program is then tested for the if. If it's zero, then the sendmail program is executed. If validsys returns a nonzero exit status, then timeok is not executed, and this is used as the exit status that is tested by the if. In that case, sendmail won't be executed.

The use of the && operator in the above case is like a "logical AND"; both programs must return an exit status of zero in order for the sendmail program to be executed. In fact, you could have even written the above if as

```
validsys "$sys"  &&  timeok  &&  sendmail "$sys!$user" < $message
```

When the || is used in an if, the effect is like a "logical OR":

```
if endofmonth || specialrequest
then
        sendreports
fi
```

If `endofmonth` returns a zero exit status, then `sendreports` is executed; otherwise `specialrequest` is executed and if its exit status is zero, `sendreports` is executed. The net effect is that `sendreports` is executed if `endofmonth` or `specialrequest` return an exit status of zero.

In the next chapter you'll learn about how to write loops in your programs. However, before proceeding to that chapter, try the exercises that follow.

◆ Exercises ◆

1. Write a program called `valid` that prints "yes" if its argument is a valid shell variable name and "no" otherwise:

   ```
   $ valid foo_bar
   yes
   $ valid 123
   no
   $
   ```

   (Hint: define a regular expression for a valid variable name and then enlist the aid of `grep` or `sed`.)

2. Write a program called `t` that displays the time of day in am or pm notation, rather than in 24-hour clock time. Here's an example showing `t` run at night:

   ```
   $ date
   Thu Sep  5 19:21:46 EDT 1985
   $ t
   7:21 pm
   $
   ```

   Use `expr` to convert from 24-hour clock time. Then rewrite the program to use a case command instead.

3. Write a program called `mysed` that applies the `sed` script given as the first argument against the file given as the second. If the `sed` succeeds (i.e., exit status of zero), then replace the original file with the modified one. So

   ```
   mysed '1,10d' text
   ```

   will use `sed` to delete the first 10 lines from `text`, and if successful, will replace `text` with the modified file.

4. Write a program called `isyes` that returns an exit status of 0 if its argument is "yes," and 1 otherwise. For purposes of this exercise, consider `y`, `yes`, `Yes`, `YES`, and `Y` all to be valid "yes" arguments:

```
$ isyes yes
$ echo $?
0
$ isyes no
$ echo $?
1
```

Write the program using an if command, and then rewrite it using a case command. This program can be useful when reading yes/no responses from the terminal (which you'll learn about in Chapter 10).

5. Use the date and who commands to write a program called conntime that prints the number of hours and minutes that a user has been logged on to the system (assume that this is less than 24 hours).

´Round and ´Round She Goes

I n this chapter you'll learn how to set up program loops. These loops will enable you to execute repeatedly a set of commands either a specified number of times or until some condition is met. There are three built-in looping commands; they are

1. the `for`;

2. the `while`; and

3. the `until`.

You'll learn about each one of these loops in separate sections of this chapter.

◆ The `for` Command ◆

The `for` command is used to execute a set of commands a specified number of times. Its basic format is as shown:

```
for var in word₁ word₂ ... wordₙ
do
          command
          command
          . . .
done
```

The commands enclosed between the `do` and the `done` form what's known as the *body* of the loop. These commands are executed for as many words as you have listed after the `in`. When the loop is executed, the first word, *word₁*, is assigned to the variable *var* and the body of the loop is then executed. Next, the second word in the list, *word₂*, is assigned to *var* and the body of the loop is executed. This process continues, with successive words in the list being assigned to *var* and the commands in the loop body executed until the last word in the list, *wordₙ*, is assigned to *var* and the body of the loop executed. At that point, there are no words left in the list, and execution of the for command is then finished. Execution then continues with the command that immediately follows the done. So if there are *n* words listed after the in, then the body of the loop will have been executed a total of *n* times after the loop has finished.

Here's a loop that will be executed a total of three times:

```
for i in 1 2 3
do
        echo $i
done
```

To try it out, you can type this in directly at the terminal, just like any other shell command:

```
$ for i in 1 2 3
> do
>         echo $i
> done
1
2
3
$
```

While the shell is waiting for the done to be typed to close off the for command it displays your secondary command prompt. Once it gets the done the shell then proceeds to execute the loop. Since there are three words listed after the in (1, 2, and 3), the body of the loop—in this case a single echo command—will be executed a total of three times.

The first time through the loop, the first word in the list, 1, is assigned to the variable i. Then the body of the loop is executed. This displays the value of i at the terminal. Then the next word in the list, 2, is assigned to i and the echo command reexecuted, resulting in the display of 2 at the terminal. The third word in the list, 3, is assigned to i the third time through the loop and the echo command executed. This results in 3 being displayed at the terminal. At that point there are no more words left in the list, so execution of the for command is then complete, and the shell displays your command prompt to let you know it's done.

Recall the run program from Chapter 7 that enabled you to run a file through tbl, nroff, and lp:

```
$ cat run
tbl $1 | nroff -mm -Tlp | lp
$
```

If you wanted to run the files memo1 through memo4 through this program, you could type the following at the terminal:

```
$ for file in memo1 memo2 memo3 memo4
> do
>            run $file
> done
request id is laser1-33 (standard input)
request id is laser1-34 (standard input)
request id is laser1-35 (standard input)
request id is laser1-36 (standard input)
$
```

The four words memo1, memo2, memo3, and memo4 will be assigned to the variable file in order, and the run program executed with the value of this variable as the argument. Execution will be just as if you typed in the four commands

```
$ run memo1
request id is laser1-33 (standard input)
$ run memo2
request id is laser1-34 (standard input)
$ run memo3
request id is laser1-35 (standard input)
$ run memo4
request id is laser1-36 (standard input)
$
```

Incidentally, the shell permits file name substitution in the list of words in the for, meaning that the previous loop could have also been written

```
for file in memo[1-4]
do
        run $file
done
```

And if you wanted to run all of the files in your current directory through run, you could type

```
for file in *
do
        run $file
done
```

If the file `filelist` contains a list of the files that you want to run through `run`, then you can type

```
files=`cat filelist`

for file in $files
do
        run $file
done
```

to run each of the files, or, more succinctly,

```
for file in `cat filelist`
do
        run $file
done
```

If you found that you were using the `run` program often to process several files at once, then you could go inside the `run` program and modify it to allow any number of files to be passed as arguments to the program.

```
$ cat run
#
# process files through nroff -- version 2
#

for file in $*
do
        tbl $file | nroff -mm -Tlp | lp
done
$
```

You'll recall that the special shell variable `$*` stands for *all* of the arguments typed on the command line. So if you executed the new version of `run` by typing

```
run memo1 memo2 memo3 memo4
```

then the `$*` in the `for`'s list would be replaced by the four arguments `memo1`, `memo2`, `memo3`, and `memo4`. Of course, you could also type

```
run memo[1-4]
```

to achieve the same results.

The $@ Variable

While we're on the subject of $*, let's look at it in a bit more detail. We'll write a program called args that displays all of the arguments typed on the command line, one per line.

```
$ cat args
echo Number of arguments passed is $#

for arg in $*
do
        echo $arg
done
$
```

Now to try it:

```
$ args a b c
Number of arguments passed is 3
a
b
c
$ args 'a b' c
Number of arguments passed is 2
a
b
c
$
```

In the second case, even though a b was passed as a single argument to args, the $* in the for command was replaced by the shell with a b c, which is three words. Thus the loop was executed three times.

Whereas the shell replaces the value of $* with $1, $2, ..., if you instead use the special shell variable "$@" it will be replaced with "$1", "$2", ... The double quotes are necessary around $@, as without them this variable behaves just like $*.

Go back to the args program and replace the $* with "$@":

```
$ cat args
echo Number of arguments passed is $#

for arg in "$@"
do
        echo $arg
done
$
```

Now try it:

```
$ args a b c
Number of arguments passed is 3
a
b
c
$ args 'a b' c
Number of arguments passed is 2
a b
c
$ args                          Try it with no arguments
Number of arguments passed is 0
$
```

In the last case, no arguments were passed to the program. So the variable "$@" was replaced by *nothing*. The net result is that the body of the loop was not executed at all.

The for without the List

A special notation is recognized by the shell when writing for commands. If you write

```
for var
do
        command
        command
        . . .
done
```

(note the absence of the in) then the shell will automatically sequence through all of the arguments typed on the command line, just as if you had written

```
for var in  "$@"
do
        command
        command
        . . .
done
```

Here's the third and last version of the `args` program:

```
$ cat args
echo Number of arguments passed is $#

for arg
do
        echo $arg
done
$ args a b c
Number of arguments passed is 3
a
b
c
$ args 'a b' c
Number of arguments passed is 2
a b
c
$
```

♦ The `while` Command ♦

The second type of looping command to be described in this chapter is the `while`. The format of this command is

```
while command_t
do
        command
        command
        . . .
done
```

$command_t$ is executed and its exit status tested. If it's zero, then the commands enclosed between the `do` and `done` are executed. Then $command_t$ is executed again and its exit status tested. If it's zero, then the commands enclosed between the `do` and `done` are once again executed. This process continues until *command*ₜ returns a nonzero exit status. At that point execution of the loop is terminated. Execution then proceeds with the command that follows the done.

Note that the commands between the do and done might never be executed if *command*ₜ returns a nonzero exit status the first time it's executed.

Here's a program called twhile that simply counts to 5:

```
$ cat twhile
i=1

while [ "$i" -le 5 ]
do
        echo $i
        i=`expr $i + 1`
done
$ twhile                              Run it
1
2
3
4
5
$
```

The variable i is used as the counting variable and is initially set equal to 1. Then the while loop is entered. It continues execution as long as i is less than or equal to 5. Inside the loop, the value of i is displayed at the terminal. Then expr is used to add one to it.

The while loop is often used in conjunction with the shift command to process a variable number of arguments typed on the command line. The next program, called prargs, prints each of the command-line arguments one per line.

```
$ cat prargs
#
# Print command line arguments one per line
#

while [ "$#" -ne 0 ]
do
        echo "$1"
        shift
done
$ prargs a b c
a
b
c
$ prargs 'a b' c
```

```
a b
c
$ prargs *
addresses
intro
lotsaspaces
names
nu
numbers
phonebook
stat
$ prargs                              No arguments
$
```

While the number of arguments is not equal to zero, the value of $1 is displayed, and then a shift executed. Recall that this shifts down the variables (i.e., $2 to $1, $3 to $2, and so on) and also decrements $#. When the last argument has been displayed and shifted out, $# will equal zero, at which point execution of the while will be terminated. Note that if no arguments are given to prargs (as was done in the last case), then the echo and shift are never executed since $# is equal to zero as soon as the loop is entered.

♦ The until Command ♦

The while command continues execution as long as the command listed after the while returns a zero exit status. The until command is similar to the while, only it continues execution as long as the command that follows the until returns a *nonzero* exit status. As soon as a zero exit status is returned, the loop is terminated. Here is the general format of the until:

```
until command_t
do
        command
        command
        . . .
done
```

Like the while, the commands between the do and done might never be executed if *command*_t returns a zero exit status the first time it's executed.

The until command is useful for writing programs that are waiting for a particular event to occur. For example, suppose you want to see if sandy is logged on because you have to give her something important. You could send her electronic mail, but you know that she usually doesn't get around to reading her mail until late in the day. One approach is to use the on program from Chapter 8 to see if sandy's logged on:

```
$ on sandy
sandy is not logged on
$
```

You could execute this program periodically throughout the day, until sandy eventually logs on, or you could write your own program to continually check until she does. Let's call the program mon and have it take a single argument: the name of the user you want to monitor. Instead of having the program continually check for that user logging on, we'll have it check only once every minute. In order to do this, you have to know about a command called sleep that suspends execution of a program for a specified number of seconds. So the UNIX command (this isn't a shell built-in)

```
    sleep n
```

suspends execution of the program for *n* seconds. At the end of that interval, the program resumes execution where it left off—with the command that immediately follows the sleep.

```
$ cat mon
#
# Wait until a specified user logs on
#

if [ "$#" -ne 1 ]
then
        echo "Usage: mon  user"
        exit 1
fi

user="$1"

#
# Check every minute for user logging on
#

until who | grep "^$user " > /dev/null
do
        sleep 60
done

#
# When we reach this point, the user has logged on
#
```

```
echo "$user has logged on"
$
```

After checking that one argument was provided, the program assigns $1 to user. Then an until loop is entered. This loop will be executed until the exit status returned by grep is zero; i.e., until the specified user logs on. As long as the user isn't logged on, the body of the loop—the sleep command—is executed. This command suspends execution of the program for one minute (60 seconds). At the end of the minute, the pipeline listed after the until is reexecuted and the process repeated.

When the until loop is exited—signaling that the monitored user has logged on—a message is displayed at the terminal to that effect.

```
$ mon sandy                            Time passes
sandy has logged on
$
```

Using the program as shown above is not very practical since it ties up your terminal until sandy logs on. A better idea is to run mon in the background so that you can use your terminal for other work:

```
$ mon sandy &                          Run it in the background
4392                                   Process id
$ nroff newmemo                        Do other work
  . . .
sandy has logged on                    Happens sometime later
```

So now you can do other work and the mon program will continue executing in the background until sandy logs on, or until you log off the system.[†]

Since mon only checks once per minute for the user's logging on, it won't be hogging the system's resources while it's running (an important consideration when submitting programs to the background for execution).

Unfortunately, once the specified user logs on, there's a chance you might miss that one line message (you may be cating a file and might not even notice it come and go right off your screen); also if you're editing a file with a screen editor like vi when the message comes, it may turn your screen into a mess, and you still might miss the message. A better alternative to writing the message to the terminal might be to mail it instead. Actually, you can let the user select his or her preference by adding an option to the program that, if selected, will indicate that the message is to be mailed. If the option is not selected, then the message can be displayed at the terminal.

[†] All of your processes are automatically terminated when you log off the system. If you want a program to continue executing after you've logged off, you can run it with the nohup command, or schedule it to run with at or from the cron. Consult your *UNIX User's Manual* for more details.

In the version of mon that follows, a −m option has been added for this
purpose.

```
$ cat mon
#
# Wait until a specified user logs on -- version 2
#

if [ "$1" = -m ]
then
        mailopt=TRUE
        shift
else
        mailopt=FALSE
fi

if [ "$#" -eq  0  -o  "$#" -gt 1  ]
then
        echo "Usage: mon  [-m] user"
        echo "        -m means to be informed by mail"
        exit 1
fi

user="$1"

#
# Check every minute for user logging on
#

until who | grep "^$user " > /dev/null
do
        sleep 60
done

#
# When we reach this point, the user has logged on
#

if [ "$mailopt" = FALSE ]
then
        echo "$user has logged on"
else
        echo "$user has logged on" | mail steve
fi
$
```

The first test checks to see if the −m option was supplied. If it was, then the characters TRUE are assigned to the variable mailopt, and shift is executed to "shift out" the first argument (moving the name of the user to be monitored to $1 and decrementing $#). If the −m option wasn't specified as the first argument, then the characters FALSE are assigned to mailopt.

Execution then proceeds as in the previous version. However, this time when the loop is exited a test is made to see if the −m option was selected. If it wasn't, then the message is written to standard output; otherwise it's mailed to steve.

```
$ mon sandy -m
Usage: mon   [-m] user
          -m means to be informed by mail
$ mon -m sandy &
5435
$ vi newmemo                        Work continues
   . . .
you have mail
$ mail
From steve Mon Jul 22 11:05 EDT 1985
sandy has logged on

?d
$
```

Of course, we could have written mon to accept the −m option as either the first or second argument, but that goes against the recommended command syntax standard, which specifies that all options should proceed any other types of arguments on the command line.[†]

You should also note that the old version of mon could have been executed as follows:

```
$ mon sandy | mail steve &
5522
$
```

to achieve the same net result as adding the −m option.

Two last points before leaving the discussion of mon: First, you'll probably always want to run this program in the background. It would be nice if mon itself could take care of that. Later you'll see how to do it.

---

† The command syntax standard consists of a set of rules as outlined in the INTRO(1) section of your *UNIX User's Reference Manual*.

Second, the program always sends mail to steve; not very nice if someone else wants to run it. A better way is to determine the user running the program and then send him or her the mail if the −m option is selected. But how do you do that? One way is to execute the who command with the am i options and get the user name that comes back. This will tell you who's logged onto the terminal that the program was run from. You can then use cut to extract the user name from who's output and use that name as the recipient of the mail. All of this can be done in the last if command of mon if it's changed to read as shown:

```
if [ "$#" -eq 1 ]
then
        echo "$user has logged on"
else
        runner=`who am i | cut -c1-8`
        echo "$user has logged on" | mail $runner
fi
```

Now the program can be run by anyone, and the mail will be properly sent.

◆ More on Loops ◆

Breaking Out of a Loop

Sometimes you may want to make an immediate exit from a loop. To just exit from the loop (and not from the program) you can use the break command, whose format is simply

```
break
```

When the break is executed, control is sent immediately out of the loop, where execution then continues as normal with the command that follows the done.

The UNIX command true serves no purpose but to return an exit status of zero. The command false also does nothing but return a nonzero exit status. If you write

```
while true
do
        . . .
done
```

then the while loop will theoretically be executed forever, since true always returns a zero exit status. By the way, the : command also does nothing but

return a zero exit status, so an "infinite" loop can also be set up with

```
while :
do

        ...

done
```

Since `false` always returns a nonzero exit status, the loop

```
until false
do

        ...

done
```

will theoretically execute forever.

The `break` command is often used to exit from these sorts of infinite loops, usually when some error condition or the end of processing is detected:

```
while true
do
        cmd=`getcmd`

        if [ "$cmd" = quit ]
        then
                break
        else
                processcmd "$cmd"
        fi
done
```

Here the `while` loop will continue to execute the `getcmd` and `processcmd` programs until `cmd` is equal to `quit`. At that point, the `break` command will be executed, thus causing the loop to be exited.

If the `break` command is used in the form

```
break n
```

then the *n* innermost loops are immediately exited, so in

```
        for file
        do
                ...
                while [ "$count" -lt 10 ]
                do
                        ...
                        if [ -n "$error" ]
                        then
                                        break 2
                        fi
                        ...
                done
                ...
        done
```

both the `while` *and* the `for` loops will be exited if `error` is nonnull.

Skipping the Remaining Commands in a Loop

The `continue` command is similar to `break`, only it doesn't cause the loop to be exited, merely the remaining commands in the loop to be skipped. Execution of the loop then continues as normal. Like the `break`, an optional number can follow the `continue`, so

```
        continue n
```

causes the commands in the innermost *n* loops to be skipped; but execution of the loops then continues as normal.

```
        for file
        do
                if [ ! -f "$file" ]
                then
                        echo "$file not found!"
                        continue
                fi

                #
                # Process the file
                #

                ...
        done
```

Each value of `file` is checked to make sure the file exists. If it doesn't, a message is printed and further processing of the file is skipped. Execution of the loop then continues with the next value in the list. Note that the above is equivalent to writing

```
for file
do
        if [ ! -f "$file" ]
        then
                echo "$file not found!"
        else
                #
                # Process the file
                #

                . . .

        fi
done
```

Executing a Loop in the Background

An entire loop can be sent to the background for execution simply by placing an ampersand after the done:

```
$ for file in memo[1-4]
> do
>            run $file
> done &                          Send it to the background
9932
$
request id is laser1-85 (standard input)
request id is laser1-87 (standard input)
request id is laser1-88 (standard input)
request id is laser1-92 (standard input)
```

I/O Redirection on a Loop

You can also perform I/O redirection on the entire loop. Input redirected into the loop applies to all commands in the loop that read their data from standard input. Output redirected from the loop to a file applies to all commands in the loop that write to standard output:

```
$ for i in 1 2 3 4
> do
>           echo $i
> done > loopout                    Redirect loop's output to loopout
$ cat loopout
1
2
3
4
$
```

You can override redirection of the entire loop's input or output by explicitly redirecting the input and/or output of commands inside the loop. To force input or output of a command to come from or go to the terminal, use the fact that /dev/tty always refers to your terminal. In the following loop, the echo command's output is explicitly redirected to the terminal to override the global output redirection applied to the loop:

```
for file
do
        echo "Processing file $file" >/dev/tty
        . . .
done > output
```

echo's output is redirected to the terminal while the rest goes to the file output.

Naturally, you can also redirect the standard error output from a loop, simply by tacking on a 2>*file* after the done:

```
while [ "$endofdata" -ne TRUE ]
do
        . . .
done 2> errors
```

Here output from all commands in the loop writing to standard error will be redirected to the file errors.

Piping Data Into and Out of a Loop

A command's output can be piped into a loop, and the entire output from a loop can be piped into another command in the expected manner. Here's a highly manufactured example of the output from a for command piped into wc:

```
$ for i in 1 2 3 4
> do
>           echo $i
> done | wc -l
      4
$
```

There is an interesting point to note about redirecting and/or piping input and output to and from loops; it has to do with the fact that the loop will be run as a *subshell*. This topic is discussed in full detail in Chapter 11.

Typing a Loop on One Line

If you find yourself frequently executing loops directly at the terminal, then you'll want to use the following shorthand notation to type the entire loop on a single line: Put a semicolon after the last item in the list, and one after each command in the loop. Don't put a semicolon after the do.

Following these rules, the loop

```
for i in 1 2 3 4
do
        echo $i
done
```

becomes

```
for i in 1 2 3 4; do echo $i; done
```

And you can type it in directly this way:

```
$ for i in 1 2 3 4; do echo $i; done
1
2
3
4
$
```

The same rules apply to while and until loops.

if commands can also be typed on the same line using a similar format:

```
$ if [ 1 = 1 ]; then echo yes; fi
yes
$ if [ 1 = 2 ]; then echo yes; else echo no; fi
no
$
```

Note that no semicolons appear after the then and the else.

♦ The getopts Command ♦

Let's extend our mon program further. We'll add a -t option to it that will specify the time interval, in seconds, to perform the check. Now our mon program will take both -m and -t options. We'll allow it to take these options in any order on the command line, provided that if they are used, they appear before the name of the user that we're monitoring. So valid mon command lines look like this:

```
mon ann
mon -m ann
mon -t 600 ann
mon -m -t 600 ann
mon -t 600 -m ann
```

and invalid ones look like this:

```
mon                      Missing user name
mon -t600 ann            Need a space after -t
mon ann -m               Options must appear first
mon -t ann               Missing argument after -t
```

If you start writing the code to allow this sort of flexibility on the command line, you will soon discover that it can start to get a bit complex. Luckily, the shell provides a built-in command called getopts that exists for the express purpose of processing command line arguments. The general format of the command is:

```
getopts options variable
```

The getopts command is designed to be executed inside a loop. Each time through the loop, getopts examines the next command line argument and determines if it is a valid option. This determination is made by checking to see if the argument begins with a minus sign and is followed by any single letter contained inside *options*. If it does, getopts stores the matching option letter inside the specified *variable* and returns a zero exit status.

If the letter that follows the minus sign is not listed in *options*, getopts stores a question mark inside *variable* before returning with a zero exit status. It also writes an error message to standard error.

If there are no more arguments left on the command line or if the next argument doesn't begin with a minus sign, getopts returns a nonzero exit status.

Suppose you want getopts to recognize the options -a, -i, and -r for a command called foo. Your getopts call might look like this:

```
getopts air option
```

Here the first argument—air—specifies the three acceptable options to the command and option specifies the variable that getopts will use as previously described.

The getopts command permits options to be "stacked" together on the command line. This is done by following a single minus sign with one or more consecutive options letters. For example, our foo command can be executed like this:

```
foo -a -r -i
```

or like this:

```
foo -ari
```

using this stacking feature.

The getopts command also handles the case where an option must be followed by an argumnet. For example, the new -t option to be added to the mon command requires a following argument. In order to handle options that take arguments, getopts requires that at least one whitespace character separate the option from the argument. Furthermore, such options cannot be stacked.

To indicate to getopts that an option takes a following argument, you write a colon character after the option letter on the getopts command line. So our mon program, which takes -m and -t options, should call getopts like this:

```
getopts mt: option
```

If getopts doesn't find an argument after an option that requires one, it will store a question mark inside the specified variable and will write an error message to standard error. Otherwise, it will store the actual argument inside a special variable called OPTARG.

One final note about getopts: Another special variable called OPTIND is used by the command. This variable is initially set to one, and is updated each time getopts returns to reflect the number of the *next* command line argument to be processed.

Here is the third version of mon that uses the getopts command to process the command line arguments. It also incorporates the previously noted change to send mail to the user running the program.

```
$ cat mon
#
# Wait until a specified user logs on -- version 3
#

# Set up default values

mailopt=FALSE
interval=60

# process command options

while getopts mt: option
do
        case "$option"
        in
                m)      mailopt=TRUE;;
                t)      interval=$OPTARG;;
                \?)     echo "Usage: mon  [-m] [-t n] user"
                        echo "    -m means to be informed by mail"
                        echo "    -t means check every n secs."
                        exit 1;;
        esac
done

# Make sure a user name was specified

if [ "$OPTIND" -gt "$#" ]
then
        echo "Missing user name!"
        exit 2
fi

shiftcount=`expr $OPTIND - 1`
shift $shiftcount
user=$1

#
# Check for user logging on
#

until who | grep "^$user " > /dev/null
do
        sleep $interval
done
```

```
#
# When we reach this point, the user has logged on
#

if [ "$mailopt" = FALSE ]
then
        echo "$user has logged on"
else
        runner=`who am i | cut -c1-8`
        echo "$user has logged on" | mail $runner
fi
```

```
$ mon -m
Missing user name!
$ mon -x fred                          Illegal option
mon: illegal option -- x
Usage: mon   [-m] [-t n] user"
    -m means to be informed by mail"
    -t means check every n secs."
$ mon -m -t 600 ann &                  Check every 10 min. for ann
5792
$
```

When the line

```
    mon -m -t 600 ann &
```

is executed, the following occurs inside the while loop in mon: getopts is executed and it stores the character m inside the variable option, sets OPTIND to two, and returns a zero exit status. The case command is then executed to determine what was stored inside option. A match on the character m indicates that the "send mail" option was selected, so mailopt is set to TRUE. (Note that the ? inside the case is quoted. This is to remove its special meaning as a pattern matching character from the shell.)

The second time getopts is executed, getopts stores the character t inside option, stores the next command line argument (600) inside OPTARG, sets OPTIND to three, and returns a zero exit status. The case command then matches the character t stored inside option. The code associated with that case copies the value of 600 that was stored in OPTARG into the variable interval.

The third time getopts is executed, getopts returns a nonzero exit status, indicating the end of options. The program then checks the value of OPTIND against $# to make sure the user name was typed on the command line. If OPTIND is greater than $#, then no more arguments remain on the command line and the user forgot the user name argument. Otherwise, the shift command is executed to move the user name argument into $1. The actual number of places to shift is one less than the value of OPTIND.

The rest of the mon program remains as before, the only change is the use of the interval variable to specify the number of seconds to sleep.

◆ Exercises ◆

1. Modify the `prargs` program to precede each argument by its number. So typing

   ```
   prargs a 'b c' d
   ```

   should give the following output:

   ```
   1: a
   2: b c
   3: d
   ```

2. Modify the `mon` program to also print the `tty` number that the user logs onto. That is, the output should say

   ```
   sandy logged onto tty13
   ```

   if `sandy` logs onto `tty13`.

3. Add a `-f` option to `mon` to have it periodically check for the existence of a file (ordinary file or directory) instead of for a user logging on. So typing

   ```
   mon -f /usr/spool/uucppublic/steve/newmemo &
   ```

   should cause `mon` to periodically check for the existence of the indicated file and inform you once it does (by displaying a message or by mail if the `-m` option is also selected).

4. Add a `-n` option to `mon` that will invert the monitoring function. So

   ```
   mon -n sandy
   ```

   will check for `sandy` logging off the system, and

   ```
   mon -n -f /tmp/dataout &
   ```

   will periodically check for the removal of the specified file.

5. Write a program called `collect` that runs in the background and counts the number of users logged in at the end of each interval and also the number of processes run during that interval. Allow the interval to be specified with a

-t option (see the previous exercise), with the default 10 minutes. Use the fact that the special shell variable $!$ is set to the process number of the last command executed in the background and that

```
:  &
```

runs a null command in the background. Also make sure that the program correctly handles the case where the process number loops back around to 1 after the maximum is reached.

So

```
collect -t 900 > stats &
```

should start up collect to gather the desired statistics every 15 minutes and write them into the file stats.

6. Write a shell program called wgrep that searches a file for a given pattern, just as grep does. For each line in the file that matches, print a "window" around the matching line. That is, print the line preceding the match, the matching line, and the line following the match. Be sure to properly handle the special cases where the pattern matches the first line of the file, and where the pattern matches the last line of the file.

7. Modify wgrep to take an optional -w option that specifies the window size; so

```
wgrep -w 3 UNIX text
```

should print three lines before and after each line from text that contains the pattern UNIX.

8. Modify wgrep to take a variable number of file names as arguments. Precede each output line with the name of the file in which the match occurs (as grep does).

CHAPTER

◆   ◆   ◆ **10** ◆   ◆   ◆

Reading Data

In this chapter you'll learn how to read data from the terminal or from a file. It's done with the read command, whose general format is

> read *variables*

When this command is executed, the shell reads a line from standard input and assigns the first word read to the first variable listed in *variables*, the second word read to the second variable, and so on. If there are more words on the line then there are variables listed, then the excess words get assigned to the last variable. So for example, the command

> read x y

will read a line from standard input, storing the first word read in the variable x, and the remainder of the line in the variable y. It follows from this that the command

> read text

will read and store an entire line into the shell variable text.

You can't perform I/O redirection on the read command unless you're running UNIX System V Release 2 or later. So

> read text < data

won't work on System V or earlier versions.[†]

[†] If you need to redirect input, you can use the UNIX system's line command, which reads an entire line from standard input and writes it to standard output; so text=`line < data` will do the same thing as the example shown. There are other alternatives (such as with the exec command) that we'll talk about later.

215

A Program to Copy Files

Let's put the read command to work. We'll write a simplified version of the cp command that will be a bit more user-friendly than the standard UNIX one. We'll call it mycp and we'll have it take two arguments: the source file and the destination file. If the destination file already exists, then we'll tell the user and then ask him (or her) if they want to proceed with the copy. If the answer is "yes," then we'll go ahead with it; otherwise, we won't.

```
$ cat mycp
#
# Copy a file
#

if [ "$#" -ne 2 ]
then
        echo "Usage: mycp from to"
        exit 1
fi

from="$1"
to="$2"

#
# See if the destination file already exists
#

if [ -f "$to" ]
then
        echo "$to already exists; overwrite (yes/no)?"
        read answer

        if [ "$answer" != yes ]
        then
                echo "Copy not performed"
                exit 0
        fi
fi

#
# Either destination doesn't exist or ''yes'' was typed
#

cp $from $to        # proceed with the copy
$
```

And now for the test:

```
$ ls                              What files are around?
addresses
intro
lotsaspaces
mycp
names
nu
numbers
phonebook
stat
$ mycp                            No arguments
Usage: mycp from to
$ mycp names names2               Make a copy of names
$ ls -l names*                    Did it work?
-rw-r--r--    1 steve     steve       43 Jul 20 11:12 names
-rw-r--r--    1 steve     steve       43 Jul 21 14:16 names2
$ mycp names numbers              Try to overwrite an existing file
numbers already exists; overwrite (yes/no)?
no
Copy not performed
$
```

To complete the test cases, you should try answering yes and ensuring that the program proceeds with the copy.

There are a few things worthy of mention with the mycp program. First, if the file already exists, then the echo command that prompts for the yes/no response is executed. The read command that follows causes the shell to wait for you to type something in. Note that the shell does not prompt you when it's waiting for you to enter data; it's up to you to add your own prompt message to the program.

The data that is typed is stored in the variable answer, and is then tested against the characters "yes" to determine if the copy is to proceed. The quotes around answer in the test

```
[ "$answer" != yes ]
```

are necessary in case the user just presses the RETURN key without typing any data. In that case, the shell would store a null value in answer and test would issue an error message if the quotes were omitted.

Special echo Escape Characters

A slight annoyance with mycp is that after the echo command is executed to alert the user that the file already exists, the response that is typed by the user appears on the next line. This happens because the echo command always automatically displays a terminating newline character after the last argument.

This can be suppressed if the last two characters given to echo are the special *escape* characters \c. This tells echo to leave the cursor right where it is after displaying the last argument, and not to go to the next line. So if you changed the echo command in mycp to read like this:

```
echo "$to already exists; overwrite (yes/no)? \c"
```

then the user's input would be typed right after the message on the same line. Bear in mind that the \c is interpreted by echo and not by the shell, meaning that it must be quoted so that the backslash makes it to echo.

There are other special characters that echo interprets. These must each be preceded by a backslash. They're summarized in Table 10-1.

TABLE 10-1. echo escape characters[†]

Character	Prints
\b	Backspace
\c	The line without a terminating newline
\f	Formfeed
\n	Newline
\r	Carriage return
\t	Tab character
\\	Backslash character
nnn	The character whose ASCII value is *nnn*, where *nnn* is a one- to three-digit octal number that starts with a zero.

An Improved Version of mycp

Suppose you have a program called prog1 in your current directory and you want to copy it into your bin directory directly below. Take another look at the mycp program and determine what happens if you type in

```
mycp prog1 bin
```

---

† These characters were added to echo as of System III. If you're running an earlier version, then you can still display tabs and newlines by enclosing these characters in quotes and passing them to echo. To suppress the terminating newline character, you have to use the -n option with echo, for example
```
echo -n "$to already exists; overwrite (yes/no)? "
```

The -f test on bin will fail (since bin is not an ordinary file) and the copy will proceed, *overwriting the copy of prog1 (if one exists) in the bin directory*!!

If the second argument is a directory, then mycp should check to see if the from file exists *inside* this directory. The next version of mycp performs this check. It also has the modified echo command that includes the \c to suppress the terminating newline.

```
$ cat mycp
#
# Copy a file -- version 2
#

if [ "$#" -ne 2 ]
then
        echo "Usage: mycp from to"
        exit 1
fi

from="$1"
to="$2"

#
# See if destination file is a directory
#

if [ -d "$to" ]
then
        to="$to/`basename $from`"
fi

#
# See if the destination file already exists
#

if [ -f "$to" ]
then
        echo "$to already exists; overwrite (yes/no)? \c"
        read answer

        if [ "$answer" != yes ]
        then
                echo "Copy not performed"
                exit 0
        fi
fi
```

```
#
# Either destination doesn't exist or ''yes'' was typed
#

cp $from $to        # proceed with the copy
$
```

If the destination file is a directory, then the program changes the variable to to more precisely identify the file inside the directory as $to/`basename $from`. This ensures that the following test on the existence of the ordinary file $to will be done on the file in the directory, not on the directory itself as the previous version of mycp did. The basename command give the base file name of its argument (e.g. basename /usr/bin/troff gives troff; basename troff gives troff). This ensures that the copy is made to the correct place. (e.g., if mycp /tmp/data bin is typed, where bin is a directory, you want to copy /tmp/data into bin/data and not into bin/tmp/data.)

Here's some sample output. Note the effect of the \c escape characters.

```
$ ls                             Check out current directory
bin
prog1
$ ls bin                         Look inside bin
lu
nu
prog1
$ mycp prog1 prog2               Simple case
$ mycp prog1 bin                 Copy into directory
bin/prog1 already exists; overwrite (yes/no)? yes
$
```

A Final Version of mycp

The last modification to mycp makes the program virtually equivalent to the standard UNIX cp command by allowing a variable number of arguments. Recall that any number of files can precede the name of a directory, as in:

```
cp prog1 prog2 greetings bin
```

To modify mycp to accept any number of files, you can use this approach:

1. Get each argument but the last from the command line and store it in the shell variable filelist.

2. Store the last argument in the variable to.

3. If $to is not a directory, then there must be exactly two arguments.

4. For each file in $filelist, check if the file already exists; if it does then ask the user if the file should be overwritten. If the answer is "yes," or if the file doesn't already exist, then add the file to the variable copylist.

5. If copylist is nonnull, copy the files in it to $to.

If this algorithm seems a bit fuzzy, perhaps the program, followed by a detailed explanation, will help clear things up. Note the modified command usage message.

```
$ cat mycp
#
# Copy a file -- final version
#

numargs=$#                     # save this for later use
filelist=
copylist=

#
#  Process the arguments, storing all but the last in filelist
#

while [ "$#" -gt 1 ]
do
        filelist="$filelist $1"
        shift
done

to="$1"

#
#  If less than two args, or if more than two args and last arg
#  is not a directory, then issue an error message
#
```

```
if [ "$numargs" -lt 2    -o   "$numargs" -gt 2   -a  ! -d "$to" ]
then
     echo "Usage: mycp file1 file2"
     echo "       mycp file(s) dir"
     exit 1
fi


#
# Sequence through each file in filelist
#

for from in $filelist
do
     #
     #  See if destination file is a directory
     #

     if [ -d "$to" ]
     then
             tofile="$to/`basename $from`"
     else
             tofile="$to"
     fi

     #
     # Add file to copylist if file doesn't already exist
     # or if user says it's okay to overwrite
     #

     if [ -f "$tofile" ]
     then
             echo "$tofile already exists; overwrite (yes/no)? \c"
             read answer

             if [ "$answer" = yes ]
             then
                     copylist="$copylist $from"
             fi
     else
             copylist="$copylist $from"
     fi
done


#
# Now do the copy -- first make sure there's something to copy
#
```

```
if [ -n "$copylist" ]
then
        cp $copylist $to         # proceed with the copy
fi
$
```

Let's look at some sample output before getting into the explanation.

```
$ ls                              See what's around
bin
lu
names
prog1
prog2
$ ls bin                          And what's in bin?
lu
nu
prog1
$ mycp                            No arguments
Usage: mycp file1 file2
       mycp file(s) dir
$ mycp names prog1 prog2          Last arg isn't a directory
Usage: mycp file1 file2
       mycp file(s) dir
$ mycp names prog1 prog2 lu bin   Legitimate use
bin/prog1 already exists; overwrite (yes/no)? yes
bin/lu already exists; overwrite (yes/no)? no
$ ls -l bin                       See what happened
total 5
-rw-r--r--    1 steve    steve        543 Jul 19 14:10 lu
-rw-r--r--    1 steve    steve        949 Jul 21 17:11 names
-rw-r--r--    1 steve    steve         38 Jul 19 09:55 nu
-rw-r--r--    1 steve    steve        498 Jul 21 17:11 prog1
-rw-r--r--    1 steve    steve        498 Jul 21 17:11 prog2
$
```

In the last case, prog1 was overwritten and lu wasn't, as per the user's request.

When the program starts execution, it saves the number of arguments in the variable numargs. This is done because it's changed later in the program by the shift command.

Next a loop is entered that is executed as long as the number of arguments is greater than one. The purpose of this loop is to get the last argument on the line. While doing this, the loop stashes away the first argument into the shell variable `filelist`, which will contain a list of all the files to be copied. The statement

```
filelist="$filelist $1"
```

says to take the previous value of `filelist`, add on a space followed by the value of `$1`, and then store the result back into `filelist`. Then the `shift` command is executed to "move" all the arguments over by one. Eventually, `$#` will be equal to one, and the loop will be exited. At that point, `filelist` will contain a space-delimited list of all the files to be copied, and `$1` will contain the last argument, which is the destination file (or directory). To see how this works, consider execution of the `while` loop when the command is executed as

```
mycp names prog1 prog2 lu bin
```

Figure 10-1 depicts the changing values of the variables through each iteration of the loop. The first line shows the state of the variables before the loop is entered.

$#	$1	$2	$3	$4	$5	filelist
5	names	prog1	prog2	lu	bin	*null*
4	prog1	prog2	lu	bin		names
3	prog2	lu	bin			names prog1
2	lu	bin				names prog1 prog2
1	bin					names prog1 prog2 lu

Fig. 10-1. Processing command line arguments

After the loop is exited, the last argument contained in `$1` is stored in the variable `to`. Next a test is made to ensure that at least two arguments were typed on the command line and if more than two were typed, that the last argument is a directory. If either condition isn't satisfied, then usage information is displayed to the user and the program exits with a status of 1.

Following this, a `for` loop is entered, for the purpose of individually examining each file in the list to see if it already exists. If it does, then the user is prompted as before. If the user wants to overwrite the file, or if the file doesn't already exist, then the file is added to the shell variable `copylist`. The technique used here is the same used to accumulate the arguments inside `filelist`.

When the `for` loop is exited, `copylist` contains a list of all of the files to be copied. This list can be null if each of the destination files exists and the user types "no" for each one. So a test is made to ensure `copylist` is nonnull, and if it is, the copy is performed.

Please take some time to review the logic of the final version of `mycp`; it does a good job at illustrating many of the features you've learned so far in this book. There are some exercises at the end of this chapter that will help test your understanding of this program.

A Menu-Driven Phone Program

One of the nice things about the `read` command is it enables you to write menu-driven shell programs. As an example, we'll return to our phone book programs `add`, `lu`, and `rem` and gather their execution together under one program which we'll call `rolo` (for rolodex program). `rolo` will display a list of choices to the user and then execute the appropriate program depending upon the selection. It will also prompt for the proper arguments to the program. Here, then, is the program:

```
$ cat rolo
#
# rolo - rolodex program to look up, add, and
#        remove people from the phone book
#


#
# Display menu
#

echo '
        Would you like to:

                1. Look someone up
                2. Add someone to the phone book
                3. Remove someone from the phone book

        Please select one of the above (1-3): \c'

#
# Read and process selection
#

read choice
echo
```

```
case "$choice"
in
        1)    echo "Enter name to look up: \c"
              read name
              lu "$name";;
        2)    echo "Enter name to be added: \c"
              read name
              echo "Enter number: \c"
              read number
              add "$name" "$number";;
        3)    echo "Enter name to be removed: \c"
              read name
              rem "$name";;
        *)    echo "Bad choice";;
esac
$
```

A single echo command is used to display the menu at the terminal, taking advantage of the fact that the quotes preserve the embedded newline characters. Then the read command is executed to get the selection from the user and store it in the variable choice.

A case statement is next entered to determine what choice was made. If choice 1 was selected, then the user wants to look someone up in the phone book. In that case, the user is asked to enter the name to be looked up, and the lu program is called, passing it the name typed in by the user as the argument. Note that the double quotes around name in

```
lu "$name"
```

are necessary to ensure that two or more words typed in by the user are handed over to lu as a single argument.

A similar sequence occurs if the user selects menu items 2 or 3.

The programs lu, rem, and add are from earlier chapters (lu is from page 140, rem from page 172, and add from page 142.)

Now here are some sample runs of rolo:

```
$ rolo

        Would you like to:

                1. Look someone up
                2. Add someone to the phone book
                3. Remove someone from the phone book

        Please select one of the above (1-3): 2
```

```
Enter name to be added: El Coyote
Enter number: 567-3232
$ rolo                              Try it again

    Would you like to:

        1. Look someone up
        2. Add someone to the phone book
        3. Remove someone from the phone book

    Please select one of the above (1-3): 1

Enter name to look up: Coyote
El Coyote          567-3232
$ rolo                              Once again

    Would you like to:

        1. Look someone up
        2. Add someone to the phone book
        3. Remove someone from the phone book

    Please select one of the above (1-3): 4
Bad choice
$
```

When an invalid choice is entered, the program simply displays `Bad choice` and then terminates. A friendlier approach would be to reprompt the user until a proper choice is made. This can be done by enclosing the entire program inside an `until` loop that will be executed until a valid selection is made. To determine when a valid choice has been made, we can test a variable in the `until` that won't be assigned a value in the program until either 1, 2, or 3 is selected by the user.

Another change to make to `rolo` involves the way it will be used. Since the most common operation performed will be one of lookup, there will probably be a tendency on the part of the user to avoid typing `rolo`, then making selection 1, and then typing the name to be found when instead he or she can still type in

```
lu name
```

directly. Given all this, it might be a good idea to allow `rolo` to take command line arguments. If any arguments are typed, then `rolo` can assume that a lookup is being requested, and just call `lu` directly. So if the user wants to perform a quick lookup, he or she can type `rolo` followed by the name. On the other hand, if the user wants to see the menu, then typing just `rolo` will cause the program to display its menu and prompt for a choice.

The above two changes (looping until a valid choice is selected and doing a quick lookup) were added to version 2 of rolo that is shown next.

```
$ cat rolo
#
# rolo - rolodex program to look up, add, and
#        remove people from the phone book -- version 2
#


#
# If arguments are supplied, then do a lookup
#

if [ "$#" -ne 0 ]
then
        lu "$@"
        exit
fi

validchoice=""             # set it null


#
# Loop until a valid selection is made
#


until [ -n "$validchoice" ]
do
        #
        # Display menu
        #

        echo '

        Would you like to:

                1. Look someone up
                2. Add someone to the phone book
                3. Remove someone from the phone book

        Please select one of the above (1-3): \c'

        #
        # Read and process selection
        #
```

```
      read choice
      echo

      case "$choice"
      in
              1)   echo "Enter name to look up: \c"
                   read name
                   lu "$name"
                   validchoice=TRUE;;
              2)   echo "Enter name to be added: \c"
                   read name
                   echo "Enter number: \c"
                   read number
                   add "$name" "$number"
                   validchoice=TRUE;;
              3)   echo "Enter name to be removed: \c"
                   read name
                   rem "$name"
                   validchoice=TRUE;;
              *)   echo "Bad choice";;
         esac
    done
    $
```

If $# is nonzero, then lu is called directly with the arguments typed on the command line. Then the program exits. Otherwise, the until loop is executed until the variable validchoice is nonnull. The only way it can ever become nonnull is if the command

```
      validchoice=TRUE
```

is executed inside the case upon selection of either 1, 2, or 3. Otherwise, the program continues to loop until one of these three choices is made.

```
$ rolo Bill                    Quick lookup
Billy Bach       331-7618
$ rolo                         Let's have the menu this time

    Would you like to:

           1. Look someone up
           2. Add someone to the phone book
           3. Remove someone from the phone book
```

```
        Please select one of the above (1-3): 4
Bad choice


        Would you like to:

            1. Look someone up
            2. Add someone to the phone book
            3. Remove someone from the phone book

        Please select one of the above (1-3): 0
Bad choice


        Would you like to:

            1. Look someone up
            2. Add someone to the phone book
            3. Remove someone from the phone book

        Please select one of the above (1-3): 1

Enter name to look up: Tony
Tony Iannino     386-1295
$
```

The $$ Variable and Temporary Files

If two or more people on your system use the rolo program at the same time, there's a potential problem that may occur. Look at the rem program and see if you can spot it. The problem occurs with the temporary file /tmp/phonebook that is used to create a new version of the phone book file.

```
grep -v "$name" phonebook > /tmp/phonebook
mv /tmp/phonebook phonebook
```

If more than one person is using rolo to remove an entry at the same time, there's a chance that their phone book file can get messed up since the same temporary file will be used by all `rolo` users.[†] Naturally, the chances of this happening (i.e., the above two commands being executed at the same time by more than one user) are rather small, but, nevertheless there still is that chance. Anyway, it brings up an important point when dealing with temporary files in general.

When writing shell programs to be run by more than one person, you should make your temporary files unique. One way is to create the temporary file in the user's home directory, for example. Another way is to choose a temporary file name that will be unique for that particular process. To do this, you can use the special `$$` shell variable, which contains the process id number of the current process:

```
$ echo $$
4668
$ ps
   PID TTY TIME COMMAND
  4668 co  0:09 sh
  6470 co  0:03 ps
$
```

As you can see, `$$` is equal to the process id number (PID) of your login shell. Since each process on the UNIX system is given a unique process id number, using the value of `$$` in the name of a file will minimize the possibility of another process using the same file. So you can replace the two lines from `rem` with these

```
grep -v "$name" phonebook > /tmp/phonebook$$
mv /tmp/phonebook$$ phonebook
```

to circumvent any potential problems. Each person running `rolo` will be running it as a different process, so the temporary file used in each case will be different.

The Exit Status from **read**

`read` always returns an exit status of zero unless an end of file condition is detected on the input. If the data is coming from the terminal, this means that *CTRL-d* has been typed. If the data is coming from a file, then it means that there's no more data to read from the file.

Knowing about the exit status returned by `read` makes it easy to write a loop that will read any number of lines of data from a file or from the terminal. The next program, called `addi`, reads in lines containing pairs of integers. Each

---

† Actually, it depends upon the users' default file creation mask (known as `umask`). If one person has created `/tmp/phonebook` and it's not writable by anyone else, then the next person who comes along and tries to create it will get an error message from the shell. The net result is that the first user's file will get properly updated while the second user's won't; neither file will get corrupted.

pair of numbers is summed, and the result written to standard output.

```
$ cat addi
#
# add pairs of integers on standard input
#

while read n1 n2
do
        expr "$n1" + "$n2"
done
$
```

The while loop is executed as long as the read command returns an exit status of zero; i.e., as long as there's still data to be read. Inside the loop, the two values read from the line (presumably integers—no error checking is done here) are summed by expr and the result written to standard output.

```
$ addi
10 25
35
-5 12
7
123 3
126
CTRL-d
$
```

It goes without saying that standard input for addi can be redirected, as can standard output:

```
$ cat data
1234 7960
593  -595
395   304
3234 999
-394 -493
$ addi < data > sums
$ cat sums
9194
-2
699
4233
-887
$
```

The following program, called `number`, is a simplified version of the standard UNIX `nl` command: it takes one or more files given as arguments and displays them preceded by line numbers. If no arguments are supplied, it uses standard input instead.

```
.$ cat number
#
# Number lines from files given as argument or from
# standard input if none supplied
#

lineno=1                  — all Variables

cat $* |
while read line
do
        echo "$lineno: $line"
        lineno=`expr $lineno + 1`
done
$
```

The variable `lineno`—the line number count—is initially set to `1`. Then the arguments typed to `number` are given to `cat` to be collectively written to standard output. If no arguments are supplied, `$*` will be null, and `cat` will be passed no arguments. This will cause it to read from standard input.

The output from `cat` is piped into the `while` loop. For each line read by `read`, the line is echoed at the terminal, preceded by the value of `lineno`, whose value is then incremented by one.

```
$ number phonebook
1: Alice Chebba      596-2015
2: Barbara Swingle 598-9257
3: Billy Bach        331-7618
4: El Coyote         567-3232
5: Liz Stachiw       775-2298
6: Susan Goldberg    338-7776
7: Teri Zak          393-6000
8: Tony Iannino      386-1295
$ who | number                     Try from standard input
1: root       console Jul 25 07:55
2: pat        tty03   Jul 25 09:26
3: steve      tty04   Jul 25 10:58
4: george     tty13   Jul 25 08:05
$
```

You should note that `number` won't work too well for lines that contain backslashes or leading whitespace characters. The following example illustrates this point.

```
$ number
            Here are some backslashes: \ \*
1: Here are some backslashes:   *
$
```

Leading whitespace characters are removed from any line that's read. The backslash characters are also interpreted by the shell when it reads the line.

In a later chapter you'll learn how to preserve the leading whitespace characters and also how to have some control over the parsing of the input data. In the next chapter you'll learn about the environment that the shell maintains for you. But first try your hand at the exercises that follow.

♦ Exercises ♦

1. What happens to `mycp` if one or more of the files to be copied doesn't exist? Can you make any suggestions to better handle the situation?

2. What happens to `mycp` if one of the file names contains a character that has a special meaning to the shell such as `;` or `|`?

3. Write a program called `mymv` that does with the `mv` command what `mycp` does with the `cp` command. How many changes did you have to make to `mycp` to produce this new program?

4. Modify `mycp` to prompt for arguments if none are supplied. A typical execution of the modified version should look like this:

   ```
   $ mycp
   Source file name? voucher
   Destination file name? voucher.sv
   $
   ```

   Be sure that the program allows one or both of the files to be specified with file name substitution characters.

5. Add a `-n` option to `mycp` that suppresses the normal check for the existence of the destination files.

6. Modify `mycp` to use `sed` instead of the `while` loop to process the arguments typed on the command line.

7. Modify the `rem` program used by `rolo` so that if multiple entries are found, then the program will prompt the user for the entry to be removed.

   Here's a sample session:

   ```
   $ rolo
       ...
        Please select one of the above (1-3): 3

   Enter name to be removed: Susan

   More than one match; please select the one to remove:
   Susan Goldberg    Remove (y/n)? n
   Susan Topple      Remove (y/n)? y
   $
   ```

8. Modify `rolo` so that the menu is redisplayed after each selection is made and processed. To allow the user to get out of this, add another selection to the menu to exit from the program.

9. What happens to the `rolo` program if just a carriage return is entered as the name for the add, look up, or remove options?

11

Your Environment

When you log onto the system, you're effectively given your own copy of the shell program. This shell maintains what's known as your *environment*—an environment that is distinct from other users on the system. This environment is maintained from the moment you log on until the moment you log off. In this chapter you'll learn about this environment in detail, and you'll see how it relates to writing and running programs.

◆ Local Variables ◆

Type the following program called `vartest` into your computer:

```
$ cat vartest
echo :$x:
$
```

`vartest` consists of a solitary `echo` command that displays the value of the variable `x`, surrounded by colons. Now assign any value you want to the variable `x` from your terminal:

```
$ x=100
```

Here we chose 100. Question: What do you think will be displayed when `vartest` is now executed? Answer:

```
$ vartest
::
$
```

`vartest` doesn't know about the value of `x`. Therefore, its value is null. The variable x that was assigned the value 100 in the login shell is known as a *local* variable. The reason why it has this name will become clear shortly.

Here's another example. This program is called vartest2:

```
$ cat vartest2
x=50
echo :$x:
$ x=100
$ vartest2                              Execute it
:50:
$
```

Now the question is: What's the value of x?

```
$ echo $x
100
$
```

So you see that vartest2 didn't change the value of x that you set equal to 100 in your login shell.

Subshells

The behavior exhibited by vartest and vartest2 is due to the fact that these two programs are run as *subshells* by your login shell. A subshell is, for all intents and purposes, an entirely new shell that is executed by your login shell in order to run the desired program. So when you ask your login shell to execute vartest, it starts up a new shell to execute the program. Whenever a new shell runs, it runs in its own environment, with its own set of local variables. *A subshell has no knowledge of local variables that were assigned values by the login shell (the "parent" shell).* Furthermore, a subshell cannot change the value of a variable in the parent shell, as evidenced by vartest2.

Let's review the process that goes on here. Before executing vartest2, your login shell has a variable called x that has been assigned the value 100 (assume for now that this is the only variable defined in the shell). This is depicted in Fig. 11-1.

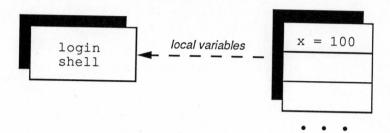

Fig. 11-1. Login shell with x=100

When you ask to have vartest2 executed, your login shell starts up a subshell to run it, giving it an empty list of local variables to start with (see Fig. 11-2).

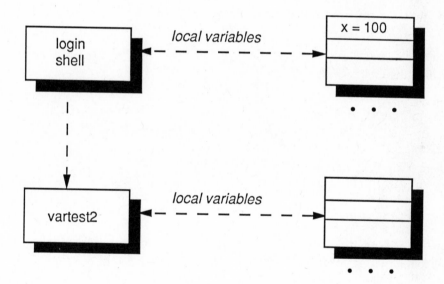

Fig. 11-2. Login shell executes vartest2

After the first command in vartest2 is executed (that assigns 50 to x), the local variable x *that exists in the subshell's environment* will have the value 50 (see Fig. 11-3). Note that this has no relation whatsoever to the variable x that still maintains its value of 100 in the login shell.

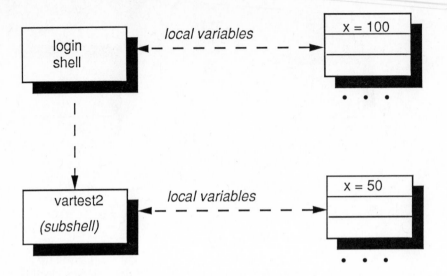

Fig. 11-3. `vartest2` executes `x=50`

When `vartest2` finishes execution, the subshell goes away, *together with any variables that were assigned values.*

◆ Exported Variables ◆

There *is* a way to make the value of a variable known to a subshell, and that's by *exporting* it with the `export` command. The format of this command is simply

```
export variables
```

where variables is the list of variable names that you want exported. For any subshells that get executed from that point on, the value of the exported variables will be passed down to the subshell.

Here's a program called `vartest3` to help illustrate the difference between local and exported variables:

```
$ cat vartest3
echo x = $x
echo y = $y
$
```

Assign values to the variables `x` and `y` in the login shell, and then run `vartest3`:

```
$ x=100
$ y=10
$ vartest3
x =
y =
$
```

x and y are both local variables, so their values aren't passed down to the sub-shell that runs `vartest3`. Now let's export the variable y and try it again:

```
$ export y                              Make y known to subshells
$ vartest3
x =
y = 10
$
```

This time `vartest3` knew about y since it is an exported variable. Conceptually, whenever a subshell is executed, the list of exported variables gets "copied down" to the subshell, while the list of local variables does not (see Fig. 11-4).

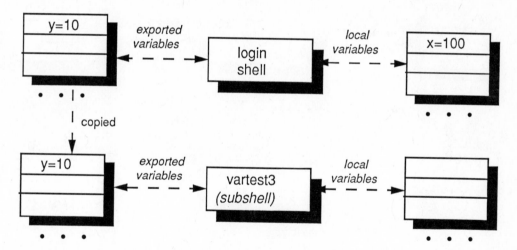

Fig. 11-4. Execution of `vartest3`

Now it's time for another question: What do you think happens if a subshell changes the value of an exported variable? Will the parent shell know about it once the subshell has finished? To answer this question, here's a program called `vartest4`:

```
$ cat vartest4
x=50
y=5
$
```

We'll assume that you haven't changed the values of x and y, and that y is still exported.

```
$ vartest4
$ echo $x $y
100 10
$
```

So the subshell couldn't even change the value of the exported variable y; it merely changed the copy of y that was passed to its environment when it was executed (see Fig. 11-5). Just as with local variables, when a subshell goes away, so do the values of the exported variables. *There is no way to change the value of a variable in a parent shell from within a subshell.*

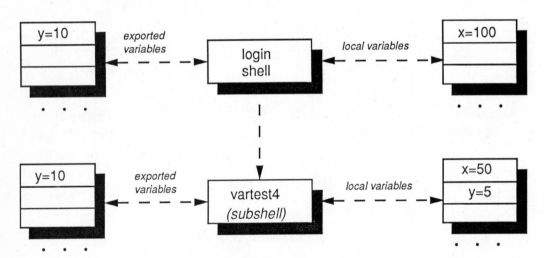

Fig. 11-5. Execution of vartest4

In Fig. 11-5 two y variables are shown for vartest4: an exported one and a local one. From a conceptual point of view, whenever you change a variable in your environment, a new local version of that variable is created. Subsequent use of the variable in the subshell always refers to the local one.

In the case of a subshell executing another subshell (e.g., the rolo program executing the lu program), the process is repeated: the exported variables from the subshell are copied to the new subshell. These exported variables may have been exported from above, or newly exported from within the subshell.

Once a variable is exported, it remains exported to all subshells that are subsequently executed.

Consider a modified version of vartest4:

```
$ cat vartest4
x=50
y=5
z=1
export z
vartest5
$
```

and also consider vartest5:

```
$ cat vartest5
echo x = $x
echo y = $y
echo z = $z
$
```

When vartest4 gets executed, the exported variable y will be copied into the subshell's environment. vartest4 sets the value of x to 50, changes the value of y to 5, and sets the value of z to 1. Then it exports z. This makes the value of z accessible to any subshell subsequently run by vartest4. vartest5 is such a subshell, and when it is executed, the shell copies into its environment the exported variables from vartest4: y and z. This should explain the following output. Note that vartest5 gets the *original* value of the exported variable y.

```
$ vartest4
x =
y = 10
z = 1
$
```

This entire operation is depicted in Fig. 11-6

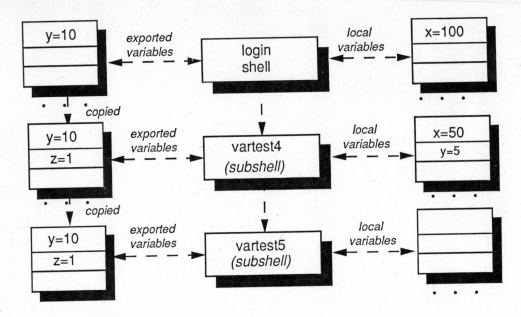

Fig. 11-6. Subshell execution

If you change `vartest4` to explicitly export the value of `y`, then the changed value of `y` *will* get passed down to `vartest5`:

```
$ cat vartest4
x=50
y=5
z=1
export y z
vartest5
$
```

Explicitly exporting `y` inside `vartest4` means that any changes made to this variable will get sent down to subshells.

```
$ vartest5
x =
y = 5
z = 1
$
```

Operation of this sequence of events is depicted in Fig. 11-7. Note that since `y` is explicitly exported by `vartest4` that there are no longer two different `y` variables in `vartest4`'s environment, just the exported one.

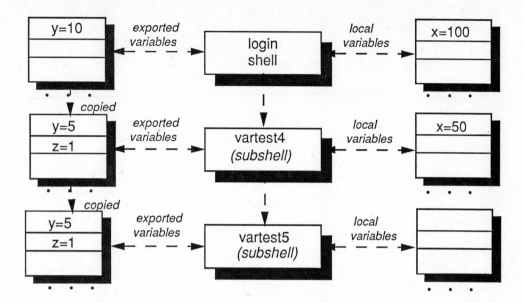

Fig. 11-7. Subshell execution

To summarize the way local and exported variables work:

1. Any variable that is not exported is a local variable whose existence will not be known to subshells.

2. Exported variables and their values are copied into a subshell's environment, where they may be accessed and changed. However, such changes have no affect on the variables in the parent shell.

3. If a subshell explicitly exports a variable, then changes made to that variable affect the exported one. If a subshell does not explicitly export a variable, then changes made to that variable affect a local one, even if the variable was exported from a parent shell.

4. Exported variables retain this characteristic not only for directly spawned subshells, but also for subshells spawned by those subshells (and so on down the line).

5. A variable can be exported any time before or after it is assigned a value.

export with No Arguments

If you simply type `export`, not followed by any arguments, you'll get a list of the variables that are exported by your shell:

```
export LOGNAME
export PATH
export TIMEOUT
export TZ
export y
$
```

As you can see, there's actually more exported variables here than you were initially led to believe. Note that y shows up on the list, together with other variables that were exported when you logged on.

Note that the variables listed are only those *explicitly* exported by the current shell, and that the list does not include those that may have been inherited from a parent shell.

◆ PS1 and PS2 ◆

The characters that the shell displays as your command prompt are stored in the variable PS1. You can change this variable to be anything you like. As soon as you change it, it'll be used by the shell from that point on.

```
$ echo :$PS1:
:$ :
$ PS1="==> "
==> pwd
/usr/steve
==> PS1="I await your next command, master: "
I await your next command, master: date
Wed Jul 24 18:52:13 EDT 1985
I await your next command, master: PS1="$ "
$                                            Back to normal
```

Your secondary command prompt, normally > , is kept in the variable PS2, where you can change it to your heart's content:

```
$ echo :$PS2:
:> :
$ PS2="=======> "
$ for x in 1 2 3
=======> do
=======> echo $x
```

```
=======> done
1
2
3
$
```

Like any other shell variables: once you log off the system, the values of those variables go with it. So if you change PS1, the shell will use the new value for the remainder of your login session. Next time you log in, however, you'll get the old value again. You can make the change yourself every time you log in, or you can have the change made automatically by adding it to your .profile file (discussed later in this chapter).

◆ HOME, James ◆

Your home directory is where you're placed whenever you log onto the system. A special shell variable called HOME is also automatically set to this directory when you log on:

```
$ echo $HOME
/usr/steve
$
```

This variable can be used by your programs to identify your home directory. It's also used by the cd command whenever you type just cd with no arguments:

```
$ pwd                          Where am I?
/usr/src/lib/libc/port/stdio
$ cd
$ pwd
/usr/steve                     There's no place like home
$
```

You can change your HOME variable to anything you like, but be warned that doing so may affect the operation of any programs that rely on it (cd being the only "official" UNIX command that does):

```
$ HOME=/usr/steve/book          Change it
$ pwd
/usr/steve
$ cd
$ pwd                           See what happened
/usr/steve/book
$
```

♦ Your PATH ♦

Return for a moment to the rolo program from Chapter 10.

```
$ rolo Liz
Liz Stachiw      775-2298
$
```

Let's see what directory this program was created in:

```
$ pwd
/usr/steve/bin
$
```

Okay, now change directory to anywhere you like:

```
$ cd                            Go home
$
```

And now try to look up Liz in the phone book:

```
$ rolo Liz
rolo: not found
$
```

Unless you already know where this discussion is leading, you are likely to get the results shown above.

Whenever you type in the name of a program to be executed, the shell searches a list of directories until it finds the requested program.[†] Once found, it initiates its execution. This list of directories is contained in a special shell variable called PATH. This variable is automatically set for you when you log onto

---

[†] This is the normal procedure. The System V, Release 2 and later shells are a bit more intelligent, as they keep track of where they find each command you execute. When you reexecute one of these commands, the shell remembers where it was found, and doesn't go searching for it again. This feature is known as *hashing*.

the system. See what it's set to now:

```
$ echo $PATH
/bin:/usr/bin::
$
```

Chances are that your PATH has a slightly different value. As noted, the PATH specifies the directories that the shell will search to execute a command. These directories are separated from one another by colons (:). In the example above, three directories are listed: /bin, /usr/bin, and a special notation : : that stands for the *current* directory. So whenever you type in the name of a program, say for example rolo, the shell searches the directories listed in PATH from left to right until it finds an executable file called lu. First it looks in /bin, then in /usr/bin, and finally in the current directory for an executable file called lu. As soon as it finds it, the shell executes it; if it doesn't find it, the shell issues its "not found" message.

The path

```
/bin::/usr/bin
```

specifies to search /bin, followed by the current directory, followed by /usr/bin. To have the current directory searched *first*, you put a single leading colon at the start of the path:

```
:/bin:/usr/bin
```

For security reasons, it's generally not a good idea to have your current directory searched before the system ones.[†]

You can always override the PATH variable by specifying a path to the file to be executed. For example, if you type

```
/bin/date
```

then the shell will go directly to /bin to execute date. The PATH in this case is ignored, as if you type in

```
../bin/lu
```

or

```
./rolo
```

[†] This is to avoid the so-called *Trojan horse* problem: Someone stores their own version of a command like su (the command that changes you to another user) in a directory they can write into and waits for another user to change to that directory and run su. If the PATH specifies that the current directory be searched first, then the horsed version of su will be executed. This version will get the password that is typed, and then print out Sorry. The user will think he just typed the wrong password.

This last case says to execute the program rolo in the current directory.

So now you understand why you couldn't execute rolo from your HOME directory: /usr/steve/bin wasn't included in your PATH, and so the shell couldn't find rolo. This is a simple matter to rectify. You can simply add this directory to your PATH:

```
$ PATH=/bin:/usr/bin::/usr/steve/bin
$
```

Now *any* program in /usr/steve/bin can be executed by you from *anywhere*:

```
$ pwd                                    Where am I?
/usr/steve
$ rolo Liz
grep: can't open phonebook
$
```

This time the shell found rolo and executed it, but grep couldn't seem to find the phonebook file. Look back at the rolo program and you'll see that the grep error message must be coming from lu. Take another look at lu:

```
$ cat /usr/steve/bin/lu
#
# Look someone up in the phone book -- version 3
#

if [ "$#" -ne 1 ]
then
        echo "Incorrect number of arguments"
        echo "Usage: lu name"
        exit 1
fi

grep "$name" phonebook
$
```

grep is trying to open the phonebook file in the current directory, which is /usr/steve (that's where the program is being executed from—the current directory has no relation to the directory in which the program itself resides).

The PATH only specifies the directories to be searched for programs to be executed, and not for any other types of files. So phonebook must be precisely located for lu. There are several ways to fix this problem—a problem which, by the way, exists with the rem and add programs as well. One approach is to have the lu program change directory to /usr/steve/bin before it does the grep. That way, grep will find phonebook since it will exist in the current directory:

```
   . . .
cd /usr/steve/bin
grep "$1" phonebook
```

This approach is a good one to take when you're doing a lot of work with different files in a particular directory: simply cd to the directory first and then you can directly reference all the files you need.

A second approach is to simply list a full path to phonebook in the grep command:

```
   . . .
grep "$1" /usr/steve/bin/phonebook
```

But suppose you want to let others use your rolo program (and associated lu, add, and rem programs)? You can give them each their own copy, and then you'll have several copies of the identical program on the system—programs that you'll probably have to maintain. And what happens if you make a small change to rolo? Are you going to update all of their copies as well? A better solution might be to keep just one copy of rolo but to give other users access to it.[†]

If you change all of the references of phonebook to explicitly reference *your* phone book, then everyone else who uses your rolo program will be using *your* phone book, and not their own. One way to solve the problem is to require that everyone have their phonebook file in their home directory; this way if the program references the file as $HOME/phonebook it will be relative to the home directory of the person running the program.

Let's try this approach: define a variable inside rolo called PHONEBOOK and set it to $HOME/phonebook. If you then export this variable, lu, rem, and add (which are executed as subshells by rolo) can use the value of PHONEBOOK to reference the file. One nice advantage of this is in case you ever decide in the future to change the location of the phonebook file. All you'll have to do is change this one variable in rolo; the other three programs can remain untouched.

Here is the new rolo program, followed by modified lu, add, and rem programs.

---

† This can be done by giving them execute permission on all of the directories leading to rolo, as well as read and execute permissions on the programs themselves. They can always copy your programs at that point, but you won't have to maintain them.

```
$ cd /usr/steve/bin
$ cat rolo
#
# rolo - rolodex program to look up, add, and
#        remove people from the phone book
#

#
# Set PHONEBOOK to point to the phone book file
# and export it so other progs know about it
#

PHONEBOOK=$HOME/phonebook
export PHONEBOOK

if [ ! -f "$PHONEBOOK" ]
then
        echo "No phone book file in $HOME!"
        exit 1
fi

#
# If arguments are supplied, then do a lookup
#

if [ "$#" -ne 0 ]
then
        lu "$@"
        exit
fi

validchoice=""              # set it null

#
# Loop until a valid selection is made
#

until [ -n "$validchoice" ]
do
        #
        # Display menu
        #

        echo '

        Would you like to:
```

```
                1. Look someone up
                2. Add someone to the phone book
                3. Remove someone from the phone book

          Please select one of the above (1-3): \c'

          #
          # Read and process selection
          #

          read choice
          echo

          case "$choice"
          in
                1)   echo "Enter name to look up: \c"
                     read name
                     lu "$name"
                     validchoice=TRUE;;
                2)   echo "Enter name to be added: \c"
                     read name
                     echo "Enter number: \c"
                     read number
                     add "$name" "$number"
                     validchoice=TRUE;;
                3)   echo "Enter name to be removed: \c"
                     read name
                     rem "$name"
                     validchoice=TRUE;;
                *)   echo "Bad choice";;
          esac
done
$ cat add
#
# Program to add someone to the phone book file
#

if [ "$#" -ne 2 ]
then
        echo "Incorrect number of arguments"
        echo "Usage: add name number"
        exit 1
fi

echo "$1        $2" >> $PHONEBOOK
```

```
      sort -o $PHONEBOOK $PHONEBOOK
$ cat lu
#
# Look someone up in the phone book
#

if [ "$#" -ne 1 ]
then
        echo "Incorrect number of arguments"
        echo "Usage: lu name"
        exit 1
fi

name=$1
grep "$name" $PHONEBOOK

if [ $? -ne 0 ]
then
        echo "I couldn't find $name in the phone book"
fi
$ cat rem
#
# Remove someone from the phone book
#

if [ "$#" -ne 1 ]
then
        echo "Incorrect number of arguments"
        echo "Usage: rem name"
        exit 1
fi

name=$1

#
# Find number of matching entries
#

matches=`grep "$name" $PHONEBOOK | wc -l`

#
# If more than one match, issue message, else remove it
#

if [ "$matches" -gt 1 ]
then
```

```
        echo "More than one match; please qualify further"
elif [ "$matches" -eq 1 ]
then
        grep -v "$name" $PHONEBOOK > /tmp/phonebook$$
        mv /tmp/phonebook$$ $PHONEBOOK
else
        echo "I couldn't find $name in the phone book"
fi
$
```

(In an effort to be more user-friendly, a test was added to the end of lu to see if the grep succeeds; if it doesn't then a message is displayed to the user.)

Now to test it out:

```
$ cd                              Return home
$ rolo Liz                        Quick lookup
No phonebook file in /usr/steve!  Forgot to move it
$ mv /usr/steve/bin/phonebook .
$ rolo Liz                        Try again
Liz Stachiw      775-2298
$ rolo                            Try menu selection

        Would you like to:

                1. Look someone up
                2. Add someone to the phone book
                3. Remove someone from the phone book

        Please select one of the above (1-3): 2

Enter name to be added: Teri Zak
Enter number: 393-6000
$ rolo Teri
Teri Zak         393-6000
$
```

rolo, lu, and add seem to be working fine. rem should also be tested to make sure it's okay as well.

If you still want to run lu, rem, or add standalone, you can do it provided you first define PHONEBOOK and export it:

```
$ PHONEBOOK=$HOME/phonebook
$ export PHONEBOOK
$ lu Harmon
I couldn't find Harmon in the phone book
$
```

If you do intend to run these programs standalone, then you'd better put checks in the individual programs to ensure that PHONEBOOK is set to some value.

◆ Your Current Directory ◆

Your current directory is also part of your environment. Take a look at this small shell program called cdtest:

```
$ cat cdtest
cd /usr/steve/bin
pwd
$
```

The program does a cd to /usr/steve/bin and then executes a pwd to verify that the change was made. Let's run it:

```
$ pwd                              Get my bearings
/usr/steve
$ cdtest
/usr/steve/bin
$
```

Now for the $64,000 question: If you execute a pwd command now, will you be in /usr/steve or /usr/steve/bin?

```
$ pwd
/usr/steve
$
```

The cd executed in cdtest had no effect on your current directory. Since the current directory is part of the environment, when a cd is executed from a subshell, the current directory of that subshell is altered. *There is no way to change the current directory of a parent shell from a subshell.*

Incidentally, cd is a shell built-in command.

CDPATH

There is a special variable that was added to the shell as of UNIX System V. The CDPATH variable works like the PATH variable: it specifies a list of directories to be searched by the shell whenever you execute a cd command. This search is done only if the specified directory is not given by a full path name and if CDPATH is not null (obviously). So if you type in

```
cd /usr/steve
```

then the shell changes your directory directly to /usr/steve; but if you type

```
cd memos
```

then the shell will look at your CDPATH variable to find the memos directory. And if your CDPATH looks like this:

```
$ echo $CDPATH
:/usr/steve:/usr/steve/docs
$
```

then the shell will first look in your current directory (the leading :) for a memos directory, and if not found will then look in /usr/steve for a memos directory, and if not found there will try /usr/steve/docs in a last ditch effort to find the directory. If the directory that it finds is not relative to your current one, then the cd command prints the full path to the directory to let you know where it's taking you:

```
$ cd /usr/steve
$ cd memos
/usr/steve/docs/memos
$ cd bin
/usr/steve/bin
$
```

Judicious use of the CDPATH variable can save you a lot of typing, especially if your directory hierarchy is fairly deep and you find yourself frequently moving around in it (or if you're frequently moving around into other directory hierarchies as well).

Unlike the PATH, you'll probably want to put your current directory first in the CDPATH list. This will give you the most natural use of CDPATH (since you're used to doing a cd x to switch to the subdirectory x). If the current directory isn't listed first, you may end up in an unexpected directory.

♦ More on Subshells ♦

It's important for you to understand the way subshells work and how they interact with your environment. You know now that a subshell can't change the value of a variable in a parent shell, nor can it change its current directory. Suppose you want to write a program to set values for some variables that you like to use whenever you log on. For example, assume you have the following file called `vars`:

```
$ cat vars
BOOK=/usr/steve/book
UUPUB=/usr/spool/uucppublic
DOCS=/usr/steve/docs/memos
DB=/usr2/data
$
```

You know that if you execute `vars` the values assigned to these variables will not be accessible by you after this program has finished executing, since `vars` will be run in a subshell:

```
$ vars
$ echo $BOOK

$
```

The . Command

Luckily, there is a shell built-in command called `.` (pronounced "dot") whose general format is

    . *file*

and whose purpose is to execute the contents of *file* in the *current* shell. That is, commands from `file` are executed by the current shell just as if they were typed at that point. A subshell is not spawned to execute the program. The shell uses your `PATH` variable to find *file*, just like it does when executing other programs.

```
$ . vars                    Execute vars in the current shell
$ echo $BOOK
  /usr/steve/book           Hoorah!
$
```

Since a subshell isn't spawned to execute the program, any variable that gets assigned a value stays even after execution of the program is completed. It follows then that if you have a program called db that has the following commands in it:

```
$ cat db
DATA=/usr2/data
RPTS=$DATA/rpts
BIN=$DATA/bin

cd $DATA
$
```

then executing db with the "dot" command

```
$ . db
$
```

will define the three variables DATA, RPTS, and BIN in the current shell and then change you to the $DATA directory.

```
$ pwd
/usr2/data
$
```

This last example brings up an interesting point of discussion. If you're one of those UNIX users who has to support a few different directory hierarchies, then you can create programs like db to execute whenever you have to work on one of your directories. In that program you can also include definitions for other variables; for example, you might want to change your prompt in PS1 to something like DB: to let you know that your data base variables have been set up. You may also want to change your PATH to include a directory that has programs related to the database, and your CDPATH variable so that directories in the data base will be easily accessible with the cd command. You can even change HOME so that a cd without any arguments will return you directly to your data base directory.

If you make these sorts of changes, then you'll probably want to execute db in a subshell and not in the current shell, since doing the latter will leave all of the modified variables around after you've finished your work on the data base. The trick to doing it right is to start up a *new* shell from inside the subshell, with all of the modified variables exported to it. Then, when you're done working with the data base, you can "log off" the new shell by typing *CTRL-d*. Let's take a look at how this works. Here is a new version of db:

```
$ cat db
#
# Set up and export variables related to the data base
#

HOME=/usr2/data
BIN=$HOME/bin
RPTS=$HOME/rpts
DATA=$HOME/rawdata

PATH=$PATH$BIN
CDPATH=:$HOME:$RPTS

PS1="DB: "

export HOME BIN RPTS DATA PATH CDPATH PS1

#
# Start up a new shell
#

/bin/sh
$
```

The HOME directory is set to /usr2/data, and then the variables BIN, RPTS, and DATA are defined relative to this HOME (a good idea in case you ever have to move the directory structure somewhere else: all you'd have to change in the program is the variable HOME).

Next the PATH is modified to include the data base bin directory, and the CDPATH variable is set to search the current directory, the HOME directory, and the RPTS directory (which presumably contains subdirectories).

After exporting these variables (which as you recall must be done to put the values of these variables into the environment of subsequently spawned sub-shells), the standard shell, /bin/sh, is started. From that point on, this new shell will process commands typed in from the terminal. When *CTRL-d* is typed to this shell, control will return back to db, which in turn will return control back to your login shell.

```
$ db                                      Run it
DB: echo $HOME
/usr2/data
DB: cd rpts                               Try out CDPATH
/usr2/data/rpts                           It works
DB: ps                                    See what processes are running
   PID TTY TIME COMMAND
   123 13  0:40 sh    Your login shell
```

```
    761 13   0:01  sh      Subshell running db
    765 13   0:01  sh      New shell run from db
    769 13   0:03  ps
DB: CTRL-d                            Done for now
$ echo $HOME
/usr/steve                            Back to normal
$
```

The execution of db is depicted in Fig. 11-8 (where we've only shown the exported variables of interest, not necessarily all that exist in the environment).

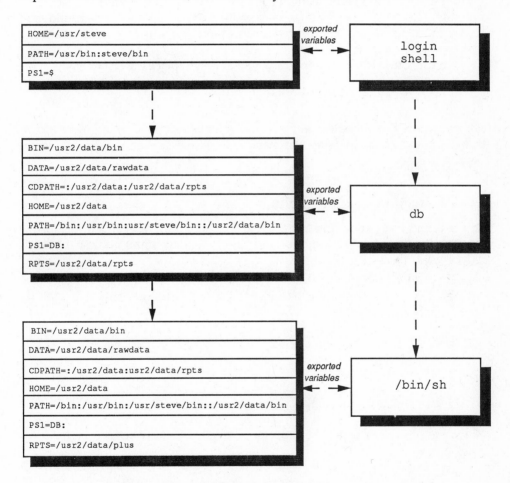

Fig. 11-8. Executing db

The exec Command

Once you started up the new shell from db, you weren't interested in doing anything further once the shell finished, as evidenced by the fact that no commands followed /bin/sh in the program. Rather than having db wait around for the new shell to finish, you can use the exec command to *replace the current program* (db) *with the new one* (/bin/sh). The general format of exec is

```
exec program
```

where *program* is the name of the program to be executed. Since the exec'ed program replaces the current one, there's one less process hanging around; also start up time of an exec'ed program is quicker, due to the way the UNIX system executes processes.

To use exec in the db program, you simply replace the last line with

```
exec /bin/sh
```

As noted, once this gets executed, db will be replaced by /bin/sh. This means that it's pointless to have any commands follow the exec, as they'll never be executed.

I/O Redirection and Subshells

You may not have known it, but the shell automatically executes in a subshell commands like if, for, while, and until if their input and/or output is redirected.

Here's an experiment to try at the terminal:

```
$ for i in 1 2 3; do echo $i; done
1
2
3
$ echo $i                              What's its value?
3
$
```

The value of i after it left the for loop was 3, which makes sense. Now try this:

```
$ for j in 1 2 3; do echo $j; done > /tmp/foo
$ echo $j

$
```

The value of j here is null. That's because the shell executed the for loop in a subshell since its output was redirected. That means that changes made to any variables by the loop are inaccessible once the loop has finished.

This information can help avoid subtle program bugs that may occur if you forget this fact. For example, consider the following program called `wcl` that counts the number of lines contained in the file typed on the command line:

```
$ cat wcl
#
# Count the number of lines in a file
#

file=$1
count=0

while read line
do
        count=`expr $count + 1`
done < $file

echo   $count
$
```

Now run it on a file:

```
$ wcl /etc/passwd
0
$ wc -l /etc/passwd                    See what wc has to say
   59 /etc/passwd
$
```

Here the `while` loop is executed in a subshell since input to it is redirected from the file `$file`. The command inside this loop tallies the number of lines read in the variable `count`. After the loop is finished, the program simply displays this value at the terminal. This value will *always* be 0, because the variable `count` used inside the loop disappears once the `while` loop finishes execution. That's because the `while` was executed in a subshell.

Subshell execution also takes place if input is piped into a `for`, `while`, `until`, `if`, or `case` command, or if the output is piped out. So changing the above `while` to read

```
cat $file |
while read line
do
        count=`expr $count + 1`
done
```

has the same effect.

The subshell that the noted commands get executed in are actually pseudo-subshells, since local variables are actually accessible by these commands, and, as you recall, that's not the case for true subshells. However, changes made to variables, and to the current directory, do behave the same.

Just in case you really need to do the sort of thing shown with the previous while command without having it run in a subshell, there is a way to do it: you can close standard input and reopen it with the file that you want to read. Then you won't have to redirect the while's input, and it won't be run as a subshell.

To change standard input to *file*, you use the exec command in the form

    exec < *file*

Any commands that subsequently read data from standard input will read from *file*.

Redirection of standard output is done similarly. The command

    exec > report

will redirect all subsequent output written to standard output to the file report. Note here that exec is not used to start up execution of a new program as previously described; here it is used to reassign standard input or standard output.

So here's a modified version of wcl that uses the exec to open the data file on standard input.

```
$ cat wcl
#
# Count the number of lines in a file -- version 2
#

file=$1
count=0

exec < $file

while read line
do
        count=`expr $count + 1`
done

echo  $count
$ wcl /etc/passwd                    Try it again
59                                   Much better
$
```

If you use `exec` to reassign standard input and later want to reassign it someplace else, you can simply execute another `exec`. To reassign standard input back to the terminal, you would write

```
exec < /dev/tty
```

The same discussion applies to reassignment of standard output.

The (. . .) and { . . . ; } Constructs

Sometimes you may want to group a set of commands together for some reason. For example, you may want to send a `sort` followed by execution of your `plotdata` program into the background for execution. You can group a set of commands together by enclosing them in a set of parentheses or braces. The first form causes the commands to be executed by a subshell, the latter form by the current shell.

Here's some examples to illustrate how they work:

```
$ x=50
$ (x=100)                    Execute this in a subshell
$ echo $x
50                           Didn't change
$ { x=100; }                 Execute this in the current shell
$ echo $x
100
$ pwd                        Where am I?
/usr/steve
$ (cd bin; ls)               Change to bin and do an ls
add
greetings
lu
number
phonebook
rem
rolo
$ pwd
/usr/steve                   No change
$ { cd bin; }                This should change me
$ pwd
/usr/steve/bin
$
```

If the commands enclosed in the braces are all to be typed on the same line, then a space must follow the left brace, and a semicolon must appear after the last command.

As the example

```
(cd bin; ls)
```

showed, the parentheses are useful for doing some commands without affecting
your current environment. You can also use them for other purposes:

```
$ (sort 1986data -o 1986data; plotdata 1986data) &
3421
$
```

The parentheses group the `sort` and `plotdata` commands together so that
they can both be sent to the background for execution, with their order of execution preserved.

Input and output can be piped to and from these constructs, and I/O can be
redirected. In the next example, a

```
.ls 2
```

`nroff` command (for double-spaced output) is effectively tacked to the beginning of the file `memo` before being sent to `nroff`.

```
$ { echo ".ls 2"; cat memo; } | nroff -Tlp | lp
```

In the command sequence

```
$ { prog1; prog2; prog3; } 2>errors
```

all messages written to standard error by the three programs are collected into
the file `errors`. You should note that even with the `{ ... }` construct the shell
will execute the enclosed commands in a subshell if I/O redirection (this includes
pipes) is used on the construct as in the example above.

As a final example, let's return to the `mon` program from Chapter 9. As
you'll recall, this program periodically checked for a user logging onto the system. One of the comments we made back then is that it would be nice if the program could somehow automatically "send itself" to the background for execution, since that's how it's really meant to be run. Now you know how to do it:
You simply enclose the `until` loop and the commands that follow inside
parentheses and send it into the background:

```
$ cat mon
#
# Wait until a specified user logs on -- version 4
#

# Set up default values
```

```
mailopt=FALSE
interval=60

# process command options

while getopts mt: option
do
        case "$option"
        in
                m)        mailopt=TRUE;;
                t)        interval=$OPTARG;;
                \?)       echo "Usage: mon  [-m] [-t n] user"
                    echo "   -m means to be informed by mail"
                    echo "   -t means check every n secs."
                     exit 1;;
        esac
done

# Make sure a user name was specified

if [ "$OPTIND" -gt "$#" ]
then
        echo "Missing user name!"
        exit 2
fi

shiftcount=`expr $OPTIND - 1`
shift $shiftcount
user=$1

#
# Send everything that follows into the background
#

(
   #
   # Check for user logging on
   #

   until who | grep "^$user " > /dev/null
   do
           sleep $interval
   done

   #
```

```
      # When we reach this point, the user has logged on
      #

      if [ "$mailopt" = FALSE ]
      then
              echo "$user has logged on"
      else
              runner=`who am i | cut -c1-8`
              echo "$user has logged on" | mail $runner
      fi
  ) &
```

The entire program could have been enclosed in parentheses, but we arbitrarily decided to do the argument checking and parsing first before sending the remainder to the background.

```
$ mon fred
$                              Prompt comes back so you can continue working
  ...
fred has logged on
```

Note that a process id number is not printed by the shell when a command is sent to the background within a shell program.

Another Way to Pass Variables to a Subshell

If you want to send the value of a variable to a subshell, there's another way to do it besides setting the variable and then exporting it. On the command line, you can precede the name of the command with the assignment of as many variables as you want. For example,

```
DBHOME=/uxn2/data DBID=452 dbrun
```

places the variables DBHOME and DBID, and their indicated values, into the environment of dbrun and then dbrun gets executed. These variables will not be known to the current shell; they're created only for the execution of dbrun. In fact, execution of the above command behaves identically to typing

```
(DBHOME=/uxn2/data; DBID=452; export DBHOME DBID; dbrun)
```

Here's a short example:

```
$ cat foo1
echo :$x:
foo2
$ cat foo2
```

```
       echo :$x:
       $ foo1
       ::
       ::                                        x not known to foo1 or foo2
       $ x=100 foo1                              Try it this way
       :100:                                     x  is known to foo1
       :100:                                     and to its subshells
       $ echo :$x:
       ::                                        Still not known to current shell
       $
```

So variables defined this way otherwise behave as normal exported variables to
the subshell.

◆ Your `.profile` File ◆

In Chapter 3 you learned about the login sequence. This sequence is completed
when your shell displays your command prompt and waits for you to type your
first command. Just before it does that, however, your login shell executes two
special files on the system. The first is `/etc/profile`. This file is set up by the
system administrator and usually does things like checking to see if you have
mail (where do you think the `You have mail.` message comes from?), setting
your default file creation mask (your *umask*), assigning values to some standard
exported variables, and anything else that the administrator wants to have executed whenever a user logs in.

The second file that gets automatically executed is `.profile` in your
home directory. Your system administrator may have given you a default
`.profile` file when you got your account. See what's in it now:

```
       $ cat $HOME/.profile
       PATH="/bin:/usr/bin:/usr/lbin::"
       export PATH
       $
```

Here you see a small `.profile` file that simply sets the PATH and exports
it.

You can change your `.profile` file to include any commands that you
want executed whenever you log in. Note that the commands in
`/etc/profile` and `.profile` are executed by your login shell (as if you
typed in

```
$ . /etc/profile
$ . .profile
$
```

as soon as you logged in), which means that changes made to your environment remain after the programs are executed.

Here's a sample .profile that sets your PATH to include your own bin, sets your CDPATH, changes your primary and secondary command prompts, changes your erase character to a backspace (*CTRL-h*) with the stty command, and prints a friendly message using the greetings program from Chapter 8:

```
$ cat $HOME/.profile
PATH=/bin:/usr/bin:/usr/lbin:$HOME/bin::
CDPATH=:$HOME:$HOME/misc:$HOME/documents

PS1="=> "
PS2="====> "

export PATH CDPATH PS1 PS2

stty echoe erase CTRL-h

echo
greetings
$
```

Here's what a login sequence would look like with this .profile:

```
login: steve
Password:

Good morning                        Output from greetings
=>                                  New PS1
```

◆ The **TERM** Variable ◆

If you tend to use more than one type of terminal, then the .profile is a good place to put some code to prompt for the terminal type and then set the TERM variable accordingly. This variable is used by screen editors like vi and other screen-based programs.

A sample section of code from a .profile file to prompt for the terminal type might look like this:

```
echo "What terminal are you using (hp-2621 is the default)? \c"
read TERM
if [ -z "$TERM" ]
then
        TERM=2621
fi
export TERM
```

Based upon the terminal type entered, you may also want to do things like set up the function keys or the tabs on the terminal.

Even if you always use the same terminal type, you should set the TERM variable in your .profile file.

♦ Exercises ♦

1. Write a program called `myrm` that takes as arguments the names of files to be removed. If the global variable `MAXFILES` is set, then take it as the maximum number of files to remove without question. If the variable is not set, then use 10 as the maximum. If the number of files to be removed exceeds this count, then ask the user for confirmation before removing the files:

```
$ ls | wc -l
      25
$ myrm *                          Remove them all
Remove 25 files (y/n)? n
files not removed
$ MAXFILES=100 myrm *
$ ls
$                                 All files removed
```

   If `MAXFILES` is set to zero, then the check should be suppressed.

2. Here are two programs called `prog1` and `prog2`:

```
$ cat prog1
e1=100
export e1
e2=200
e3=300 prog2
$ cat prog2
echo $e1 $e2 $e3 $e4
$
```

   What output would you expect after typing the following:

```
$ e2=20; export e2
$ e4=40 prog1
```

3. Modify `rolo` from this chapter so that a person running the program can keep his or her phonebook file in any directory and not just in the home directory. This can be done by requiring that the user set an exported variable called `PHONEBOOK` to the name of the phonebook file before executing `rolo`. Check to make sure that this variable is set to a valid file. If the variable is not set, then have the program assume that the phonebook file is in the user's home directory as before.

Here are some examples:

```
$ PHONEBOOK=/usr/steve/personal lu Leela
Leela           747-0370
$ PHONEBOOK=/usr/pat/phonebook lu Toritos
El Toritos      945-2236
$
```

In the last example, we assume that the user `steve` has been granted read access to `pat`'s phonebook file.

More on Parameters

I n this chapter, you'll learn some more about parameters. Technically speaking, parameters include the arguments passed to a program (the *positional* parameters), the special shell variables like `$#` and `$?`, and ordinary variables, also known as *keyword* parameters.

Positional parameters cannot be assigned values directly; however, they can be reassigned values with the `set` command. Keyword parameters are assigned values simply by writing

variable=value

The format is a bit more general than that shown; actually, you can assign several keyword parameters at once using the format

variable=value variable=value ...

as the following example illustrates:

```
$ x=100 y=200 z=50
$ echo $x $y $z
100 200 50
$
```

◆ Parameter Substitution ◆

In the simplest form, to have the value of a parameter substituted, you simply precede the parameter with a dollar sign, as in `$i` or `$9`.

${parameter}

If there's a potential conflict caused by the characters that follow the parameter name, then you can enclose the name inside curly braces, as in

```
mv $file ${file}x
```

This command would add an x to the end of the file name specified by $file, and could not be written as

```
mv $file $filex
```

since the shell would substitute the value of filex for the second argument.

${parameter:-value}

This construct says to substitute the value of *parameter* if it is not null, and to substitute *value* otherwise. For example, in the command line

```
echo Using editor ${EDITOR:-/bin/vi}
```

the shell will substitute the value of EDITOR if it's not null, and the value /bin/vi otherwise. It has the same effect as writing

```
if [ -n "$EDITOR" ]
then
        echo Using editor $EDITOR
else
        echo Using editor /bin/vi
fi
```

The command line

```
${EDITOR:-/bin/ed} /tmp/edfile
```

will start up the program stored in the variable EDITOR (presumably a text editor), or /bin/ed if EDITOR is null.

Here's a simple test of this construct from the terminal:

```
$ EDITOR=/bin/ed
$ echo ${EDITOR:-/bin/vi}
/bin/ed
$ EDITOR=                          Set it null
$ echo ${EDITOR:-/bin/vi}
/bin/vi
$
```

${ *parameter* := *value* }

This version is similar to the last, only if *parameter* is null, not only is *value* used, but it is also assigned to *parameter* as well (note the = in the construct). You can't assign values to positional parameters this way (that means that *parameter* can't be a number).

     A typical use of this construct would be in testing to see if an exported variable has been set and, if not, setting it to a default value, as in

```
${PHONEBOOK:=$HOME/phonebook}
```

This says that if PHONEBOOK is set to some value, then leave it alone; otherwise, set it to $HOME/phonebook.

     You should note that the above could not stand alone as a command, since after the substitution was performed the shell would attempt to execute the result:

```
$ PHONEBOOK=
$ ${PHONEBOOK:=$HOME/phonebook}
sh: /usr/steve/phonebook: cannot execute
$
```

In order to use this construct as a "standalone" command, the null command is often employed. If you write

```
: ${PHONEBOOK:=$HOME/phonebook}
```

the shell will still do the substitution (it evaluates the rest of the command line), yet execute nothing (the null command).

```
$ PHONEBOOK=
$ : ${PHONEBOOK:=$HOME/phonebook}
$ echo $PHONEBOOK                    See if it got assigned
/usr/steve/phonebook
$ : ${PHONEBOOK:=foobar}             Shouldn't change it
$ echo $PHONEBOOK
/usr/steve/phonebook                 It didn't
$
```

${parameter:?value}

If *parameter* is not null, the shell substitutes its value; otherwise, the shell writes *value* to standard error and then exits (don't worry—if it's done from your login shell, you won't be logged off). If *value* is omitted, then the shell writes the message

> *prog*: *parameter*: `parameter null or not set`

Here's an example from the terminal:

```
$ PHONEBOOK=
$ : ${PHONEBOOK:?"No PHONEBOOK file!"}
No PHONEBOOK file!
$ : ${PHONEBOOK:?}                        Don't give a value
sh: PHONEBOOK: parameter null or not set
$
```

With this construct, you can easily check to see if a set of variables needed by a program are all set and not null, as in

```
: ${TOOLS:?}   ${EXPTOOLS:?}   ${TOOLBIN:?}
```

${parameter:+value}

This one substitutes *value* if *parameter* is not null; otherwise it substitutes nothing.

```
$ traceopt=T
$ echo options: ${traceopt:+"trace mode"}
options: trace mode
$ traceopt=
$ echo options: ${traceopt:+"trace mode"}
options:
$
```

The *value* part for any of the constructs in this section can be a back-quoted command; it's executed by the shell only if its value is to be used. In

```
WORKDIR=${DBDIR:-`pwd`}
```

WORKDIR is assigned the value of DBDIR if it's not null; otherwise the pwd command is executed and the result assigned to WORKDIR. pwd is executed *only if* DBDIR is null.

Each of the parameter substitution constructs described in this section is summarized in Table A-3 in Appendix A.

♦ The $0 Variable ♦

Whenever you execute.a shell program, the shell automatically stores the name of the program inside the special variable $0. This can be used to advantage when you have two or more programs that are linked under different names and you want to know which one was executed. It's also useful for displaying error messages since it removes the dependency of the file name from the program. If the name of the program is referenced by $0, then subsequently renaming the program will not require the program to be edited:

```
$ cat lu
#
# Look someone up in the phone book
#

if [ "$#" -ne 1 ]
then
        echo "Incorrect number of arguments"
        echo "Usage: $0 name"
        exit 1
fi

name=$1
grep "$name" $PHONEBOOK

if [ $? -ne 0 ]
then
        echo "I couldn't find $name in the phone book"
fi
$ PHONEBOOK=$HOME/phonebook
$ export PHONEBOOK
$ lu Teri
Teri Zak        393-6000
$ lu Teri Zak
Incorrect number of arguments
Usage: lu name
$ mv lu lookup                    Rename it
$ lookup Teri Zak                 See what happens now
Incorrect number of arguments
Usage: lookup name
$
```

◆ The set Command ◆

The shell's set command is a dual-purpose command: it's used both to set various shell options as well as to reassign the positional parameters $1, $2, ...

The -x Option

This option turns on trace mode in the shell. It does to the current shell what the command

```
sh -x ctype a
```

did for the execution of the ctype program in Chapter 8. From the point that the

```
set -x
```

command is executed, all subsequently executed commands will be printed by the shell, after file name, variable, and command substitution and I/O redirection have been performed. The traced commands are preceded by plus signs, although variable assignments are not.

```
$ x=*
$ set -x                          Set command trace option
$ echo $x
+ echo add greetings lu rem rolo
add greetings lu rem rolo
$ cmd=wc
cmd=wc
$ ls | $cmd -l
+ ls
+ wc -l
        5
$
```

You can turn off trace mode at any time simply by executing set with the +x option:

```
$ set +x
+ set +x
$ ls | wc -l
        5                          Back to normal
$
```

You should note that the trace option is *not* passed down to subshells. But you can trace a subshell's execution either by running the shell with the -x option followed by the name of the program to be executed, as in

```
sh -x rolo
```

or you can insert a `set -x` command inside the file itself. In fact, you can insert any number of `set -x` and `set +x` commands inside your program to turn trace mode on and off as desired.

set with No Arguments

If you don't give any arguments to `set`, you'll get an alphabetized list of all of the variables that exist in your environment, be they local or exported:

```
$ set                            Show me all variables
CDPATH=:/usr/steve:/usr/spool
EDITOR=/bin/vi
HOME=/usr/steve
IFS=

LOGNAME=steve
MAIL=/usr/spool/mail/steve
MAILCHECK=600
PATH=/bin:/usr/bin:/usr/steve/bin::
PHONEBOOK=/usr/steve/phonebook
PS1=$
PS2=>
PWD=/usr/steve/misc
SHELL=/bin/sh
TERM=hp2621
TMOUT=0
TZ=EST5EDT
cmd=wc
x=*
$
```

Using set to Reassign Positional Parameters

There is no way to directly assign a value to a positional parameter; e.g.,

```
1=100
```

does not work. These parameters are initially set upon execution of the shell program. The only way they may be changed is with the `shift` or the `set` commands. If words are given as arguments to `set` on the command line, then the positional parameters $1, $2, ... will be assigned to those words. The previous values stored in the positional parameters will be lost forever. So

```
set a b c
```

assigns a to $1, b to $2, and c to $3. $# also gets set to 3.

```
$ set one two three four
$ echo $1:$2:$3:$4
one:two:three:four
$ echo $#                        This should be 4
4
$ echo $*                        What does this reference now?
one two three four
$ for arg; do echo $arg; done
one
two
three
four
$
```

So after execution of the set, everything seems to work consistently: $#, $*, and the for loop without a list.

set is often used in this fashion to "parse" data that is read from a file or the terminal. Here's a program called words that counts the number of words typed on a line (using the shell's definition of a "word"):

```
$ cat words
#
# Count words on a line
#

read line
set $line
echo $#
$ words                          Run it
Here's a line for you to count.
7
$
```

The program stores the line read in the shell variable line and then executes the command

```
set $line
```

This causes each word stored in line to be assigned to the positional parameters. The variable $# is also set to the number of words assigned, which is the number of words on the line.

The -- Option

Try typing in a line to words that begins with a – and see what happens:

```
$ words
-1 + 5 = 4
words: -1: bad option(s)
$
```

After the line was read and assigned to line, the command

```
set $line
```

was executed. After the shell did its substitution, the command line looked like this:

```
set -1 + 5 = 4
```

When set executed, it saw the – and thought that an option was being selected, thus explaining the error message.

Another problem with words occurs if you give it a line consisting entirely of whitespace characters, or if the line is null:

```
$ words
                                            Just RETURN is pressed
CDPATH=:/usr/steve:/usr/spool
EDITOR=/bin/vi
HOME=/usr/steve
IFS=

LOGNAME=steve
MAIL=/usr/spool/mail/steve
MAILCHECK=600
PATH=/bin:/usr/bin:/usr/steve/bin::
PHONEBOOK=/usr/steve/phonebook
PS1=$
PS2=>
PWD=/usr/steve/misc
SHELL=/bin/sh
TERM=hp2621
TMOUT=0
TZ=EST5EDT
cmd=wc
x=*
0
$
```

To protect against both of these problems occurring, you can use the `--` option to `set`. This tells `set` not to interpret any subsequent arguments on the command line as options. It also prevents `set` from displaying all of your variables if no other arguments follow, as was the case when you typed a null line.

So the `set` command in `words` should be changed to read

```
set -- $line
```

With the addition of a `while` loop and some help from `expr`, the `words` program can be easily modified to count the total number of words on standard input, giving you your own version of `wc -w`:

```
$ cat words
#
# Count all of the words on standard input
#

count=0

while read line
do
        set -- $line
        count=`expr $count + $#`
done

echo $count
$
```

After each line is read, the `set` command is executed to take advantage of the fact that `$#` will be assigned the number of words on the line. The `--` option is supplied to `set` just in case any of the lines read begins with a `-`, or consists entirely of whitespace characters.

The value of `$#` is then added into the variable `count`, and the next line is read. When the loop is exited, the value of `count` is displayed. This represents the total number of words read.

```
$ words < /etc/passwd
567
$ wc -w < /etc/passwd                    Check against wc
     567
$
```

(Our version is a lot slower than wc, since the latter is written in C.)
Here's a quick way to count the number of files in your directory:[†]

```
$ set *
$ echo $#
8
$
```

This is much faster than

```
ls | wc -l
```

since the first method uses only shell built-in commands (echo became a built-in as of System V). In general, your shell programs will run a lot faster if you try to get as much done as you can using the shell's built-in commands.

Other Options to set

There are several other options that set accepts, each of them enabled by preceding the option with a -, and disabled by preceding it with a +. The -x option that we have described here is perhaps the most commonly used. Others are summarized in Table A-8 in Appendix A.

♦ The IFS Variable ♦

There is a special shell variable called IFS, which stands for *Internal Field Separator*. The shell uses the value of this variable when parsing input from the read command, output from command substitution (the back-quoting mechanism), and when performing variable substitution. If it's typed on the command line, then the shell treats it like a normal whitespace character (i.e., as a word delimiter).

See what it's set to now:

```
$ echo "$IFS"


$
```

Well, that wasn't very illuminating! To determine the actual characters that are stored in there, pipe the output from echo into the od (*octal dump*) command

---

[†] This technique may not work on very large directories as you may exceed the limit on the length of the command line (the precise length varies between UNIX systems). Working with such directories may cause problems when using file name substitution in other commands as well, such as echo *, or for file in *.

with the −b (byte display) option:

```
$ echo "$IFS" | od -b
0000000 040 011 012 012
0000004
$
```

The first column of numbers shown is the relative offset from the start of the input. The following numbers are the octal equivalents of the characters read by od. The first such number is 040, which is the ASCII value of the space character. It's followed by 011, the tab character, and then by 012, the newline character. The next character is another newline; this was written by the echo. These characters for IFS come as no surprise; they're the "whitespace" characters we've talked about throughout the book.

   You can change your IFS to any character or characters you like. This is useful when you want to parse a line of data whose fields aren't delimited by the normal whitespace characters. For example, we noted that the shell normally strips any leading whitespace characters from the beginning of any line that you read with the read command. You can change your IFS to just a newline character before the read is executed, which will have the effect of preserving the leading whitespace (since the shell won't consider it a field delimiter):

```
$ read line                          Try it the "old" way
            Here's a line
$ echo "$line"
Here's a line
$ IFS="
> "                                  Set it to a just a newline
$ read line                          Try it again
            Here's a line
$ echo "$line"
            Here's a line            Leading spaces preserved
$
```

To change the IFS to just a newline, an open quote was typed, followed immediately by the pressing of the RETURN key, followed by the closed quote on the next line. No additional characters can be typed inside those quotes, as they'll be stored inside IFS and then used by the shell.

   Now let's change the IFS to something more visible, like a colon:

```
$ IFS=:
$ read x y z
123:345:678
$ echo $x
123
$ echo $z
```

```
678
$ list="one:two:three"
$ for x in $list; do echo $x; done
one
two
three
$ var=a:b:c
$ echo "$var"
a:b:c
$
```

Since the IFS was changed to a colon, when the line was read, the shell divided the line into three words: 123, 345 and 678, which were stored into the three variables x, y, and z, respectively. In the next to last example the shell used the IFS when substituting the value of list in the for loop. The last example shows that the shell doesn't use the IFS when performing variable assignment.

Changing the IFS is often done in conjunction with execution of the set command.

```
$ line="Micro Logic Corp.:Box 174:Hackensack, NJ 07602"
$ IFS=:
$ set $line
$ echo $#                           How many parameters were set?
3
$ for field; do echo $field; done
Micro Logic Corp.
Box 174
Hackensack, NJ 07602
$
```

This technique is a very powerful one; it uses all built-in shell commands, which also makes it very fast. (An alternate approach might have been to echo the value of $line into the tr command, where all colons could have been translated into newlines, an approach that would have been much slower.) This technique is used in a final version of the rolo program that's presented in Chapter 14.

Since the IFS has quite an influence on the way things are interpreted by the shell, if you're going to change it in your program it's usually wise to save the old value first in another variable (like OIFS) and then restore it once you've finished the operations that depend upon the changed IFS.

♦ The **readonly** Command ♦

The `readonly` command is used to specify variables whose values cannot be subsequently changed. For example,

```
readonly PATH HOME
```

makes the `PATH` and `HOME` variables readonly. Subsequently attempting to assign a value to these variables will cause the shell to issue an error message:

```
$ PATH=/bin:/usr/bin::
$ readonly PATH
$ PATH=$PATH:/usr/steve/bin
PATH: is read-only
$
```

Here you see that after the variable `PATH` was made readonly, the shell printed an error message when an attempt was made to assign a value to it.

To get a list of your readonly variables, type `readonly` without any arguments:

```
$ readonly
readonly PATH
$
```

You should be aware of the fact that the readonly variable attribute is not passed down to subshells. Also, once a variable has been made readonly in a shell, there is no way to "undo" it.

♦ The **unset** Command ♦

Sometimes you may wish to remove the definition of a variable from your environment. To do so, you type `unset` followed by the names of the variables.

```
$ x=100
$ echo $x
100
$ unset x                        Remove x from the environment
$ echo $x

$
```

You can't `unset` a readonly variable. Furthermore, the variables `IFS`, `MAIL-CHECK`, `PATH`, `PS1`, and `PS2` cannot be unset.

`unset` can also be used to remove the definition of a function.

♦ Exercises ♦

1. Given the following variable assignments:

   ```
   $ EDITOR=/bin/vi
   $ DB=
   $ EDITFLAG=yes
   $ PHONEBOOK=
   $
   ```

   What will be the results of the following commands?

   ```
   echo ${EDITOR}              echo ${DB:=/usr/pat/db}

   echo ${EDITOR:-/bin/ed}  echo ${PHONEBOOK:?}

   echo ${DB:-/usr/pat/db}  ed=${EDITFLAG:+${EDITOR:-/bin/ed}}
   ```

2. Rewrite the home program from Exercise 5, Chapter 7 to use the set command and the IFS to extract the home directory from /etc/passwd. What happens to the program if one of the fields in the file is null, as in

   ```
   steve:okI.yL3Wf8OEs,2.YA:203:100::/usr/steve:/bin/ksh
   ```

   Here the fifth field is null (: :).

13

Loose Ends

We've put commands and features into this chapter that for one reason or another did not logically fit into earlier chapters. There's no particular rationale for their order of presentation.

◆ The `eval` Command ◆

This section describes another of the more unusual commands in the shell: `eval`. Its format is as follows:

eval   *command-line*

where *command-line* is a normal command line that you would type at the terminal. When you put `eval` in front of it, however, the net effect is that the shell scans the command line *twice* before executing it.[†] For the simple case, this really has no effect:

```
$ eval echo hello
hello
$
```

But consider the following example without the use of `eval`:

---

† Actually, what happens is that `eval` simply executes the command passed to it as arguments; so the shell processes the command line when passing the arguments to `eval`, and then once again when `eval` executes the command. The net result is that the command line is scanned twice by the shell.

```
$ pipe="|"
$ ls $pipe wc -l
| not found
wc not found
-l not found
$
```

Those errors come from ls. The shell takes care of pipes and I/O redirection *before* variable substitution, so it never recognizes the pipe symbol inside pipe. The result is that the three arguments |, wc, and -l are passed to ls as arguments.

Putting eval in front of the command sequence gives the desired results:

```
$ eval ls $pipe wc -l
      16
$
```

The first time the shell scans the command line, it substitutes | as the value of pipe. Then eval causes it to rescan the line, at which point the | is recognized by the shell as the pipe symbol.

The eval command is frequently used in shell programs that build up command lines inside one or more variables. If the variables contain any characters that must be seen by the shell directly on the command line (i.e., not as the result of substitution), then eval can be useful. Command terminator (;, |, &), I/O redirection (<, >) and quote characters are among the characters that must appear directly on the command line to have any special meaning to the shell.

For the next example, consider writing a program last whose sole purpose is to display the last argument passed to it. You needed to get at the last argument in the mycp program in Chapter 10. There you did so by shifting all of the arguments until the last one was left. You can also use eval to get at it as shown:

```
$ cat last
eval echo \$$#
$ last one two three four
four
$ last *                          Get the last file
zoo_report
$
```

The first time the shell scans

```
echo \$$#
```

the backslash tells it to ignore the $ that immediately follows. After that, it encounters the special parameter `$#`, so it substitutes its value on the command line. The command now looks like this:

```
echo $4
```

(the backslash is removed by the shell after the first scan). When the shell rescans this line, it will substitute the value of `$4` and then execute `echo`.

This same technique could be used if you had a variable called `arg`, that contained a digit, for example, and you wanted to display the positional parameter referenced by `arg`. You could simply write

```
eval echo \$$arg
```

The only problem is that just the first nine positional parameters can be accessed this way, since it's not possible to explicitly reference parameters 10 and greater (recall what happens if you write `$10`). This problem is also shared with the `last` program: it can't be used with more that nine arguments.

Here's how the `eval` command can be used to effectively create "pointers" to variables.

```
$ x=100
$ ptrx=x
$ eval echo \$$ptrx            Dereference ptrx
100
$ eval $ptrx=50               Store 50 in var that ptrx points to
$ echo $x                      See what happened
50
$
```

♦ The wait Command ♦

If you submit a command line to the background for execution, then that command line runs in a subshell that is independent of your current shell (the job is said to run *asynchronously*). At times, you may want to wait for the background process (also known as a *child* process since it's spawned from your current shell—the *parent*) to finish execution before proceeding. For example, you may have sent a large `sort` into the background and now want to wait for the `sort` to finish because you need to used the sorted data.

The `wait` command is for such a purpose. Its general format is

```
wait process-id
```

where *process-id* is the process id number of the process you want to wait for. If omitted, then the shell waits for all child processes to complete execution. Execution of your current shell will be suspended until the process or processes finish execution. You can try the `wait` command at your terminal:

```
$ sort bigdata > sorted_data &      Send it to the background
3423                                Process id printed by the shell
$ date                              Do some other work
Mon Aug  5 12:23:25 EDT 1985
$ wait 3423                         Now wait for the sort to finish
$                                   When sort finishes, prompt is returned
```

The $! Variable

If you only have one process running in the background, then `wait` with no argument suffices. However, if you're running more than one command in the background and you want to wait on a particular one, then you can take advantage of the fact that the shell stores the process id of the last command executed in the background inside the special variable `$!`. So the command

```
wait $!
```

will wait for the last process sent to the background to complete execution. As mentioned, if you send several commands to the background, then you can save the value of this variable for later use with `wait`:

```
prog1 &
pid1=$!
...
prog2 &
pid2=$!
...
wait $pid1        # wait for prog1 to finish
...
wait $pid2        # wait for prog2 to finish
```

♦ The trap Command ♦

When you hit the DELETE or BREAK key at your terminal during execution of a shell program, normally that program is immediately terminated and your command prompt returned. This may not always be a desirable action. For instance, you may end up leaving around a bunch of temporary files that won't get cleaned up.

The pressing of the DELETE key at the terminal sends what's known as a *signal* to the executing program. The program can specify the action that should be taken upon receipt of the signal. This is done with the trap command, whose general format is

    trap *commands signals*

where *commands* is one or more commands that will be executed whenever any of the signals specified by *signals* is received.

Numbers are assigned to the different types of signals, and the more commonly used ones are summarized in Table 13-1. A more complete list is given under the trap command in Appendix A.

TABLE 13-1. Commonly used signal numbers

Signal	Generated for
0	Exit from the shell
1	Hangup
2	Interrupt (e.g., Delete key)
15	Software termination signal (sent by kill by default)

As an example of the trap command, the following shows how you can remove some files and then exit if someone tries to abort the program from the terminal:

    trap "rm $WORKDIR/work1$$ $WORKDIR/dataout$$; exit" 2

From the point in the shell program that this trap is executed, the two files work1$$ and dataout$$ will be automatically removed if signal number 2 is received by the program. So if the user interrupts execution of the program after this trap is executed, then you can be assured that these two files will be cleaned up. The exit that follows the rm is necessary, since without it execution would continue in the program at the point that it left off when the signal was received.

Signal number 1 is generated for hangup: either someone intentionally hangs up the line, or gets accidentally disconnected. You can modify the above trap to also remove the two specified files in this case by adding signal number 1 to the list of signals:

    trap "rm $WORKDIR/work1$$ $WORKDIR/dataout$$; exit" 1 2

Now these files will be removed if the line gets hung up or if the DELETE key gets pressed.

The commands that are specified to trap must be enclosed in quotes if they contain more than one command. Also note that the shell scans the command line at the time that the trap command gets executed and also again when one of the listed signals is received. So in the last example, the value of WORKDIR and $$ will be substituted at the time that the trap command is executed. If you wanted this substitution to occur at the time that either signal 1 or 2 were received (for example, WORKDIR may not have been defined yet), then you can put the commands inside single quotes:

```
trap 'rm $WORKDIR/work1$$ $WORKDIR/dataout$$; exit'  1 2
```

The trap command can be used to make your programs more user-friendly. In the next chapter, when we revisit the rolo program, the signal generated by the DELETE key is caught by the program and brings the user back to the main menu. In this way, this key can be used to abort the current operation without exiting from the program.

trap with No Arguments

Executing trap with no arguments results in the display of any traps that you have changed.

```
$ trap 'echo logged off at `date` >>$HOME/logoffs' 0
$ trap                          List changed traps
0: echo logged off at `date` >>$HOME/logoffs
$ CTRL-d                        Log off

login: steve                    Log back in
Password:
$ cat $HOME/logoffs             See what happened
logged off at Mon Aug 5 13:12:47 EDT 1985
$
```

A trap was set to be executed whenever signal 0 was received by the shell. This signal is generated whenever the shell is exited. Since this was set in the login shell, the trap will be taken when you log off. The purpose of this trap is to write the time you logged off into the file $HOME/logoffs. The command is enclosed in single quotes to prevent the shell from executing date when the trap is defined.

The trap command is then executed with no arguments, which results in the display of the changed action to be taken for signal 0. Next, steve logs off and then back on again to see if the trap works. Displaying the contents of $HOME/logoffs verifies that the echo command was executed when steve logged off.

Ignoring signals

If the command listed for trap is null, then the specified signal will be ignored when received. For example, the command

```
trap "" 2
```

specifies that the interrupt signal is to be ignored. You might want to ignore certain signals when performing some operation that you don't want interrupted.

Note that the first argument must be specified for a signal to be ignored, and is not equivalent to writing the following, which has a separate meaning of its own:

```
trap 2
```

If you ignore a signal, then all subshells also ignore that signal. However, if you specify an action to be taken upon receipt of a signal, then all subshells will still take the default action upon receipt of that signal. For the signals we've described, this means the subshells will be terminated.

Suppose you execute the command

```
trap "" 2
```

and then execute a subshell, which in turn executes other shell programs as subshells. If an interrupt signal is then generated it will have no effect on the shells or subshells that are executing, since they will all ignore the signal.

If instead of executing the previous trap command you execute

```
trap : 2
```

and then execute your subshells, then upon receiving the interrupt signal the current shell will do nothing (it will execute the null command), but all active subshells will be terminated (they will take the default action—termination).

Resetting Traps

Once you've changed the default action to be taken upon receipt of a signal, you can change it back again with trap if you simply omit the first argument; so

```
trap 1 2
```

will reset the action to be taken upon receipt of signals 1 or 2 back to the default.

◆ More on I/O ◆

You know about the standard constructs `<`, `>`, and `>>` for input redirection, output redirection, and output redirection with append, respectively. You also know that you can redirect standard error from any command simply by writing

   command `2>`*file*

Sometimes you may want to explicitly write to standard error in your program. You can redirect the standard output for a command to standard error by writing

   command `>& 2`

The notation `>&` specifies output redirection to a file associated with the *file descriptor* that follows. File descriptor 0 is standard input, descriptor 1 is standard output, and descriptor 2 is standard error. Note that no space is permitted between the `>` and the `&`.

So to write an error message to standard error, you write

```
echo "Invalid number of arguments" >& 2
```

Frequently you may want to collect the standard output and the standard error output from a program into the same file. If you know the name of the file, then this is straightforward enough:

   command `>foo 2>>foo`

Here both the standard output and the standard error output from *command* will be written to `foo`.

You can also write

   command `>foo 2>&1`

to achieve the same effect; standard output is redirected to `foo`, and standard error is redirected to standard output (which has already been redirected to `foo`). Note that since the shell evaluates redirection from left to right on the command line, that the last example cannot be written

   command `2>&1 >foo`

as this would first redirect standard error to standard output (your terminal by default) and then standard output to `foo`.

You recall that you can also dynamically redirect standard input or output in a program using the `exec` command:

```
exec < datafile
```

redirects standard input from the file `datafile`. Subsequent commands executed that read from standard input will read from `datafile` instead. The command

```
exec > /tmp/output
```

does the same thing with standard output: all commands that subsequently write to standard output will write to `/tmp/output` (unless explicitly redirected elsewhere). Naturally, standard error can be reassigned this way as well:

```
exec 2>/tmp/errors
```

Here all output to standard error will go to `/tmp/errors`.

<&- and >&-

The characters `>&-` have the effect of closing standard output. If preceded by a file descriptor, then the associated file is closed instead. So writing (the impractical)

```
ls >&-
```

causes the output from `ls` to go nowhere since standard output is closed by the shell before `ls` is executed.

The same thing applies for input using `<&-`.

```
$ wc <&-
       0       0       0
$
```

In-line Input Redirection

If the `<<` characters follow a command in the format

command *<<word*

then the shell will use the lines that follow as the standard input for *command*, up until a line that contains just *word* is found. Here's a small example at the terminal:

```
$ wc -l <<ENDOFDATA          Use lines up to ENDOFDATA as standard input
> here's a line
> and another
> and yet another
> ENDOFDATA
       3
$
```

Here the shell fed every line typed into the standard input of wc until it encountered the line containing just ENDOFDATA.

In-line input redirection is a very powerful feature when used inside shell
programs. It lets you specify the standard input to a command directly in the
program, thus obviating the need to write it into a separate file first, or to use
echo to get it into the standard input of the command.

```
$ cat mailmsg
mail $* <<END-OF-DATA

Attention:

        Our monthly computer users group meeting
        will take place on Friday, December 13, 1985 at
        8am in Room 1A-308.  Please try to attend.

END-OF-DATA
$
```

To execute this program for all members of the group that are contained in
the file users_list, you could write

```
mailmsg `cat users_list`
```

The shell performs parameter substitution for the redirected input data,
executes back-quoted commands, and recognizes the backslash character. How-
ever, any other special characters like *, |, and " are ignored. If you have dol-
lar signs, back quotes, or backslashes in these lines that you don't want interpreted by the shell, then you can precede them with a backslash character. Alternatively, if you want the shell to leave the input lines completely untouched,
then you can precede the word that follows the << with a backslash.

```
$ cat <<FOOBAR
> $HOME
> *****
>     \$foobar
> `date`
> FOOBAR                       Terminates the input
```

```
/usr/steve
*****
    $foobar
Mon Aug  5 16:46:12 EDT 1985
$
```

Here the shell supplies all of the lines up to FOOBAR as the input to cat. It substitutes the value for HOME but not for foobar since it's preceded by a backslash. The date command is also executed since back quotes are interpreted.

```
$ cat <<\FOOBAR
> \\\\
> `date`
> $HOME
> FOOBAR
\\\\
`date`
$HOME
$
```

The backslash before FOOBAR told the shell to leave the following lines alone. So it ignored the dollar signs, the backslashes, and the back quotes.

Care should be used when selecting the word that follows the <<. Generally, just make sure it's weird enough so that the chances of it accidentally appearing in the following lines are remote.

If the first character that follows the << is a dash (–), then leading tab characters in the input will be removed by the shell. This is useful for visually indenting the redirected text.

```
$ cat <<-END
>           Indented lines
>           So there you have it
> END
Indented lines
So there you have it
$
```

Shell Archives

One of the best uses of the in-line input redirection feature is for creating shell *archive* files. With this technique, one or more related shell programs can be put into a single file and then shipped to someone else using the standard UNIX mail or uucp commands. When the archive is received, it can be easily "unpacked" by simply running the shell on it.

For example, here's an archived version of the `lu,` `add,` and `rem` programs used by `rolo:`

```
$ cat rolosubs
#
# Archived programs used by rolo.
#

echo Extracting lu
cat >lu <<\THE-END-OF-DATA
#
# Look someone up in the phone book
#

if [ "$#" -ne 1 ]
then
        echo "Incorrect number of arguments"
        echo "Usage: lu name"
        exit 1
fi

name=$1
grep "$name" $PHONEBOOK

if [ $? -ne 0 ]
then
        echo "I couldn't find $name in the phone book"
fi
THE-END-OF-DATA

echo Extracting add
cat >add <<\THE-END-OF-DATA
#
# Program to add someone to the phonebook file
#

if [ "$#" -ne 2 ]
then
        echo "Incorrect number of arguments"
        echo "Usage: add name number"
        exit 1
fi

echo "$1        $2" >> $PHONEBOOK
sort -o $PHONEBOOK $PHONEBOOK
```

```
THE-END-OF-DATA

echo Extracting rem
cat >rem <<\THE-END-OF-DATA
#
# Remove someone from the phone book
#

if [ "$#" -ne 1 ]
then
        echo 'Incorrect number of arguments"
        echo 'Usage: rem name"
        exit 1
fi

name=$1

#
# Find number of matching entries
#

matches=`grep "$name" $PHONEBOOK | wc -l`

#
# If more than one match, issue message, else remove it
#

if [ "$matches" -gt 1 ]
then
        echo 'More than one match; please qualify further'
elif [ "$matches" -eq 1 ]
then
        grep -v "$name" $PHONEBOOK > /tmp/phonebook
        mv /tmp/phonebook $PHONEBOOK
else
        echo "I couldn't find $name in the phone book"
fi
THE-END-OF-DATA
$
```

To be complete, this archive should probably include `rolo` as well, but we didn't here to conserve space.

Now you have one file, `rolosubs`, that contains the source for the three programs `lu`, `add`, and `rem`, which can be sent to someone else using `mail` or `uucp`:

```
$ mail whuxb!tony < rolosubs        Mail the archive
$ mail whuxb!tony                   Mail tony a message
Tony,
     I mailed you a shell archive containing the programs
     lu, add, and rem.  rolo itself will be sent along shortly.
Pat
CTRL-d
$
```

When tony receives the file in his mail, he can extract the three programs simply by running the shell on the file (after having first removed some header lines that mail sticks at the beginning of the file):

```
$ sh rolosubs
Extracting lu
Extracting add
Extracting rem
$ ls lu add rem
add
lu
rem
$
```

The shar program that was used to create the rolosubs archive file is simple:

```
$ cat shar
#
# Program to create a shell archive
# from a set of files
#

echo "#"
echo "# To restore, type sh archive"
echo "#"

for file
do
    echo
    echo "echo Extracting $file"
    echo "cat >$file <<\THE-END-OF-DATA"
    cat $file
    echo "THE-END-OF-DATA"
done
```

Refer back to the contents of the `rolosubs` file when studying the operation of this `shar` program. Remember, `shar` actually creates a shell program.

More sophisticated archiving programs allow entire directories to be archived and also check to make sure that no data is lost in the transmission (see Exercises 2 and 3 at the end of this chapter). The UNIX `sum` command can be used to generate a checksum for a program. This checksum can be generated on the sending end for each file in the archive, and then commands included in the shell archive can verify the sum on the receiving end. If they don't match, then an error message can be displayed.

◆ Functions ◆

As of UNIX System V Release 2, functions were added to the shell. To define a function, you use the general format:

name () { *command;* ... *command;* }

where *name* is the name of the function, the parentheses denote to the shell that a function is being defined, and the commands enclosed between the curly braces define the body of the function. These commands will be executed whenever the function is executed. Note that at least one whitespace character must separate the { from the first command, and that a semicolon must separate the last command from the closing brace if they occur on the same line.

The following defines a function called `nu` that displays the number of logged-in users:

```
nu () { who | wc -l; }
```

You execute a function the same way you execute an ordinary command: simply by typing its name to the shell:

```
$ nu
    22
$
```

Arguments listed after the function on the command line are assigned to the positional parameters `$1`, `$2`, ..., just as with any other command. Here's a function called `nrrun` that runs `tbl`, `nroff`, and `lp` on the file given as its argument:

```
$ nrrun () { tbl $1 | nroff -mm -Tlp | lp; }
$ nrrun memo1                              Run it on memo1
$
```

Functions exist only in the shell in which they're defined; that is, they can't be passed down to subshells. Further, since the function is executed in the current shell, changes made to the current directory or to variables remain after the function has completed execution:

```
$ db () {
>        PATH=$PATH:/uxn2/data
>        PS1=DB:
>        cd /uxn2/data;
>        }
$ db                          Execute it
DB:
```

As you see, a function definition can continue over as many lines as necessary. The shell displays your secondary command prompt until you close the definition with the }.

You can put definitions for commonly used functions inside your .pro-file so that they'll be available whenever you log in. Alternatively, you can group the definitions in a file, say myfuncs, and then execute the file in the current shell by typing

```
. myfuncs
```

This will have the effect of causing any functions defined inside myfuncs to be read in and defined to the current shell.

The following function, called mycd, takes advantage of the fact that functions are run in the current environment. It mimics the operation of the Korn shell's cd command, which allows a – to be given as the argument to switch back to the *previous* directory.

```
$ cat myfuncs                      See what's inside
#
# new cd function:
#       mycd dir  Switches to dir
#       mycd -    Switches to previous dir
#
```

```
mycd ()
{
        CURDIR=`pwd`

        if [ "$1" = "-" ]
        then
                echo $OLDDIR
                cd $OLDDIR
        else
                cd "$1"
        fi

        OLDDIR=$CURDIR
}
```

```
$ . myfuncs                              Read in definition
$ pwd
/usr/steve
$ mycd /usr/spool/uucppublic             Change directory
$ pwd                                    Did it work?
/usr/spool/uucppublic
$ mycd -                                 Go back to previous directory
/usr/steve
$ mycd -                                 Ditto
/usr/spool/uucppublic
$
```

Once a function has been defined, its execution will be faster than an equivalent shell program file. That's because the shell won't have to: Search the disk for the program, open the file, and read its contents into memory.

Another advantage of functions is the ability to group all of your related shell programs in a single file if desired. For example, the add, lu, and rem programs from Chapter 11 can be defined as functions inside rolo. The template for such an approach is shown:

```
$ cat rolo
#
# rolo program written in function form
#

#
# Function to add someone to the phonebook file
#

add () {
        # put commands from add program here
}

#
# Function to look someone up in the phone book
#


lu () {
        # put commands from lu program here
}

#
# Function to remove someone from the phone book
#

rem () {
        # put commands from rem program here
}

#
# rolo - rolodex program to look up, add, and
#        remove people from the phone book
#

# put commands from rolo here
$
```

None of the commands inside the original add, lu, rem, or rolo programs would have to be changed. These first three programs are turned into functions by including them inside rolo, sandwiched between the function header and the closing curly brace. Note that defining them as functions this way now makes them inacessible as standalone commands.

Removing a Function Definition

In order to remove the definition of a function from the shell, you use the `unset` command. This is the same command you use to remove the definition of a variable to the shell.

```
$ unset nu
$ nu
nu: not found
$
```

The `return` Command

If you execute an `exit` command from inside a function, its effect is not only to terminate execution of the function, but also of the shell program that called the function. If you instead would like to just terminate execution of the function, you can use the `return` command, whose format is

```
return n
```

The value *n* is used as the return status of the function. If omitted, then the status returned is that of the last command executed. This is also what gets returned if you don't execute a `return` at all in your function. The return status is in all other ways equivalent to the exit status: you can access its value through the shell variable `$?`, and you can also test it in `if`, `while`, and `until` commands.

♦ The `type` Command ♦

When you type in the name of a command to execute, it's frequently useful to know where that command is coming from. In other words, is the command actually defined as a function? Is it a shell program? Is it a shell built-in? Is it a standard UNIX command? This is where the `type` command comes in handy. The type command takes one or more command names as its argument and tells you what it knows about it. Here's some examples:

```
$ nu () { who | wc -l; }
$ type pwd
pwd is a shell built-in
$ type troff
troff is /usr/bin/troff
$ type cat
cat is /bin/cat
$ type nu
nu is a function
nu () {
who | wc -l
}
$
```

♦ The Restricted Shell rsh ♦

The restricted shell is almost the same as the regular shell, but it's designed to *restrict* a user's capabilities by disallowing certain actions that the standard shell allows. It is found in /bin/rsh and is usually started as the login shell for a user who should not have full capabilities on a system, e.g., a game user or data-entry clerk. The list of actions disallowed is very short:

1. Cannot change directory (cd)

2. Cannot change PATH or SHELL variables

3. Cannot specify a path to a command

4. Cannot redirect output (> and >>)

5. Cannot exec programs

These restrictions are enforced *after* the .profile is executed when logging in, and the user is logged off if he hits BREAK or DELETE while the .profile is being interpreted.

These simple restrictions allow the writer of a restricted user's .profile to have control over what commands that user can use. The example that follows shows a simple setup for a restricted environment.

```
$ cat .profile                           User restrict's .profile
PATH=/usr/rbin:/usr/restrict/bin
export PATH
SHELL=/bin/rsh                           Some commands use SHELL variable
```

```
export SHELL
cd /usr/restrict/restdir                    Don't leave user in HOME directory
$ ls -l .profile                            Restricted user shouldn't own his .profile
-rw-r--r--  1 pat   group1  179 Apr 14 17:50 .profile
$ ls /usr/rbin                              Directory of restricted commands
cat                                         Harmless commands
echo
ls
mail                                        Let them send us mail
red                                         Restricted editor
write
$ ls /usr/restrict/bin                      restrict's command directory
adventure                                   Lots of games
backgammon
chess
hearts
poker
rogue
$
```

Here we have a restricted environment for a user. When this user logs in, his PATH is changed to search just the directories /usr/rbin and /usr/restrict/bin. He can only run commands found in these two directories. Any other command will get a *command: not found* response. The user is effectively bottled up in the directory /usr/restrict/restdir and cannot cd out of it. The .profile is owned by a user other than the restricted one, and the permissions are such that only the owner can change the file. (Don't let a restricted user alter his or her .profile since the .profile is executed before any restrictions are applied.)

One quick note about the commands in /usr/rbin: they were simply copied from the /bin and /usr/bin directories. You can put almost any command from /bin and /usr/bin in /usr/rbin; just use common sense in choosing the commands you allow restricted users to use. For example, don't give them access to the shell, a compiler, or chmod, as these may be used to bypass the restricted shell. The mail and write commands are safe even though they have shell escapes because the shell looks at the SHELL variable and runs restricted if the first character of its name is "r." The restricted editor red is the same as ed, except it doesn't allow shell escapes, and it only allows editing of files in the current directory.

You should note that the System V restricted shell is not really very secure. It should not be used to contain hostile users. The System V, Release 2 restricted shell is more secure, but if you give a restricted user certain commands (like env), he will be able to break out into a nonrestricted shell.

We have now covered virtually every feature of the standard shell. Descriptions of some other commands like umask and ulimit have been relegated to Appendix A. In the next chapter we'll take a look at a more sophisticated version of the rolo program.

♦ Exercises ♦

1. Using `eval`, write a program called `recho` that prints its arguments in reverse order. So

   ```
   recho one two three
   ```

   should produce

   ```
   three two one
   ```

   Assume that no more than 9 arguments will be passed to the program.

2. Modify the `shar` program presented in this chapter to handle directories. `shar` should recognize input files from different directories and should make sure the directories are created if necessary when the archive is unpacked. Also allow `shar` to be used to archive an entire directory.

   ```
   $ ls rolo
   lu
   add
   rem
   rolo
   $ shar rolo/lu rolo/add rolo/rem  > rolosubs.shar
   $ shar rolo > rolo.shar
   ```

   In the first case, `shar` was used to archive three files from the `rolo` directory. In the last case, `shar` was used to archive the entire `rolo` directory.

3. Modify `shar` to include in the archive the character count for each file and commands to compare the count of each extracted file against the count of the original file. If a discrepancy occurs, an error should be noted, as in

   ```
   add: expected 345 characters, extracted 343.
   ```

4. Write a function called `sw` to replace `cd`. If the argument to `sw` is `-`, then have it `cd` you to your previous directory. Like `cd`, if no argument is given to `sw`, have it change you to your HOME directory. Here's some sample uses of `sw`:

   ```
   $ pwd
   /usr/steve/docs/memos
   $ sw /usr/steve
   ```

```
$ pwd
/usr/steve
$ sw -                          Change to previous directory
$ pwd
/usr/steve/docs/memos
$
```

14

Rolo Revisited

This chapter presents a final version of the `rolo` program. This version is enhanced with additional options and also allows for more general types of entries (other than just names and numbers). The sections in this chapter discuss the individual programs in `rolo`, starting with `rolo` itself. At the end of this chapter, sample output is shown.

♦ Design Considerations ♦

A more practical type of rolodex program would permit more than just the names and numbers to be stored in the phone book. You'd probably want to keep addresses (maybe even electronic mail addresses) there as well. The new `rolo` program allows entries in the phone book to consist of multiple lines. For example, a typical entry might be:

```
Steve's Ice Cream
444 6th Avenue
New York City 10003
495-3021
```

In order to increase the flexibility of the program, we're allowing an individual entry to contain as many lines as desired. So another entry in the phone book might read

```
YMCA
(201) 965-2344
```

To logically separate one entry from the next inside the phone book file, each entry is "packed" into a single line. This is done by replacing the terminating newline characters in an entry with a special character. We arbitrarily chose the caret ^. The only restriction here is that this character not be used as part of the entry itself.

Using this technique, the first entry shown would be stored in the phone book file as:

```
Steve's Ice Cream^444 6th Avenue^New York City 10003^495-3021^
```

and the second entry shown as

```
    YMCA^(201) 965-2344^
```

You'll shortly see how convenient it becomes to process the entries once they're stored in this format. Now we'll describe each program written for the rolodex program.

◆ rolo ◆

```
#
# rolo - rolodex program to look up, add,
#        remove and change entries from the phone book
#

#
# Set PHONEBOOK to point to the phone book file
# and export it so other progs know about it
# if it's set on entry, then leave it alone
#

: ${PHONEBOOK:=$HOME/phonebook}
export PHONEBOOK

if [ ! -f "$PHONEBOOK" ]
then
        echo "$PHONEBOOK does not exist or is not an ordinary file!"
        echo "Should I create it for you (y/n)? \c"
        read answer

        if [ "$answer" != y ]
        then
                exit 1
        fi

        > $PHONEBOOK || exit 1      # exit if the creation fails
fi
```

```
#
# If arguments are supplied, then do a lookup
#

if [ "$#" -ne 0 ]
then
        lu "$@"
        exit
fi

#
#  Set trap on interrupt (DELETE key) to continue the loop
#

trap "continue" 2

#
#  Loop until user selects 'exit'
#

while true
do
        #
        # Display menu
        #

        echo '
        Would you like to:

                1. Look someone up
                2. Add someone to the phone book
                3. Remove someone from the phone book
                4. Change an entry in the phone book
                5. List all names and numbers in the phone book
                6. Exit this program

        Please select one of the above (1-6): \c'

        #
        # Read and process selection
        #

        read choice
        echo
```

```
         case "$choice"
         in
               1)   echo "Enter name to look up: \c"
                    read name

                    if [ -z "$name" ]
                    then
                            echo "Lookup ignored"
                    else
                            lu "$name"
                    fi;;
               2)   add;;
               3)   echo "Enter name to remove: \c"
                    read name
                    if [ -z "$name" ]
                    then
                            echo "Removal ignored"
                    else
                            rem "$name"
                    fi;;
               4)   echo "Enter name to change: \c"
                    read name
                    if [ -z "$name" ]
                    then
                            echo "Change ignored"
                    else
                            change "$name"
                    fi;;
               5)   listall;;
               6)   exit 0;;
               *)   echo "Bad choice\007";;
         esac
   done
```

Instead of requiring that the user have a phonebook file in his or her home directory, the program checks upon startup to see if the variable PHONE-BOOK has been set. If it has, then it's assumed that it contains the name of the phone book file. If it hasn't, then it's set to $HOME/phonebook as the default. In either case, the program then checks to see if the file exists, and if it doesn't, rather than immediately exiting, asks the user if he would like to have an initial file created. This was added so that first-time users of rolo can have an empty phone book file created for them by the program.

This version of rolo also has a couple of new items added to the menu. Since individual entries can be rather long, an editing option has been added to allow you to edit a particular entry. Formerly, the only way to change an entry was to first remove it and then add a new one, a strategy that was perfectly acceptable when the entries were small.

Another option allows for listing of the entire phone book. With this option, just the first and last lines of each entry are displayed. This assumes that the user follows some convention such as putting the name on the first line, and the number on the last.

The entire menu selection process was placed inside a `while` loop so that `rolo` will continue to display menus until the "exit" option is picked from the menu.

A `trap` command is executed before the loop is entered. This `trap` specifies that a `continue` command is to be executed if signal number 2 is received. So if the user presses the DELETE key in the middle of an operation (such as listing the entire phone book), the program won't exit but will abort the current operation and simply continue with the loop. This will result in the redisplay of the menu.

Since entries can now span as many lines as desired, the action performed when `add` is selected has been changed. Instead of asking for the name and number, `rolo` executes the `add` program to get the entry from the user.

For the lookup, change, and remove options, a check is made to ensure that the user doesn't simply press the carriage return key when asked to type in the name. This avoids the `RE error` that `grep` issues if it's given a null first argument.

Now let's look at the individual programs that `rolo` executes. Each of the original programs has been changed to accommodate the new entry format and also to be more user-friendly.

♦ **add** ♦

```
#
# Program to add someone to the phonebook file
#

echo "Type in your new entry"
echo "When you're done, type just a single RETURN on the line."

first=
entry=
```

```
while   true
do
        echo ">> \c"
        read line

        if [ -n "$line" ]
        then
                entry="$entry$line^"

                if [ -z "$first" ]
                then
                        first=$line
                fi
        else
                break
        fi
done


echo "$entry" >> $PHONEBOOK
sort -o $PHONEBOOK $PHONEBOOK
echo
echo "$first has been added to the phone book"
```

This program adds an entry to the phone book. It continually prompts the user to enter lines until a line with just a carriage return is typed (i.e., a null line). Each line that is entered is concatenated to the variable entry, with the special ^ character used to logically separate one line from the next.

When the while loop is exited, the new entry is added to the end of the phone book, and the file is sorted.

♦ lu ♦

```
#
# Look someone up in the phone book
#

name=$1
grep "$name" $PHONEBOOK > /tmp/matches$$

if [ ! -s /tmp/matches$$ ]
then
        echo "I can't find $name in the phone book"
```

```
      else
              #
              # Display each of the matching entries
              #

              while read line
              do
                      display "$line"
              done < /tmp/matches$$
      fi

      rm /tmp/matches$$
```

This is the program to look up an entry in the phone book. The matching entries are written to the file /tmp/matches$$. If the size of this file is zero, then no match was found. Otherwise, the program enters a loop to read each line from the file (remember an entry is stored as a single line in the file) and then display it at the terminal. A program called display is used for this purpose. This program is also used by the rem and change programs to display entries at the terminal.

◆ **display** ◆

```
#
# Display entry from the phonebook
#

echo
echo "----------------------------------------"

entry=$1
IFS="^"
set $entry

for line in "$1" "$2" "$3" "$4" "$5" "$6"
do
        echo "                                    |\r| $line"
done

echo "|          O                    O       |"
echo "----------------------------------------"
echo
```

As noted, this program displays an entry passed as its argument. To make the output more aesthetically pleasing, the program actually "draws" a rolodex card. So typical output from display would look like this:

```
-------------------------------------
| Steve's Ice Cream                 |
| 444 6th Avenue                    |
| New York City   10003             |
| 495-3021                          |
|                                   |
|                                   |
|         O                 O       |
-------------------------------------
```

After skipping a line and then displaying the top of the card[†], display changes IFS to ^ and then executes the set command to assign each "line" to a different positional parameter. For example, if entry is equal to

Steve's Ice Cream^444 6th Avenue^New York City 10003^495-3021^

then executing the set command will assign Steve's Ice Cream to $1, 444 6th Avenue to $2, New York City 10003 to $3, and 495-3021 to $4.

After executing the set, the program enters a for loop that will be executed exactly six times, no matter how many lines are contained in the entry (this assures uniformity of our rolodex cards—the program can be easily modified to "draw" larger-sized cards if needed). If the set command were executed on Steve's Ice Cream as shown above, then $5 and $6 would be null, thus resulting in two blank lines to "fill out" the bottom of the card.

The echo command

```
echo "                               |\r| $line"
```

requires some explanation. The problem here is to get the right side of the rolodex card to line up. To do this, the right side is drawn first at the terminal, and then the special escape characters \r send the cursor back to beginning of the *same* line. Having drawn the right side, the left side and the value of line are then displayed on the line. Note that you can't ensure that the right side of the card will line up by using tab characters unless you require that each line of the rolodex entry be the same length (modulo 8—the typical tab setting on a terminal). Other tricks can be used—cut, awk, or the tabs command can be enlisted to achieve the proper alignment—although the method used here is certainly the quickest. If it doesn't work on your terminal for some reason, try

---

† On older versions of the UNIX system (before System III) and on some versions of Xenix, you may have to specify a -- option to echo to get it to print a line of dashes.

substituting one of the mentioned alternates.

♦ **rem** ♦

```
#
# Remove someone from the phone book
#

name=$1

#
# Get matching entries and save in temp file
#

grep "$name" $PHONEBOOK > /tmp/matches$$

if [ ! -s /tmp/matches$$ ]
then
        echo "I can't find $name in the phone book"
        exit 1
fi


#
# Display matching entries one at a time and confirm removal
#

exec < /tmp/matches$$              # reassign standard input

while read line
do
        display "$line"
        echo "Remove this entry (y/n)? \c"
        read answer < /dev/tty   # use 'line' if not supported

        if [ "$answer" = y ]
        then
                break
        fi
done

rm /tmp/matches$$
```

```
if [ "$answer" = y ]
then
        if grep -v "^$line$" $PHONEBOOK > /tmp/phonebook$$
        then
                mv /tmp/phonebook$$ $PHONEBOOK
                echo "Selected entry has been removed"
        else
                echo "Entry not removed"
        fi
fi
```

The rem program collects all matching entries into a temporary file. If the size of the file is zero, then no match was found and an appropriate message is issued. Otherwise, for each matching entry the program displays the entry and asks the user if that entry is to be removed. This provides reassurance to the user that the entry the user intended to remove is the same one that the program intends to remove, even in the single match case.

Before entering the while loop, the program executes an exec to reassign standard input to the file containing the matches. This is so that the variables set inside the loop (line and answer) can be accessed by the program once the loop has finished execution.

Once a y has been typed to the program, a break command is executed to exit from the loop. Outside the loop, the program tests the value of answer to determine how the loop was exited. If its value is not equal to y, then the user doesn't want to remove an entry after all (for whatever reason). Otherwise, the program proceeds with the removal by greping out all lines but the desired one (and here the pattern specified to grep is made to match only entire lines by anchoring it to the start and end of the line).

♦ change ♦

```
#
# Change an entry in the phone book
#

name=$1

#
# Get matching entries and save in temp file
#

grep "$name" $PHONEBOOK > /tmp/matches$$

if [ ! -s /tmp/matches$$ ]
then
        echo "I can't find $name in the phone book"
        exit 1
fi
```

```
#
# Display matching entries one at a time and confirm change
#

exec < /tmp/matches$$                    # reassign standard input

while read line
do
        display "$line"
        echo "Change this entry (y/n)? \c"
        read answer < /dev/tty   # use 'line' if not supported

        if [ "$answer" = y ]
        then
                break
        fi
done

rm /tmp/matches$$

if [ "$answer" != y ]
then
        exit
fi

#
# Start up editor on the confirmed entry
#

exec < /dev/tty      # reassign standard input for editing
echo "$line\c" | tr '^' '\012' > /tmp/ed$$

echo "Enter changes with ${EDITOR:=/bin/ed}"
trap "" 2           # don't abort if DELETE hit while editing
$EDITOR /tmp/ed$$

#
# Remove old entry now and insert new one
#

grep -v "^$line$" $PHONEBOOK > /tmp/phonebook$$
{ tr '\012' '^' < /tmp/ed$$; echo; } >> /tmp/phonebook$$
# last echo was to put back trailing new line translated by tr

sort /tmp/phonebook$$ -o $PHONEBOOK
rm /tmp/ed$$ /tmp/phonebook$$
```

The `change` program allows the user to edit an entry in the phone book. The initial code is virtually identical to `rem`: it finds the matching entries, and then prompts the user to select the one to be changed.

After an entry has been confirmed, standard input is reassigned back to the terminal with `exec`. This is needed so that the editor will read its input from the terminal (otherwise the editor would read its input from `/tmp/matches$$`). The selected entry is then written into the temporary file `/tmp/ed$$`, with the `^` characters translated to newlines. This "unfolds" the entry into separate lines for convenient editing. The program then displays the message

```
echo "Enter changes with ${EDITOR:=/bin/ed}"
```

which serves a dual purpose: it tells the user what editor will be used to make the change while at the same time setting the variable `EDITOR` to `/bin/ed` if it's not already set. This technique allows the user to use his or her preferred editor by simply assigning its name to the variable `EDITOR` and exporting it before executing `rolo`:

```
$ EDITOR=vi; export EDITOR; rolo
```

The signal generated by the DELETE key (2) is ignored so that if the user hits this key while in the editor, the `change` program won't abort. The editor is then started to allow the user to edit the entry. Once the user makes his changes, writes the file, and quits the editor, control is given back to `change`. The old entry is then removed from the phone book with `grep`, and the modified entry is converted into the special internal format with `tr` and tacked onto the end. An extra newline character must be added here to make sure that a real newline is stored in the file after the entry. This is done with an `echo` with no arguments.

The phone book file is then sorted, and the temporary files removed.

♦ listall ♦

```
#
# list all of the entries in the phone book
#

IFS='^'    # to be used in set command below

echo "------------------------------------------------------------"
while read line
```

```
do
    #
    # Get the first and last fields, presumably names and numbers
    #

    set $line

    #
    # display 1st and last fields (in reverse order!)
    #

    eval echo "\"                              \$$#\r$1\""
done < $PHONEBOOK
echo "-------------------------------------------------------------"
```

The `listall` program lists all entries in the phone book, printing just the first and last line of each entry. The internal field separator characters (`IFS`) is set to a ^, to be used later inside the loop. Each line from the phone book file is then read and assigned to the variable `line`. The `set` command is used to assign each field to the positional parameters.

The trick now is to get the value of the first and last positional parameter, since that's what we want to display. The first one is easy, as it can be directly referenced as `$1`. To get the last one, you use `eval` as you saw in the last chapter. The command

```
eval echo \$$#
```

has the effect of displaying the value of the last positional parameter (provided there are less than 10 parameters). The command

```
eval echo "\"                              \$$#\r$1\""
```

gets evaluated to

```
echo "                              $4\rSteve's Ice Cream"
```

using the entry shown previously as the example, and then the shell rescans the line to substitute the value of `$4` before executing `echo`. The `\r` escape characters are used as in the `display` program to get the two columns of data to line up.

♦ Sample Output ♦

Now it's time to see how `rolo` works. We'll start with an empty phone book and add a few entries to it. Then we'll list all of the entries, look up a particular one, and change one (using the default editor `ed`—remember that the variable `EDITOR` can always be set to a different editor and then exported). To conserve space, we'll only show the full menu that `rolo` displays the first time.

```
$ PHONEBOOK=/usr/steve/misc/book
$ export PHONEBOOK
$ rolo                                    Start it up
/usr/steve/misc/book does not exist or is not an ordinary file!
Should I create it for you (y/n)? y

        Would you like to:

                1. Look someone up
                2. Add someone to the phone book
                3. Remove someone from the phone book
                4. Change an entry in the phone book
                5. List all names and numbers in the phone book
                6. Exit this program

        Please select one of the above (1-6): 2

Type in your new entry
When you're done, type just a single RETURN on the line.
>> Steve's Ice Cream
>> 444 6th Avenue
>> New York City 10003
>> 495-3021
>>

Steve's Ice Cream has been added to the phone book

        Would you like to:
            ...
        Please select one of the above (1-6): 2

Type in your new entry
When you're done, type just a single RETURN on the line.
>> YMCA
>> (201) 965-2344
>>

YMCA has been added to the phone book
```

```
        Would you like to:
          ...
        Please select one of the above (1-6): 2

Type in your new entry
When you're done, type just a single RETURN on the line.
>> Maureen Connelly
>> Hayden Book Company
>> 10 Mulholland Drive
>> Hasbrouck Heights, N.J. 07604
>> (201) 393-6000
>>


Maureen Connelly has been added to the phone book

        Would you like to:
          ...
        Please select one of the above (1-6): 2

Type in your new entry
When you're done, type just a single RETURN on the line.
>> Teri Zak
>> Hayden Book Company
>> (see Maureen Connelly for address)
>> (201) 393-6060
>>


Teri Zak has been added to the phone book

        Would you like to:
          ...
        Please select one of the above (1-6): 5


     -----------------------------------------------------------
     Maureen Connelly                    (201) 393-6000
     Steve's Ice Cream                   495-3021
     Teri Zak                            (201) 393-6060
     YMCA                                (201) 965-2344
     -----------------------------------------------------------

        Would you like to:
          ...
        Please select one of the above (1-6): 1
```

Enter name to look up: **Maureen**


```
----------------------------------------
| Maureen Connelly                     |
| Hayden Book Companu                  |
| 10 Mulholland Drive                  |
| Hasbrouck Heights, NJ   07604        |
| (201) 393-6000                       |
|                                      |
|        O                   O         |
----------------------------------------
```


```
----------------------------------------
| Teri Zak                             |
| Hayden Book Company                  |
| (see Maureen Connelly for address)   |
| (201) 393-6060                       |
|                                      |
|                                      |
|        O                   O         |
----------------------------------------
```


        Would you like to:
          ...
        Please select one of the above (1-6): **4**

Enter name to change: **Maureen**


```
----------------------------------------
| Maureen Connelly                     |
| Hayden Book Companu                  |
| 10 Mulholland Drive                  |
| Hasbrouck Heights, NJ   07604        |
| (201) 393-6000                       |
|                                      |
|        O                   O         |
----------------------------------------
```


Change this person (y/n)? **y**
Enter changes with /bin/ed
101
1,$p
Maureen Connelly

```
Hayden Book Companu
10 Mulholland Drive
Hasbrouck Heights, NJ   07604
(201) 393-6000
2s/anu/any                          Change the misspelling
Hayden Book Company
w
101
q


        Would you like to:
          ...
        Please select one of the above (1-6):  6
    $
```

The only function not tested here is removal of an entry.

Hopefully this example has given you some insight on how to develop larger shell programs, and how to use the many different programming tools provided by the system. Other than the shell built-ins, `rolo` relies upon `tr`, `grep`, an editor, `sort`, and the standard file system commands like `mv` and `rm` to get the job done. The simplicity and elegance that enables you to easily tie all of these tools together accounts for the deserved rapid rise in popularity of the UNIX system.

The next chapter introduces you to a different shell that has some nice features not found in the standard shell.

◆ Exercises ◆

1. (System V, Release 2 and later users.) Modify `rolo` so that upper and lower case letters are not distinguished when doing a look up in the phone book.

2. Add a `-m` command-line option to `rolo` to send mail to the person that follows on the command line. Have `rolo` look up the person in the phone book and then look for the string `mail:`*mailaddr* in the matching entry, where *mailaddr* is the person's mail address. Then start up an editor (as in change mode) to allow the user to enter the mail message. When the editing is complete, mail the message to the user. If no mail address is found in the phone book, prompt for it.

   Also add a mail option to the menu so that it can be selected interactively. Prompt for the name of the person to send mail to.

3. After adding the `-m` option, add a `-f` option to specify that the mail message is to be taken from the file that follows on the command line. So

   ```
   rolo -m tony -f memo
   ```

   should look up `tony`, and mail him the contents of the file `memo`.

4. Can you think of other ways to use `rolo`? For example, can it be used as a small general-purpose data base program (e.g., for storing recipes, or employee data)?

5. Modify `rolo` to use the following convention instead of the exported PHONE-BOOK variable: the file `.rolo` in each `rolo` user's home directory contains the path name to that user's phone book file (e.g.,

   ```
   $ cat $HOME/.rolo
   /usr/steve/misc/phonebook
   $
   ```

). Then add an option to `rolo` to allow you to look someone up in another user's phonebook (provided you have read access to it). This option should be added to the command line (as a `-u` option) as well as to the menu. For example,

   ```
   $ rolo -u pat Pizza
   ```

   would look up `Pizza` in `pat`'s phonebook, no matter who is running `rolo`. The program can find `pat`'s phone book by looking at `.rolo` in `pat`'s home directory.

6. What happens with `rolo` if the user adds an entry containing a ^ or [character?

15

Using the Korn Shell

The Korn shell is a relatively new shell developed by David Korn of AT&T Bell Laboratories. He designed this shell to be "upwards compatible" with the System V Bourne shell, so that programs written for the Bourne shell also run under the Korn shell. Except for a few minor differences, the Korn shell provides you with all of the Bourne shell's features, as well as many new ones. To give you an idea of the compatibility of the Korn shell with Bourne's, all shell programs in the previous chapters work under both the Bourne and Korn shells.

The main features added to the Korn shell are:

- Built-in command-line editor that simulates emacs or vi.

- History mechanism that allows previously entered commands to be recalled, edited, and executed.

- Built-in integer arithmetic.

- New pattern matching capabilities.

- New parameter substitution capabilities.

- Arrays.

- Command aliasing.

- Job control (BSD 4.1 and later Berkeley UNIX distributions, and System V Release 2 and later AT&T releases).

We'll cover these features in this chapter as well as a few others in the section labelled "Miscellaneous Features."

• Running the Korn Shell •

Normally, when you log in, you will be running the Bourne shell. Some systems do, however, have the Korn shell installed as the standard shell. As a quick test to see if you are already running the Korn shell, type the following:

```
$ echo $RANDOM $RANDOM
```

If you are running the Bourne shell, you will get a blank line displayed as the output from the above command:

```
$ echo $RANDOM $RANDOM

$
```

If two different numbers are displayed, you're already running the Korn shell:

```
$ echo $RANDOM $RANDOM
10113 17515
$
```

Since the Korn shell isn't yet a standard feature of the UNIX system, not all systems have it, and those that do may not keep it in a standard directory such as /bin or /usr/bin.

The Korn shell is usually called ksh, so you can try to run it by typing in

```
$ ksh
```

If you get the message ksh: not found, you may have to go hunting for it. Likely hiding places are in /usr/lbin, /usr/local, /usr/add-on, and the like. If you search for it for a while and can't find it, you may want to ask your system administrator where the Korn shell is on your system.

Once you've found it, you can either add the directory it's in to your PATH, or you can invoke it by typing its full path name, e.g.,

```
$ /usr/lbin/ksh
```

If you don't have the Korn shell on your system, you can obtain a copy and have it installed (or install it yourself).

Once you've been using the Korn shell for a while, you may want to make it your default login shell. Talk to your system administrator about how this can be done.

The ENV File

Whenever you start a Korn shell, one of the first things it does is to look in your environment for a variable called ENV. If it finds it, the file specified by ENV will be executed, much like the .profile is executed when logging in. The ENV file usually contains commands to set up the Korn shell's environment. Throughout this chapter, we'll mention various things that you may want to put into this file.

If you do decide to have an ENV file, then you should set and export the ENV variable inside your .profile file: The ENV variable

```
$ cat .profile
 . . .
ENV=$HOME/.alias
export ENV
 . . .
$
```

You should also set and export inside your .profile file a variable called SHELL.

```
$ cat .profile
 . . .
SHELL=/usr/lbin/ksh
export SHELL
 . . .
$
```

This variable is used by certain applications (such as vi) to determine what shell to start up when you execute a shell escape. In such cases, you want to make sure that each time you start up a new shell, that you get a Korn shell and not a Bourne shell.

◆ Command Line Editing ◆

Line edit mode is a feature of the Korn shell that allows you to edit a command line using built-in commands that mimic those found in two popular screen editors. Currently, the Korn shell provides the capability to mimic vi or emacs. (A gmacs line edit mode is also provided, but it differs from emacs mode in only one command, which isn't discussed here.)

If you've used either of these screen editors, you'll find the built-in line editors in the Korn shell are faithful reproductions of their full screen counterparts; you may want to read just the next few paragraphs to see how to turn on these modes, then refer to Appendix B for the table of commands that are supported under each line edit mode. If you've never used a screen editor, don't be intimidated. This capability is one of the most useful features in the Korn shell. In fact, after learning how to use one of the Korn shell's built-in editors, you'll be able to learn `vi` or `emacs` with little effort.

There are a several different ways to turn on a line edit mode:

1.   When the shell variable `VISUAL` is assigned a value, if it ends with the string `vi`, `emacs`, or `gmacs`, then that mode is turned on.

2.   If `VISUAL` isn't set, and `EDITOR` is assigned a string containing one of the above, then that mode is turned on. The Korn shell also checks these variables in this order when it starts.

3.   The `set` command with the `-o` *mode* option may be used to turn on one of the line edit modes. A `set -o` will override the mode previously set via the `VISUAL` or `EDITOR` variable.

Examples:

```
$ EDITOR=vi                 Turn on vi mode
$ VISUAL=emacs              Turn on emacs mode
$ set -o vi                 Turn on vi mode
```

Note that any of the above methods may be used in your `ENV` file to automatically start up the Korn shell with one of the edit modes turned on; `VISUAL` or `EDITOR` can also be set and exported in your `.profile`.

♦ Command History ♦

As we said before, the Korn shell keeps a history of previously entered commands. Each time you press the `RETURN` key to execute a command, that command gets added to the end of this history list. This command list is actually stored inside a file, which means you can access previously entered commands across login sessions. By default, the history list is kept in a file in your home directory under the name `.sh_history`. You can change this file name to anything you like by setting the variable `HISTFILE` to the name of your history file. This variable can be set and exported in your `.profile` file.

Naturally, there is a limit to the number of commands the Korn shell records. This limit is set to 128 by default. Each time you login, the Korn shell automatically truncates your history file to this length.

You can control the size of your history file through the `HISTSIZE` variable. You may find that 128 commands isn't adequate for your needs, in which case you may want to set the `HISTSIZE` variable to a larger value, such as 500 or 1000. The value you assign to `HISTSIZE` can be set and exported in your `.profile` file:

```
$ cat .profile
  . . .
HISTSIZE=500
export HISTSIZE
  . . .
$
```

Be reasonable about the values that you assign to HISTSIZE. The larger the value, the more disk space you will need to store the history file, and the longer it will take the Korn shell to search through the entire history file.

♦ The vi Line Edit Mode ♦

After turning on the vi line editor, you will be placed in *input* mode. You probably won't even notice anything different about input mode, as you can type in and execute commands almost exactly the same as before you started the vi line editor:

```
$ set -o vi
$ echo hello
hello
$ pwd
/usr/pat
$
```

To make use of the line editor, you must enter *command* mode by pressing the ESCAPE or ESC key, usually in the upper left-hand corner of the keyboard. When you enter command mode, the cursor will move to the left one space, to the last character typed in. The *current character* is whatever character the cursor is on; we'll say more about the current character in a moment. Once in command mode, you can enter vi commands. *Note that vi commands are not followed by a RETURN*.

One of the problems often encountered when typing in long commands is that you may notice an error in a command line after you finish typing it in. Invariably, the error is at the beginning of the line. In command mode, you can move the cursor around *without disturbing the command line*. Once you've moved the cursor to the place where the error is, you can change the letter or letters to whatever you want.

In the examples that follow, the underline (_) represents the cursor. A command line will be shown, followed by one or more keystrokes, followed by what the line looks like after applying the keystrokes:

before   *keystrokes*   *after*

First, let's look at moving the cursor around. The h key will move the cursor to the left and the l key will move it to the right. You should try this out by entering command mode and pressing the h and l keys a few times. The cursor should move around on the line. If you try to move the cursor past the left or right side of the line, the Korn shell will "beep" at you.

```
$ mary had a little larb_    ESC    $ mary had a little larb
$ mary had a little larb     h      $ mary had a little larb
$ mary had a little larb     h      $ mary had a little larb
$ mary had a little larb     l      $ mary had a little larb
```

Once the cursor is on the character you want to change, you can use the x command to delete the current character ("X" it out).

```
$ mary had a little larb     x      $ mary had a little lab
```

Note that the b moved to the left when the r was deleted and is now the current character.

To add characters to the command line, you can use the i and a commands. The i command adds characters *before* the current character, and the a command adds characters *after* the current character. Both of these commands put you back into input mode; you must press ESC again to go back to command mode.

```
$ mary had a little lab      im     $ mary had a little lamb
$ mary had a little lamb     m      $ mary had a little lammb
$ mary had a little lammb    ESC    $ mary had a little lammb
$ mary had a little lammb    x      $ mary had a little lamb
$ mary had a little lamb     a      $ mary had a little lamb_
$ mary had a little lamb_    da     $ mary had a little lambda_
```

If you think that moving the cursor around by repeatedly hitting h and l is slow, you're right. The h and l commands may be preceded by a number that specifies the number of spaces to move the cursor.

```
$ mary had a little lambda_   ESC    $ mary had a little lambda
$ mary had a little lambda    10h    $ mary had a little lambda
$ mary had a little lambda    13h    $ mary had a little lambda
$ mary had a little lambda    5x     $ had a little lambda
```

As you see, the x command can also be preceded by a number to tell it how many characters to delete.

You can easily move to the end of the line by typing the $ command:

```
$ had a little lambda         $      $ had a little lambda
```

To move to the beginning of the line, you use the 0 (that's a zero) command:

```
$ had a little lambda            0              $ had a little lambda
```

Two other commands useful in moving the cursor are the w and b commands. The w command moves the cursor forward to the beginning of the next word, where a word is a string of letters, numbers, and underscores delimited by blanks or punctuation. The b command moves the cursor backward to the beginning of the previous word. These commands may also be preceded by a number to specify the number of words to move forward or backward.

```
$ had a little lambda            w              $ had a little lambda
$ had a little lambda            2w             $ had a little lambda
$ had a little lambda            3b             $ had a little lambda
```

At any time you can enter RETURN and the current line will be executed as a command.

```
$ had a little lambda                 Hit RETURN
ksh: had:  not found
$ _
```

After a command is executed, you are placed back in input mode.

Accessing Commands From Your History

So far, you've learned how to edit the current line. You can use the vi commands k and j to retrieve commands from your history. The k command replaces the current line on your terminal with the previously entered command, putting the cursor at the beginning of the line. Let's assume that these commands have just been entered:

```
$ pwd
/usr/pat
$ cd /tmp
$ echo this is a test
this is a test
$ _
```

Now go into command mode and use k to access them:

```
$ _                      ESC k       $ echo this is a test
```

Every time k is used, the current line is replaced by the previous line from the command history.

```
$ echo this is a test          k          $ cd /tmp
$ cd /tmp                       k          $ pwd
```

To execute the command being displayed, just press the RETURN key.

```
$ pwd                                      Hit RETURN
/tmp
$ _
```

The j command is the reverse of the k command and is used to display the next command in the history.

The / command is used to search through the command history for a command containing a string. If the / is entered, followed by a string, then the Korn shell will search backward through its history to find the most recently executed command that contains that string anywhere on the command line. The command will then be displayed. If there is no line in the history containing the string, the Korn shell will "beep" the terminal. When the / is entered, the current line is replaced by a /.

```
/tmp
$ _                            ESC /test      /test_
```

The search is begun when the RETURN key is pressed.

```
/test_                         RETURN       $ echo this is a test
```

To execute the command that results from the search, RETURN must be pressed again.

```
$ echo this is a test          Hit RETURN again
this is a test
$ _
```

If the command that's displayed isn't the one you're interested in, then you can continue the search through the command history by simply typing in / and pressing RETURN. The shell will use the string that you entered the last time you executed the search command.

When you've found the command in the history (either by k, j, or /) you can edit the command using the other vi commands we've already discussed. Note that you don't actually change the command in the history: that command cannot be changed once it is entered. Instead, you are editing a copy of the command in the history, which will itself be entered in the history when you hit RETURN.

Table 15-1 summarizes the basic vi line edit commands.

TABLE 15-1. Basic vi line edit commands

Command	Meaning
h	Move left one character
l	Move right one character
b	Move left one word
w	Move right one word
0	Move to start of line
$	Move to end of line
x	Delete character at cursor
dw	Delete word at cursor
r*c*	Change character at cursor to *c*
a	Enter input mode and enter text after the current character
i	Enter input mode and insert text before the current character
k	Get previous command from history
j	Get next command from history
/*string*	Search history for the most recent command containing *string*; if *string* is null the previous string will be used

♦ The emacs Line Edit Mode ♦

After turning on the emacs line editor, you probably won't even notice anything different, as you can type in and execute commands almost the same way as before:

```
$ set -o emacs
$ echo hello
hello
$ pwd
/usr/pat
$
```

To make use of the line editor, you enter emacs *commands*. emacs commands are either *control* characters, i.e., characters typed in by holding down the CTRL key and pressing another character, or they are characters preceded by the ESCAPE or ESC key. You may enter emacs commands anytime you wish; there are no separate modes like the vi line editor. *Note that* emacs *commands are not followed by a* RETURN. We'll cover a few of them here; for a complete list of commands, refer to Appendix B.

First, let's look at moving the cursor around. The *CTRL-b* command will move the cursor to the left and the *CTRL-f* command will move it to the right. You should try this out by pressing *CTRL-b* and *CTRL-f* a few times. The cursor should move around on the line. If you try to move the cursor past the left or right side of the line, the Korn shell will simply ignore you.

```
$ mary had a little larb_      CTRL-b      $ mary had a little larb
$ mary had a little larb       CTRL-b      $ mary had a little larb
$ mary had a little larb       CTRL-b      $ mary had a little larb
$ mary had a little larb       CTRL-f      $ mary had a little larb
```

Once the cursor is on the character you want to change, you can use the *CTRL-d* command to delete the current character.

```
$ mary had a little larb       CTRL-d      $ mary had a little lab
```

Note that the b moved to the left when the r was deleted and is now the current character.

To add characters to the command line, you simply type them in. The characters are inserted *before* the current character.

```
$ mary had a little lab        m           $ mary had a little lamb
$ mary had a little lamb       m           $ mary had a little lammb
$ mary had a little lammb      CTRL-h      $ mary had a little lamb
```

Note that the current erase character (usually either # or *CTRL-h* will *always* delete the character to the left of the cursor.

The *CTRL-a* and *CTRL-e* commands may be used to move the cursor to the beginning and end of the command line, respectively.

```
$ mary had a little lamb       CTRL-a      $ mary had a little lamb
$ mary had a little lamb       CTRL-e      $ mary had a little lamb_
```

Note that the *CTRL-e* command places the cursor one space to the right of the last character on the line. (When you're not in emacs mode, the cursor is always at the end of the line, one space to the right of the last character typed in.) Once you're at the end of the line, anything you type will be appended to the line.

```
$ mary had a little lamb_      da          $ mary had a little lambda_
```

Two other commands useful in moving the cursor are the ESC f and ESC b commands. The ESC f command moves the cursor forward to the end of the current word, where a word is a string of letters, numbers, and underscores delimited by blanks or punctuation. The ESC b command moves the cursor backward to the beginning of the previous word.

```
$ mary had a little lambda_    ESC b     $ mary had a little lambda
$ mary had a little lambda     ESC b     $ mary had a little lambda
$ mary had a little lambda     ESC b     $ mary had a little lambda
$ mary had a little lambda     ESC f     $ mary had a little lambda
$ mary had a little lambda     ESC f     $ mary had a little lambda
```

At any time you can press the RETURN key and the current line will be executed as a command.

```
$ mary had a little_lambda          Hit RETURN; enter command
ksh: mary:  not found
$
```

Accessing Commands From Your History

So far, you've learned how to edit the current line. As we said before, the Korn shell keeps a history of recently entered commands. To access these commands, you can use the emacs commands *CTRL-p* and *CTRL-n*. The *CTRL-p* command replaces the current line on your terminal with the previously entered command, putting the cursor at the end of the line. Let's assume that these commands have just been entered:

```
$ pwd
/usr/pat
$ cd /tmp
$ echo this is a test
this is a test
$ _
```

Now use *CTRL-p* to access them:

```
$ _                    CTRL-p     $ echo this is a test_
```

Every time *CTRL-p* is used, the current line is replaced by the previous line from the command history.

```
$ echo this is a test_    CTRL-p     $ cd /tmp_
$ cd /tmp_                CTRL-p     $ pwd_
```

To execute the command being displayed, just hit RETURN.

```
$ pwd                         Hit RETURN
/tmp
$ _
```

The *CTRL-n* command is the reverse of the *CTRL-p* command and is used to display the next command in the history.

The *CTRL-r* command is used to search through the command history for a command containing a string. The *CTRL-r* is entered followed by the string to search for, followed by the RETURN key. The Korn shell then searches the command history for the most recently executed command that contains that string on the command line. If found, the command line is displayed; otherwise, the Korn shell "beeps" the terminal. When the *CTRL-r* is typed, the current line is replaced by a ^R.

```
$_                          CTRL-r test   $ ^Rtest_
```

The search is initiated when RETURN is pressed.

```
$ ^Rtest_                   RETURN        $ echo this is a test_
```

To execute the command that is displayed as a result of the search, RETURN must be pressed again.

```
$ echo this is a test              Hit RETURN again
this is a test
$ _
```

To continue the search through the command history, you simply type *CTRL-r* followed by a RETURN.

When you've found the command in the history (either by *CTRL-p*, *CTRL-n*, or *CTRL-r*) you can edit the command using the other emacs commands we've already discussed. Note that you don't actually change the command in the history: that command cannot be changed once it is entered. Instead, you are editing a copy of the command in the history, which will itself be entered in the history when you hit RETURN.

Table 15-2 summarizes the basic emacs line edit commands.

TABLE 15-2. Basic emacs line edit commands

Command	Meaning
CTRL-b	Move left one character
CTRL-f	Move right one character
ESC f	Move forward one word
ESC b	Move back one word
CTRL-a	Move to start of line
CTRL-e	Move to end of line
CTRL-d	Delete current character
ESC d	Delete current word
erase char	(User defined erase character, usually # or CTRL-h), delete previous character
CTRL-p	Get previous command from history
CTRL-n	Get next command from history
CTRL-r string	Search history for the most recent command line containing string

◆ Other Ways to Access Your History ◆

There are several other ways to access your command history that are worth noting. The `history` command writes your last 16 commands to standard output:

```
$ history
507    cd /u1/shell
508    cd ch15
509    vi int
510    ps
511    echo $HISTSIZE
512    cat $ENV
513    cp int int.sv
514    history
515    exit
516    cd /u1/shell
517    cd ch16
518    vi all
519    run -n5 all
520    ps
521    lpr all.out
522    history
```

The numbers to the left are simply relative command numbers (command number 1 would be the first, or oldest, command in your history).

The `fc` Command

The `fc` command allows you to start up an editor on one or more commands from your history or to simply write a list of history commands to your terminal. In the latter form, which is indicated by giving the `-l` option to `fc`, it is like typing in `history`, only more flexible (you can specify a range of commands to be listed or can get fewer or more than the last 16 commands listed). For example, the command

```
fc -l 510 515
```

writes commands 510 through 515 to standard output, while the command

```
fc -n -l -20
```

writes the last 20 commands to standard output, not preceded by line numbers (`-n`). Suppose you've just executed a long command line and then decide that it would be nice to turn that command line into a shell program called `runx`. You can use `fc` to get the command from your history and I/O redirection to write that command to a file:

```
fc -n -l -1 > runx
```

(That's the letter l followed by the number -1.)   `fc` is described in full detail in Appendix B.

The `r` Command

There is a simple Korn shell command that allows you to re-execute previous commands using even a fewer number of keystrokes than described. If you simply type in the `r` command, the Korn shell will re-execute your last command:

```
$ date
Tue Jan 10 21:56:47 EDT 1989
$ r                                    Re-execute previous command
date
Tue Jan 10 21:57:13 EDT 1989
$
```

When you type in the `r` command, the Korn shell redisplays the previous command and then immediately executes it.

If you give the `r` command the name of a command as an argument, the Korn shell will re-execute the most recent command line from your history that *begins* with the specified argument:

```
$ cat docs/planA
```

```
    . . .
$ pwd
/usr/steve
$ r cat                          Rerun last cat command
cat docs/planA
    . . .
$
```

Once again, the Korn shell redisplays the command line from its history before automatically re-executing it.

The final form of the r command allows you to substitute the first occurrence of one string with the next. To re-execute the last cat command on the file planB instead of planA you could type:

```
$ r cat planA=planB
cat docs/planB
    . . .
$
```

or even more simply, you could have typed:

```
$ r cat A=B
cat docs/planB
    . . .
$
```

◆ Functions ◆

Korn shell functions are slightly different from Bourne shell functions. First, the function command can be used to specify a function, as well as the *name* ( ) { ... ; } format.

Second, Korn shell functions can have local variables, making recursive functions possible. They are defined with the typeset command, as in

```
typeset i j
```

If a variable of the same name as a local function variable exists, it is saved when the typeset is executed and restored when the function exits.

The following defines a function called nu in the Korn shell to count the number of logged-in users:

```
$ function nu
> {
>       who | wc -l
> }
$ nu
      13
$
```

After using the Korn shell for a while, you may develop a set of functions that you like to use during your interactive work sessions. A good place to define such functions is inside your ENV file so that they will be defined whenever you start up a new Korn shell.

Exported Functions

You should note that function definitions are not normally passed down to subshells. However, the Korn shell does allow you to export the definition of a function by using the following command:

typeset -fx *functions*

where *functions* is a list of one or more functions to be exported. After executing this typeset command, the definition for all noted functions will be passed down to subshells.

You can use typeset with just the -f option to get a list of all functions you have defined:

```
$ typeset -f
function nu
{
      who | wc -l
}
$
```

(If you had other functions defined, they would be listed here as well.)

typeset with just the -fx option will give you a list of just your exported functions.

The autoload Option

The Korn shell allows you to set up a special variable called FPATH that is similar to your PATH variable. If you try to execute a function that is not yet defined, the Korn shell will search the colon-delimited list of directories in your FPATH variable for a file that matches the function name. If it finds such a file, it will place it in the current shell. Presumably, somewhere inside the file will be a definition for the specified function.

In order to use this feature, two things must be done in addition to setting up your `FPATH` variable:

1. You must turn on the `autoload` option (use `set -o autoload`).

2. You must tell the Korn shell in advance the names of all functions that you want to be defined this way. This is done by using the `typeset` command with the `-f` option, followed by one or more function names.

Removing a Function Definition

In order to remove a function's definition, you use the `unset` command with the `-f` option.

```
$ type nu
nu is a function
$ unset -f nu
$ type nu
ksh: nu: not found
$
```

See Appendix B for a complete list of differences between Korn and Bourne shell functions.

♦ Built-in Integer Arithmetic ♦

You learned in previous chapters how to perform integer arithmetic in the shell using the `expr` command inside back quotes, e.g.,

```
i=`expr $i + 1`
```

Besides being a clumsy way to do arithmetic, this method is also slow, because the shell must execute the `expr` command to evaluate `$i + 1` (this involves creating a new process for `expr` and may also include finding `expr` in the `PATH` and loading the `expr` program in from disk).

The `let` Command

The Korn shell provides a mechanism for performing integer arithmetic without using the `expr` command: the `let` command. The `let` command is built-in to the Korn shell, so there is no new process created, no searching, and no loading of a program. The format of the `let` command is let *expressions*

where *expressions* are arithmetic expressions using shell variables and operators. Valid shell variables are those that contain numeric values. Valid operators are taken from the C programming language, and are listed in decreasing order of precedence in Table 15-3.

TABLE 15-3. Korn shell arithmetic operators

Operator	*Meaning*
−	Unary minus
!	Logical negation
~	Bitwise negation
* / %	Multiplication, division, remainder
+ −	Addition, subtraction
<< >>	Left shift, right shift
<= >= < > == !=	Comparison
&	Bitwise and
^	Bitwise exclusive or
|	Bitwise or
&&	Logical and
||	Logical or
= *= /= %= += −= <<= >>= &= ^= |=	Assignment

For example,

```
let i=i+1
```

adds one to the shell variable i and is equivalent to the previous use of expr. Notice that the variable i doesn't have to be preceded by a dollar sign on the right-hand side of the assignment operator. That's because the Korn shell knows that the only valid items that can appear in a let are operators, numbers, and variables.

Multiple expressions may be evaluated simply by giving each expression as a separate argument to the `let` command. If any individual expression contains spaces, the expression should be quoted.

```
let "i = i + 1"  "j = j * 10"
```

Using quotes has the added effect of removing the special meaning of the characters like `*`, `&`, `<`, and `>` from the shell.

Parentheses may be used freely inside `let` expressions to force grouping, as in

```
let "i = (i + 10) * j"
```

There is an alternate format to `let` which is effected by enclosing the integer expression inside a double pair of adjacent parentheses. So the format

```
(( expression ))
```

is equivalent to

```
let "expression"
```

We prefer the alternate form of `let` since it produces more readable statements.

So to multiply the variable `i` by 5 and assign the result back to `i` you can write

```
(( i = i * 5 ))
```

Finally, to test to see if `i` is greater than or equal to 0 and less than or equal to 100, you write

```
(( i >= 0  &&  i <= 100 ))
```

Remember, the parentheses act as a quoting mechanism here, so you can freely include whitespace characters and don't have to worry about special characters like `*`, `&`, `<`, and `>`.

Recall the `number` program from Chapter 10:

```
$ cat number
#
# Number lines from files given as argument or from
# standard input if none supplied
#

lineno=1

cat $* |
while read line
do
        echo "$lineno: $line"
        lineno=`expr $lineno + 1`
done
$
```

This program can be rewritten in the Korn shell using built-in integer arithmetic:

```
$ cat number1
#
# Number lines from files given as argument or from
# standard input if none supplied (Korn shell version)
#

(( lineno = 1 ))

cat $* |
while read line
do
        echo "$lineno: $line"
        (( lineno = lineno + 1 ))
done
$
```

Would you believe that `number1` runs five to ten times faster than `number`? It does because `let` is actually 10 to 30 times faster than `expr` (depending on the speed of your computer), and this difference accounts for the relative speed of `number1` versus `number`.

An expression need not contain an assignment. The exit status of the `let` command is zero if the last expression evaluates to a nonzero number and is one otherwise. The comparison operators set the exit status to a nonzero value if the result of the comparison is false and to a zero value if the result is true. So writing

```
(( i == 100 ))
```

has the effect of testing i to see if it is equal to 100 and setting the exit status appropriately. This knowledge makes let ideal for inclusion in if, while, and until commands:

```
if   (( i == 100 ))
then
         . . .
fi
```

The ((i == 100)) will return an exit status of zero (true) if i equals 100, and one (false) otherwise, and has the same effect as writing

```
if [ "$i" -eq 100 ]
then
         . . .
fi
```

The following program prints out the first 15 numbers in the Fibonacci series. (The Fibonacci series is a sequence of numbers where each number is the sum of the two previous numbers in the series. The first two numbers of the series are defined to be one.)

```
$ cat fibonacci
#
# Fibonacci number generator
# prints first 15 Fibonacci numbers
#

(( count = 0 ))
(( fib = 1 ))
(( oldfib = 0 ))

while (( count < 15 ))
do
        echo $fib

        #
        # Compute next number in series
        # First save fib for next iteration,
        # then compute next value of fib.
        # Finally, assign the saved value of fib to oldfib
        #
```

```
        (( save = fib ))
        (( fib = fib + oldfib ))
        (( oldfib = save ))

        #
        # increment count
        #

        (( count = count + 1 ))
done
```

```
$ fibonacci
1
1
2
3
5
8
13
21
34
55
89
144
233
377
610
$
```

The command

```
(( count < 15 ))
```

returns an exit status of zero while count is less than 15 and an exit status of one when it reaches 15.

The test Built-in

The Korn shell's test built-in supports some new operators (described in Appendix B) and also allows expressions to be used as arguments to the integer comparison operators -eq, -ge, -gt, -le, -lt, and -ne. So the test command

```
[ i -lt "j + 5" ]
```

will be true if the value stored in i is less than j plus 5, false otherwise. Note that, as with the let command, dollar signs need not precede the variables here.

As you learned, this test can also be written as

```
let "i < j + 5"
```

or as

```
(( i < j + 5 ))
```

Don't confuse things here. If you're using the test built-in to perform your integer comparisons, you must use the test comparison operators -eq, -ge, etc. And if you're using the let command (in either of its two forms), then you must use its comparison operators ==, >=, etc.

The Integer Type

The Korn shell supports some limited data types; one of these is the integer data type. You can declare variables to be integers by using the integer command in the form

```
integer variables
```

where *variables* are any valid shell variable names. Initial values can be assigned to the variables at the time they are declared.

Arithmetic performed on integer variables with the let command is slightly faster than on noninteger ones because the Korn shell internally stores the value of an integer variable as a binary number and not as a character string.

An integer variable cannot be assigned anything but an integer value or an integer expression. If you attempt to assign a noninteger to it, the message bad number will be printed by the Korn shell:

```
$ integer i
$ i=hello
ksh: i: bad number
$ i=10+15
$ echo $i
25
$
```

The last example shows that integer-valued expressions can be assigned to an integer variable, without even having to use the let command.

A Simple Replacement for `expr`

The following function is a simple version of `expr` using Korn shell integer arithmetic. With the exception of the : operator, this version of `expr` will perform the same functions as those described in Chapter 6.

```
$ cat kexpr
#
# simple Korn shell replacement for 'expr'
#
function expr {
        integer local="$*"     # local integer variable
        echo $local            # print out result
}
$ . kexpr                              Read in function definition
$ expr 1 + 2
3
$ expr 1000 / 7
142
$ expr 17+18
35
$
```

The argument list that is passed to the function version of `expr` is assigned to the integer variable called `local`. This forces the expression to be evaluated. The result of the evaluation is then written to standard output using `echo`.

As you can see, the function version of `expr` is more robust than the `expr` command: it doesn't require spaces between its operators and operands.

Numbers in Different Bases

The Korn shell allows you to perform arithmetic in different bases. To write a number in a different base you use the notation

base#number

For example, to express the value 100 in base 8 (octal) you write

```
8#100
```

You can write constants in different bases anywhere an integer value is permitted. To assign octal 100 to the integer variable `i` you can write

```
integer i=8#100
```

You should note that the base of the first value assigned to an integer variable fixes the base of all subsequent substitutions of that variable. In other words, if the first value you assign to the integer variable i is an octal number, each time you subsequently substitute the value of i on the command line, the Korn shell will substitute the value as an octal number using the notation 8#*value*.

```
$ integer i=8#100
$ echo $i
8#100
$ i=50
$ echo $i
8#62
$ (( i = 16#a5 + 16#120 ))
$ echo $i
8#705
$
```

Since the first value assigned to i in this example is an octal number (8#100), all further substitutions of i will be in octal. When the base 10 value of 50 is next assigned to i and then i is subsequently displayed, we get the value 8#62, which is the octal equivalent of 50 in base 10.

In the last example, the let command is used to add together the two hexadecimal values a5 and 120. The result is then displayed, once again in octal.

As you can see, with the Korn shell its easy to work with different bases. This makes it possible to easily write functions to perform base conversion and arithmetic, for example.

♦ Pattern Substitution ♦

The Korn shell provides more powerful pattern matching capabilites than the standard shell. As you know, patterns can be specified for file name expansion and in case constructs. The Korn shell also accepts patterns in the new [[...]] construct (see Appendix B) and the new parameter substitution constructs (see the next section).

The standard pattern match constructs (* for zero or more characters, ? for any single character, and [...] for any single character in the specified range) are treated similarly by both shells. The Korn shell adds five new pattern matching constructs, all of the following form:

c (*pattern*)

where *c* is any of the characters *, ?, +, @, or !.

The * is used to match zero or more occurrences of the parenthesized *pattern*; ? matches zero or one occurrence; @ matches exactly one occurrence; +

matches one or more occurrences; and ! is used to match anything except the specified *pattern*.

The pattern

```
*([0-9])
```

says to match zero or more consecutive digit characters. The pattern

```
?([A-Z])
```

says to match zero or one uppercase letters. The pattern

```
+([0-9])
```

says to match one or more consecutive digits. Finally,

```
!(test)*
```

says to match anything that doesn't begin with the word test. (An example with the @(...) pattern construct will follow shortly.)

The vertical bar | can be used inside the parentheses to achieve a logical ORing of the patterns. In that case, the general format of the pattern matching constructs becomes

$$c\ (pattern_1 \,|\, pattern_2 \,|\, \ldots)$$

So, for example, the pattern

```
?(docs|letters)
```

says to match either docs or letters. The pattern

```
?([0-9]|xx)
```

says to match either a digit or two consecutive x's. The pattern

```
*!([0-9][0-9]|.bk)
```

says to match anything that doesn't end with two digits or with the characters .bk

As you can see, the patterns can get quite complex! Here are some more simple examples.

```
$ ls abc*
abc
abc1
```

```
abc1a
abcdef
abcdefdefdef
abczzz
$ echo abc?(def)
abc abcdef
$ echo abc@(def|ggg|zzz)
abcdef abczzz
$ echo abc*(def|ggg|zzz)
abc abcdef abcdefdefdef abczzz
$ echo abc!(def)
abc abc1 abc1a abczzz
$
```

♦ Parameter Substitution ♦

The Korn shell provides several new parameter substitution capabilities including substring and truncation operations. Each of these new capabilities is described in this section.

${n}

You will recall that the only way to access positional parameters 10 and above in the Bourne shell is to `shift` them down to a position below 10. That's because the Bourne shell only allows the dollar sign to be followed by a single digit 0-9.

The Korn shell permits you to directly access any command line argument by number. If the number is greater than 9, the format

${n}

must be used. So to directly access argument 10, you can write

${10}

in your program.

The following program, called `last`, is a rewrite of the program presented in Chapter 13. It prints the last argument to the program and does not have the "maximum of nine arguments" limitation that the Bourne shell program had.

```
$ cat last
eval echo \${$#}
$ last 1 2 3 4 5 6 7 8 9 10 11 12
12
$
```

${#variable}

This Korn shell construct gives you the ability to count the number of characters stored inside a variable. For example,

```
$ text='Korn shell'
$ echo ${#text}
10
$
```

Pattern Matching Constructs

The Korn shell provides four new parameter substitution constructs that perform pattern matching. In each case, the construct takes two arguments: a variable name (or parameter number) and a pattern. The Korn shell searches through the contents of the specified variable to match the supplied pattern. If the pattern is matched, the shell substitutes the value of the variable on the command line, *with the matching portion of the pattern deleted*. If the pattern is not matched, the entire contents of the variable is substituted on the command line. In any case, the contents of the variable remains unchanged.

The term *pattern* is used here because the Korn shell allows you to use the same pattern matching characters that it accepts in file name substitution and case values: * to match zero or more characters, ? to match any single character, [...] to match any single character from the specified set, [!...] to match any single character not in the specified set, plus the new pattern pattern matching constructs described in the previous section.

When you write the construct

$ {*variable%pattern* }

the shell looks inside *variable* to see if it *ends* with the specifed *pattern*. If it does, the contents of *variable* is substituted on the command line with the matching *pattern* removed from the right.

If you use the construct

$ {*variable%%pattern* }

then the shell once again looks inside *variable* to see if it ends with *pattern*. This time, however, it removes the *longest* matching pattern from the right. This is only relevant if the * or + is used in *pattern*. Otherwise, the % and %% behave the same way.

The # is used in a similar way to force the pattern matching to occur on the left instead of the right. So, the construct

$ {*variable#pattern*}

tells the shell to substitute the value of *variable* on the command line, with *pattern* removed from the left.

Finally, the shell construct

$ {*variable##pattern*}

works like the # form, only the longest occurrence of *pattern* is removed from the left.

Remember, that in all four cases, no permanent changes are made to the variable itself; you are only affecting what gets substituted on the command line. Also, remember that the pattern matches are *anchored*. In the case of the % and %% constructs, the variables must *end* with the specified pattern; in the case of the # and ## constructs, the variable must *begin* with it.

Here are some simple examples to show how these constructs work:

```
$ var=testcase
$ echo $var
testcase
$ echo ${var%e}                    Remove e from right
testcas
$ echo $var                        Variable is unchanged
testcase
$ echo ${var%s*e}                  Remove smallest match from right
testca
$ echo ${var%%s*e}                 Remove longest match
te
$ echo ${var%%+([a-s])}            Longest match from right
test
$ echo ${var#?e}                   Remove smallest match from left
stcase
$ echo ${var#*s}                   Remove smallest match from left
tcase
$ echo ${var##*s}                  Remove longest match from left
e
$ echo ${var#test}                 Remove test from left
case
$ echo ${var#teas}                 No match
testcase
$
```

There are many practical uses for these constructs, even though these examples don't seem to show it. For example, the following tests to see if the file name stored inside the variable `file` ends in the two characters `.o`:

```
if [ ${file%.o} != $file ]
then
    # file ends in .o
         ...
fi
```

As another example, here's a function called `basename` that works just like the UNIX system's `basename` command:

```
function basename {
    echo ${1##*/}
}
```

The function displays its argument with all the characters up to the last `/` removed. This example displays the base file name of a path given as its argument:

```
$ basename /usr/spool/uucppublic
uucppublic
$ basename $HOME
steve
$ basename memos
memos
$
```

Fixed Length Strings

The `typeset` command can be used to create shell variables of fixed length. The command

```
typeset -Ln variables
```

defines *variables* to be left justified and *n* characters long. If *n* isn't specified, the length is taken from the values assigned to the variables on the `typeset` command line.

```
$ typeset -L5 five          five will hold up to five chars
$ five=123456xxx            Assign it more than five
$ echo $five                See what happened
12345                       Truncated on the right
$ five=x                    Assign less than five chars
```

```
$ echo ":$five:"
:x     :                        Padded with spaces
$ typeset -L any=abc            Assignment fixes length at three chars
$ echo $any
abc
$ any=hello                     Assign more than three chars
$ echo $any
hel
$
```

The command

```
typeset -Rn variables
```

declares *variables* to be right justified, *n* characters long. Again, if *n* isn't specified, the size is taken from the length of the values assigned to the variables.

```
$ typeset -R6 Rsix
$ Rsix=test
$ echo ":$Rsix:"
:  test:                        Right justified
$ Rsix=12345678
$ echo ":$Rsix:"
:345678:                        Truncated on the left
$
```

Truncation is often used like cut to remove the first or last part of a line or to
format output lines. If you want output to line up in columns, you can make use
of fixed size shell variables:

```
$ typeset -R20 name1 name2 name3
$ name1="Leslie King"
$ name2="Leela Kochan"
$ name3="George Stachiw"
$ echo "$name1\n$name2\n$name3"
        Leslie King
       Leela Kochan
     George Stachiw
$
```

Here fixed length variables are used to force the three names to align on the right
side in a field width of 20 characters.

The listall program from rolo can be rewritten using fixed length
variables:

```
#
# list all of the entries in the phone book
#

typeset -L37 first

IFS='^'    # to be used in set command below

echo "-----------------------------------------------------------------"
while read line
do
      #
      # Get the first and last fields, presumably names and numbers
      #

      set $line

      #
      # display 1st and last fields
      #

      first=$1
      eval echo "\"$first \$$#\""
done < $PHONEBOOK
echo "-----------------------------------------------------------------"
```

This version is better than the old version, as it handles very long first lines (it truncates them); the Bourne shell version will overwrite the phone number with the end of the first line. (Recall that the Bourne shell version of `listall` prints the right side of the line first, then returns and prints the left side.)

```
...                          Bourne shell version
        Please select one of the above (1-6): 5


-----------------------------------------------------------------
pat wood                                386-3193
this is a very long line let's see how it works
-----------------------------------------------------------------
...



...                          Korn shell version
        Please select one of the above (1-6): 5


-----------------------------------------------------------------
pat wood                                386-3193
```

```
this is a very long line let's see ho 386-3972
-----------------------------------------------------------
...
```

You can also declare variables to be upper- or lowercase only. For example,

```
typeset -u name
```

declares `name` to be an uppercase only variable, and

```
typeset -l answer
```

declares `answer` to be lowercase only. If you assign a value that contains lowercase letters to an uppercase only variable, the Korn shell will automatically convert all lowercase letters to uppercase on the assignment. All other characters will be left alone. Similarly, assigning a value that contains one or more uppercase letters to a lowercase only variable cause the shell to convert the uppercase letters to lowercase on the assignment:

```
$ typeset -u name
$ typeset -l answer
$ name="Ann Baker"
$ echo $name
ANN BAKER
$ answer=NO
$ echo $answer
no
$ read answer
Yes
$ echo $answer
yes
$
```

The shell does the automatic conversion every time a value is assigned to an uppercase or lowercase only variable, even if it is the result of a `read` operation.

Naturally, uppercase or lowercase attributes can be combined with left or right fixed length variable declarations. So the declaration

```
typeset -uR20 name
```

declares `name` to be a right-justified uppercase only variable that is exactly 20 characters in length. The declaration

```
typeset -lL1 answer
```

declares `answer` to be lowercase only, left justified, one character in length. The code sequence

```
typeset -1L1 answer
echo "Remove $file? \c"
read answer

if [ "$answer" = y ]
then
    rm $file
fi
```

asks the user a question and reads the answer into the variable `answer`. The program takes any response that begins with the letter `y` (or `Y`) as a "yes" response. The declaration for the variable `answer` makes it easy to test for this.

♦ The alias Command ♦

An *alias* is a shorthand notation provided by the Korn shell to allow customization of commands. The Korn shell keeps a list of aliases that is searched when a command is entered. If the first word of a command line is an alias, then it is replaced by the text of the alias. An alias is defined by using the `alias` command. The format is

```
alias name=string
```

where *name* is the name of the alias, and *string* is any string of characters. For example,

```
alias ll='ls -l'
```

assigns `ls -l` to the alias `ll`. Now when the alias `ll` is typed in, the Korn shell replaces it with `ls -l`. You can type arguments after the alias name on the command line, as in

```
ll *.c
```

which will look like this after alias substitution has been performed

```
ls -l *.c
```

The shell performs its normal command line processing both when the alias is set and when it is used, so quoting can be tricky. For example, the Korn shell keeps track of your current working directory inside a variable called PWD:

```
$ cd /usr/steve/letters
$ echo $PWD
/usr/steve/letters
$ cd ..
$ echo $PWD
/usr/steve
```

You can create an alias called `dir` that gives you the base directory of your current working directory by using the PWD variable and one of the parameter substitution constructs described in an earlier section of this chapter:

```
alias dir="echo ${PWD##*/}"
```

Let's see how this alias works.

```
$ alias dir="echo ${PWD##*/}"     Define alias
$ pwd                             Where are we?
/usr/steve
$ dir                             Execute alias
steve
$ cd letters                      Change directory
$ dir                             Execute alias again
steve
$ cd /usr/spool                   One more try
$ dir
steve
$
```

It seems that no matter what the current directory is, the `dir` alias prints out `steve`. That's because we weren't careful about our quotes when we defined the `dir` alias. Recalling that the shell performs parameter substitution inside double quotes, the shell evaluated

```
${PWD##*/}
```

at the time the alias was defined. This means, that for all intents and purposes, the `dir` alias was defined as though we typed in the following:

```
$ alias dir="echo steve"
```

The solution is to use single instead of double quotes when defining the `dir` alias to defer the parameter substitution until the time the alias is executed:

```
$ alias dir='echo ${PWD##*/}'          Define alias
$ pwd                                   Where are we?
/usr/steve
$ dir                                   Execute alias
steve
$ cd letters                            Change directory
$ dir                                   Execute alias again
letters
$ cd /usr/spool                         One more try
$ dir
spool
$
```

Now the alias works just fine.

If an alias ends with a blank, the word following the alias is also checked for alias substitution. For example,

```
alias nohup="/bin/nohup "
nohup ll
```

will cause the Korn shell to perform alias checking on the string `ll` after replacing `nohup` with `/bin/nohup`.

The format

```
alias name
```

causes the value of the alias *name* to be listed, and the `alias` command without arguments causes all aliases to be listed.

The `-x` option to the `alias` command can be used to create *exported* aliases. An exported alias is accessible to subshells in a similar fashion to exported variables. The following aliases are automatically exported when the Korn shell starts up:

```
false=let 0
functions=typeset -f
hash=alias -t
history=fc -l
integer=typeset -i
nohup=nohup
r=fc -e -
suspend=kill -STOP $$
true=:
type=whence -v
```

You will note from the above that `integer` is actually an alias for the `typeset` command with the `-i` option.

Command Tracking

Aliasing can be used by the Korn shell to reduce the amount of time spent searching the PATH. The command

```
set -o trackall
```

turns on command *tracking*. This means that the first time a command is entered, a special alias is created for it. This alias (called a *tracked alias*) is set to the full path name of the command. This way, the next time the command is entered, the PATH isn't searched at all; instead, the alias is used.[†]

```
$ set -o trackall
$ alias wc                            Print alias for wc
wc alias not found                    No such animal
$ wc /etc/passwd
      15      43     794 /etc/passwd
$ alias wc                            Print alias for wc again
wc=/bin/wc                            Found it this time
$
```

As you use the system with the alias tracking on, you build up a working set of commands that are tracked. Thus, the startup time for ed, ls, and any other command is reduced after the first use. This feature can help shell programs to run faster, particularly if many commands are executed within a loop. You can list all of your tracked aliases by typing in

```
alias -t
```

The set -o trackall command may be put in your ENV file to cause command tracking to be turned on when the Korn shell starts, and you can force a command to be tracked using the format

```
alias -t command
```

This can also be put in your ENV file so that you automatically have certain tracked aliases initialized.

Note that the standard Bourne shell has a feature similar to this called *hashing*. In general, these two methods are equivalent.

[†] This isn't completely true. Any *relative* directories in the PATH (such as : :) that are listed before the directory that the command was located in are still searched.

Removing Aliases

The `unalias` command is used to remove aliases from the alias list. The format is

```
unalias name
```

Whenever the `PATH` is changed, all tracked aliases are automatically removed. This is because a change in the `PATH` may also change the directory where a command will be found. For example, the `PATH`

```
:/bin:/usr/bin:/usr/lbin
```

searches the current directory, `/bin`, `/usr/bin`, and `/usr/lbin`. If you execute the command `rolo` and the shell finds it in `/usr/lbin`, the tracked alias for `rolo` will be set to `/usr/lbin/rolo`. Should the `PATH` be changed to

```
:/bin:/usr/bin
```

then the `rolo` program shouldn't be found anymore; therefore the `rolo` alias must be removed. The Korn shell doesn't perform any checking to determine which tracked aliases will be affected by a change of the `PATH` variable. It simply removes them all.

This concludes this section on aliases. If you develop a set of alias definitions that you like to use during your login sessions, you may want to define them inside your `ENV` file so they will always be available for you to use.

◆ Arrays ◆

The Korn shell provides a limited array capability. Arrays may contain up to 512 elements (128 on some older versions); and array indexing starts at zero. An array element is accessed with a *subscript*, which is an integer-valued expression enclosed inside a pair of brackets. You don't declare the maximum size of a Korn shell array; you simply assign values to elements as you need them. The values that you can assign are the same as for ordinary variables.

```
$ arr[0]=hello
$ arr[1]="some text"
$ arr[2]=/usr/steve/memos
$
```

To retrieve an element from an array, you write the array name followed by the element number, enclosed inside a pair of brackets as before. The entire construct must be enclosed inside a pair of curly braces, which is then preceded by a dollar sign.

```
$ echo ${array[0]}
hello
$ echo ${array[1]}
some text
$ echo ${array[2]}
/usr/steve/memos
$ echo $array
hello
$
```

As you can see from the last example, if no subscript is specified element zero is used.

If you forget the curly braces when performing the substitution, here's what happens:

```
$ echo $array[1]
hello[1]
$
```

In the above example, the value of array is substituted (hello—the value inside array[0]) and then echoed along with [1]. (Note that since the shell does file name substitution after variable substitution, the shell would attempt to match the pattern hello[1] against the files in your current directory.)

The construct [*] can be used as a subscript to substitute all of the elements of the array on the command line, with each element delimited by a single space character.

```
$ echo ${array[*]}
hello some text /usr/steve/memos
$
```

The construct ${#array[*]} can be used to substitute the number of elements in the array *array*.

```
$ echo ${#array[*]}
3
$
```

Note that the number reported here is not the actual number of values stored inside the array, but the largest subscript used to store an element inside the array, plus one.

```
$ array[10]=foo
$ echo ${array[*]}                  Display all elements
hello some text /usr/steve/memos foo
$ echo ${#array[*]}                 Number of elements
11
$
```

You can declare an array of integers to the Korn shell simply by giving the array name to the integer command:

```
integer data
```

Integer calculations can be performed on array elements using the `let` command:

```
$ integer array
$ array[0]=100
$ array[1]=50
$ (( array[2] = array[0] + array[1] ))
$ echo ${array[2]}
150
$
```

Note that not only can you omit the dollar signs, but the curly braces can be dropped as well when referencing an array element inside a `let`.

Simply as an exercise with arrays, the following program calculates and stores the first 15 Fibonacci numbers into the array `fibs`. Then it displays the values at the terminal.

```
$ cat fibonacci
#
# Calculate the first 15 Fibonacci numbers with arrays
#

integer index=2 fibs

(( fibs[0] = 1 ))
(( fibs[1] = 1 ))


#
# Calculate and store the values
#

while (( index < 15 ))
do
        (( fibs[index] = fibs[index-1] + fibs[index-2] ))
```

```
        (( index = index + 1 ))
done

#
# Now display the values
#

(( index = 0 ))

while (( index < 15 ))
do
        echo ${fibs[index]}
        (( index = index + 1 ))
done
$


$ fibonacci
1
1
2
3
5
8
13
21
34
55
89
144
233
377
610
$
```

Note that dollar signs are not needed before variables used in subscript expressions.

The following program, called reverse, reads in up to 512 lines from standard input and then writes them back out to standard output in reverse order.

```
$ cat reverse
# read lines to array buf

integer line=0

while (( line < 512 )) && read buf[line]
do
    (( line = line + 1 ))
done

# now print the lines in reverse order

while (( line > 0 ))
do
    (( line = line - 1 ))
    echo "${buf[line]}"
done


$ reverse

line one
line two
line three
CTRL-d
line three
line two
line one
$
```

The first `while` loop executes as long as 512 or less lines have been read and there is more data to be read from standard input (recall the `&&` described at the end of Chapter 8).

Table 15-4 summarizes the various array constructs in the Korn shell.

TABLE 15-4. Array constructs

Construct	Meaning
${array[i]}	Substitute value of element i
$array	Substitue value of first element (array[0])
${array[*]}	Substitute value of all elements
${#array[*]}	Substitute number of elements
array[i]=val	Store val into array[i] .

♦ Job Control ♦

The Korn shell provides facilities for controlling *jobs*. A job is any command sequence, e.g.,

```
who | wc
```

If the command

```
set -o monitor
```

is executed, the *job monitor* is turned on, and the Korn shell associates a number with each job. When a command is started in the background (i.e., with &), the Korn shell prints out the job number inside brackets ([]) as well as the process number:

```
$ set -o monitor
$ who | wc &
    [1] 832
$
```

When a job finishes, the Korn shell prints the message

```
[n]  +  Done         sequence
```

where *n* is the job number of the finished job, and *sequence* is the text of the command sequence used to create the job.

The `jobs` command may be used to print the status of jobs that haven't yet finished.

```
$ jobs
[3] +  Running          make ksh &
[2] -  Running          monitor &
[1]    Running          pic chapt2 | troff > aps.out &
```

The + and − after the job number mark the current and previous jobs, respectively. The current job is the last job sent to the background, and the previous job is the next to the last job sent to the background. Several built-in commands may be given a job number or the current or previous job as arguments.

The Korn shell's built-in `kill` command can be used to terminate a job running in the background. The argument to it can be a process number or a percent sign (%) followed by a job number, a + or a −.

```
$ pic chapt1 | troff > aps.out &
    [1] 886
$ jobs
[1] +  Running            pic chapt1 | troff > aps.out &
$ kill %1
[1] +  Terminated         pic chapt1 | troff > aps.out &
$
```

The above `kill` could have used `%+` to refer to the same job. Note that the Korn shell printed out `Terminated` instead of `Done` when this pipeline finished, since it was killed by the user.

The first few characters of the pipeline can also be used to refer to a job, e.g., `kill %pic` would have worked in the above example.

Stopped Jobs and the `fg` and `bg` Commands

This section only applies to systems that support the stopping and restarting of jobs.

If you are running a job in the foreground (without an `&`) and you wish to suspend it, you can hit the *CTRL-z* key. The job stops executing, and the Korn shell prints the message

```
[n] +  Stopped      sequence
```

The stopped job is made the current job. To have it continue executing, you must use the `fg` or `bg` command. The `fg` command with no arguments causes the current job to resume execution in the foreground, and `bg` causes the current job to resume execution in the background. You can also use the job number, a `+`, or a `–` preceded by a `%` to specify any job to the `fg` and `bg` commands. These commands print out the command sequence to remind you what is being brought to the foreground or sent to the background.

```
$ troff memo | photo
CTRL-z
[1] +  Stopped         troff memo | photo
$ bg
[1]        troff memo | photo &
$
```

The above sequence is one of the most often used with job control: sending a job mistakenly started in the foreground to the background.

If a job running in the background tries to read from the terminal, it is stopped, and on Berkeley systems, the message

```
[n] -  Stopped (tty input)   pipeline
```

is printed. It can then be brought to the foreground with the `fg` command. After entering input to the job, it can be stopped (with the *CTRL-z*) and returned to the background until it again requests input from the terminal.

On Berkeley UNIX systems, output from a background job normally goes directly to the terminal. The command

```
stty tostop
```

will cause any background job that attempts to write to the terminal to be stopped and the message

```
[n]  -   Stopped(tty output)  pipeline
```

to be printed. Under System V, Release 2, background jobs that write to the terminal are always stopped.

The following shows how job control might be used:

```
$ rundb                                  Start up data base program
??? find green red                       Find green and red objects
CTRL-z                                   This may take a while
[1] +  Stopped          rundb
$ bg                                     So put it in the background
[1]           rundb &
...                                      Do some other stuff
$ jobs
[1] +  Stopped(tty output)    rundb &
$ fg                                     Bring back to foreground
rundb
1973  Ford     Mustang       red
1975  Chevy    Monte Carlo   green
1976  Ford     Granada       green
1980  Buick    Century       green
1983  Chevy    Cavalier      red
??? find blue                            Find blue objects
CTRL-z                                   Stop it again
[1] +  Stopped          rundb
$ bg                                     Back to the background
[1]           rundb &
...                                      Keep working until it's ready
```

◆ Miscellaneous Features ◆

New Features of the cd Command

Two new features have been added to the cd command. The first allows you to
cd to your previous directory without specifying it by name. The − argument to
cd always means "the previous directory."

```
$ pwd
/usr/src/cmd
$ cd /usr/spool/uucp
$ pwd
/usr/spool/uucp
$ cd -                              cd to previous directory
/usr/src/cmd                        cd prints out name of new directory
$ cd -
/usr/spool/uucp
$
```

As you can see, the cd command can be used to toggle between two directories
with no effort at all.

The second feature added to cd is the ability to substitute portions of the
current directory's path with something else. The format is

cd *old* *new*

cd will attempt to replace the first occurence of the string *old* in the current
directory's path with the string *new*.

```
$ pwd
/usr/spool/uucppublic/pat
$ cd pat steve                      Change pat to steve and cd
/usr/spool/uucppublic/steve         cd prints out name of new directory
$ pwd                               Confirm location
/usr/spool/uucppublic/steve
$
```

Tilde Substitution

If a word on a command line begins with the tilde (~) character, the Korn shell
scans the rest of the word and performs the following substitutions: If the tilde is
the only character in the word or if the character following the tilde is a slash (/),
then the value of the HOME variable is substituted:

```
$ echo ~
/usr/pat
$ grep Korn ~/shell/chapter9/ksh
The Korn shell is a new shell developed
by David Korn at AT&T
for the Bourne shell would also run under the Korn
the one on System V, the Korn shell provides you with
idea of the compatibility of the Korn shell with Bourne's,
the Bourne and Korn shells.
The main features added to the Korn shell are:
$
```

If the rest of the word up to a slash is a user's login name in /etc/passwd, then the tilde and the user's login name are substituted with the HOME directory of that user.

```
$ echo ~steve
/usr/steve
$ echo ~pat
/usr/pat
$ grep Korn ~pat/shell/chapter9/ksh
The Korn shell is a new shell developed
by David Korn at AT&T
for the Bourne shell would also run under the Korn
the one on System V, the Korn shell provides you with
idea of the compatibility of the Korn shell with Bourne's,
the Bourne and Korn shells.
The main features added to the Korn shell are:
$
```

If the ~ is followed by a + or a − then the value of the variable PWD or OLDPWD is substituted, respectively. PWD and OLDPWD are set by cd and are the full path names of the current and previous directories, respectively.

```
$ pwd
/usr/spool/uucppublic/steve
$ cd
$ pwd
/usr/pat
$ echo ~+
/usr/pat
$ echo ~-
/usr/spool/uucppublic/steve
$
```

In addition to the above substitutions, the shell also checks for a tilde after a colon (:) and performs tilde substitution on that as well (for PATH interpretation).

Command Substitution: The $(...) Construct

You're certainly familiar enough by now with the back quoting mechanism to perform command substitution; that is, to execute a command and insert its standard output onto the command line. Here are a couple of examples to refresh your memory:

```
$ users=`who | wc -l`
$ echo $users
27
$ echo You have `ls | wc -l `files in `pwd`
You have 11 files in /usr/steve/letters
$
```

The Korn shell supports an alternate way to perform command substitution. This is done by enclosing the command list inside a pair of parentheses and preceding that by a dollar sign (after all, you are performing command line substitution here, so the dollar sign actually makes more sense than the back quotes):

```
$ users=$(who | wc -l)
$ echo $users
27
$ echo You have $(ls | wc -l) files in $(pwd)
You have 11 files in /usr/steve/letters
$
```

Advanced programmers will be happy to know that this new construct can be nested.

The read Command

Several new options were added to the read command. They are all described in Appendix B. The -r option is useful for preventing the shell from interpreting backslash characters at the end of the line. Normally, whenever you read a line with the read command (either the Bourne or Korn shell's), several things happen:

1. The shell strips leading whitespace characters from the line.

2. The Bourne shell interprets backslash characters within the line.

3.   The shell treats a trailing backslash character as a line continuation and merges the current line with the next line of input

The first problem is remedied by setting the IFS variable to just a newline character. The second problem doesn't exist in the Korn shell. The third problem is fixed by using the -r option to the read command. We'll show a program that can be used to faithfully copy standard input to standard output after the following discussion on the print command.

The print Command

The Korn shell's print command behaves similarly to echo, except, once again, it takes some addtional arguments. One useful argument is the -r option, which tells the Korn shell to print its arguments to standard output without performing any special interpretation of backslash characters. This option is important if you want to write some output that may contain embedded backslash characters.

The following program, called number2 is a final version of the line numbering program presented earlier. This program will faithfully print the input lines to standard output, preceded by a line number. Notice the use of a fixed-length variable to right-align the line numbers.

```
$ cat number2
#
# Number lines from files given as argument or from
# standard input if none supplied (final Korn shell version)
#

# lineno is a fixed-width variable to line the numbers up

typeset -R5 lineno

# Modify the IFS to preserve leading whitespace on input

IFS='
'       # Just a newline appears between the quotes

(( lineno = 1 ))

cat $* |
while read -r line
do
        print -r "$lineno: $line"
        (( lineno = lineno + 1 ))
done
```

Here's a sample execution of `number`:

```
$ number2 add
    1:  #
    2:  # Program to add someone to the phonebook file
    3:  #
    4:
    5:  echo "Type in your new entry"
    6:  echo "When done, type just a single RETURN on the line."
    7:
    8:  first=
    9:  entry=
   10:
   11:  while   true
   12:  do
   13:          echo ">> \c"
   14:          read line
   15:
   16:          if [ -n "$line" ]
   17:          then
   18:                  entry="$entry$line^"
   19:
   20:                  if [ -z "$first" ]
   21:                  then
   22:                          first=$line
   23:                  fi
   24:          else
   25:                  break
   26:          fi
   27:  done
$
```

Order of Search

It's worthwhile listing the order of searching the Korn shell uses when you type a command name:

1. The Korn shell first checks to see if the command is a reserved word (such as `for` and `do`).

2. If it's not a reserved word, the Korn shell next checks its alias list, and if it finds a match, performs the substitution. If the alias definition ends in a space, it attempts alias substitution on the result. The final result is then checked against the reserved word list, and if it's not a reserved word, the shell proceeds to Item 3.

3.   The shell checks to see if the command is a built-in command (such as cd and pwd).

4.   Next, the Korn shell checks the command against its function list, and executes it if found.

5.   Finally, the Korn shell searches the PATH to locate the command.

6.   If the command still isn't found, a "command not found" error message is issued.

As noted earlier, if the alias is a tracked one, the Korn shell may still end up searching the PATH (but only relative directories that occur earlier in the PATH rather than the directory containing the command).

◆ Exercises ◆

1. Using the Korn shell's substring capabilities, write a program that "cuts" columns out of its standard input, where its first argument is the beginning column and the second is the ending column, e.g.,

```
$ mycut 10 20
this is a test of the mycut program
 test of th
$
```

2. Rewrite the `display` program from `rolo` to truncate lines wider than the rolo-dex card.

3. Using only shell built-in commands, write a function that prints all file names in a specified directory hierarchy. Its output should be similar to the output of the `find` command:

```
$ myfind /usr/pat
/usr/pat
/usr/pat/bin
/usr/pat/bin/ksh
/usr/pat/bin/lf
/usr/pat/bin/pic
/usr/pat/chapt1
/usr/pat/chapt1/intro
/usr/pat/rje
/usr/pat/rje/file1
...
```

Hint: Korn shell functions can be recursive.

4. The `-l` option to the `typeset` command declares a shell variable to be lower-case. Any subsequent assignments to such a variable containing uppercase letters will be converted to lowercase. Use this option in conjuction with trunca-tion to write a Korn shell program, `isyes`, that has an exit status of zero if its argument begins with `Y` or `y`, one otherwise:

```
$ isyes YES
$ echo $?
0
$
```

5. Using the fact that the special Korn shell construct ${#var} gives the number of characters stored in *var*, rewrite wc in the Korn shell. Be sure to use integer arithmetic! (Notes: Change your IFS variable to just a newline character so that leading whitespace characters on input are preserved, and also use the -r option to the Korn shell's read command so that terminating backslash characters on the input are ignored.)

6. Write a function called rightmatch that takes two arguments as shown:

   rightmatch *value pattern*

   where *value* is a sequence of one or more characters and *pattern* is a shell pattern that is to be removed from the right side of *value*. The *shortest* matching pattern should be removed from *value* and the result written to standard output. Here is some sample output:

   ```
   $ rightmatch test.c .c
   test
   $ rightmatch /usr/spool/uucppublic '/*'
   /usr/spool
   $ rightmatch /usr/spool/uucppublic o
   /usr/spool/uucppublic
   $
   ```

   The last example shows that the rightmatch function should simply echo its first argument if it does not end with the specified pattern.

7. Write a function called leftmatch that works similarly to the rightmatch function developed in the previous exercise. It's two arguments should be as follows:

   leftmatch *pattern value*

   Here's some example uses:

   ```
   $ leftmatch /usr/spool/ /usr/spool/uucppublic
   uucppublic
   $ leftmatch s. s.main.c
   main.c
   $
   ```

8. Write a function called substring that uses the leftmatch and rightmatch function developed in Exercises 6 and 7 to remove a pattern from the left and right side of a value. It should take three arguments as shown:

```
$ substring /usr/ /usr/spool/uucppublic /uucppublic
spool
$ substring s. s.main.c .c
main
$ substring s. s.main.c .o        Only left match
main.c
$ substring x. s.main.c .o        No matches
s.main.c
$
```

9. Modify the `substring`, `leftmatch`, and `rightmatch` functions developed in the previous exercises to take options that allow you to remove the *largest* possible matches of the specified pattern from the left or right side of the specified value.

Shell Summary

This appendix summarizes the main features of the standard Bourne shell as of System V Release 3.

◆ Startup ◆

If the shell is started with `exec`, and the first character of the command name (argument 0) is a dash (-), then the shell will first execute the commands in `/etc/profile` and in the file `.profile` in the user's home directory. The shell can be given the same options on the command line as can be specified with the `set` command. In addition, the following options can be specified:

`-c` *commands*	*commands* are executed.
`-i`	The shell is interactive. Signals 2, 3, and 15 are ignored.
`-r`	A restricted shell is started.
`-s`	Commands are read from standard input.

◆ Commands ◆

The general format of a command typed to the shell is

   command arguments

where *command* is the name of the program to be executed, and *arguments* are its arguments. The command name and the arguments are delimited by *whitespace* characters, normally the space, tab, and newline characters (changing the variable IFS will affect this).

Multiple commands can be typed on the same line if they're separated by semicolons (;).

Every command that gets executed returns a number known as the *exit status*; zero is used to indicate success, and nonzero indicates a failure.

The pipe symbol | (or ^) can be used to connect the standard output from one command to the standard input of another, as in

```
who | wc -l
```

The exit status is that of the last command in the pipeline.

If the command sequence is terminated by an ampersand character (&), then it is run asynchronously in the background. The shell displays the process number of the command at the terminal.

Typing of a command can continue to the next line if the last character on the line is a backslash character (\).

The characters && cause the command that follows to be executed only if the preceding command returns a zero exit status. The characters || cause the command that follows to be executed only if the preceding command returns a nonzero exit status. As an example, in

```
who | grep "fred" > /dev/null  &&  echo "fred's logged on"
```

the echo is executed only if the grep returns a zero exit status.

♦ Comments ♦

If a word begins with the character #, then the shell treats the remainder of the line as a comment and simply ignores it.

♦ Shell Variables ♦

There are three different "types" of shell variables, also known as *parameters*: *keyword* parameters, *positional* parameters, and special shell parameters.

Keyword Parameters

A keyword parameter name must start with an alphabetic or underscore (_) character, and can be followed by any number of alphanumeric or underscore characters. Values are assigned to keyword parameters by writing *variable=value   variable=value ...*

File name substitution is not performed on *value*.

Positional Parameters

Whenever a shell program is executed the name of the program is assigned to the variable `$0`, and the arguments typed on the command line to the variables `$1`, `$2`, ..., respectively. Positional parameters can also be assigned values with the `set` command. Only parameters 1 through 9 can be explicitly referenced.

Other Special Parameters

The special shell parameters are summarized in Table A-1.

TABLE A-1. Special parameter variables

Parameter	Meaning
`$#`	The number of arguments passed to the program; or the number of parameters set by executing the `set` statement
`$*`	Collectively references all of the positional parameters as `$1`, `$2`, ...
`$@`	Same as `$*`, except when double-quoted (`"$@"`) collectively references all of the positional parameters as `"$1"`, `"$2"`, ...
`$0`	The name of the program being executed
`$$`	The process id number of the program being executed
`$!`	The process id number of the last program sent to the background for execution
`$?`	The exit status of the last command not executed in the background
`$-`	The current options in effect (see the `set` statement)

In addition to these parameters, the shell has some other variables that it uses. These variables are summarized in Table A-2.

TABLE A-2. Other variables used by the shell

Variable	Meaning
CDPATH	The directories to be searched whenever cd is executed without a full path as argument
HOME	The directory that cd changes to when no argument is supplied
IFS	The Internal Field Separator characters; used by the shell to delimit words when parsing the command line, for the read and set commands, when substituting the output from a back-quoted command, and when performing parameter substitution. Normally, it contains the three characters space, horizontal tab, and newline
MAIL	The name of a file that the shell will periodically check for the arrival of mail. If new mail arrives, then the shell will display its You have mail message. *See also* MAILCHECK *and* MAILPATH
MAILCHECK	The number of seconds specifying how often the shell is to check for the arrival of mail in the file in MAIL or in the files listed in MAILPATH. The default is 600. A value of 0 causes the shell to check before displaying each command prompt
MAILPATH	A list of files to be checked for the arrival of mail. Each file is delimited by a colon, and can be followed by a percent sign (%) and a message to be displayed when mail arrives in the indicated file (You have mail is the default)
PATH	A colon delimited list of directories to be searched when the shell needs to find a command to be executed. The current directory is specified as : : (if it heads the list, : suffices)
PS1	The primary command prompt, normally "$ "
PS2	The secondary command prompt, normally "> "
SHACCT	The name of a file that the shell will use to write accounting information for commands that it executes. This information can later be analyzed using the acctcom command (see your *UNIX System Administrator's Manual* for details)
SHELL	The name of the shell (e.g. /bin/sh). This variable is used by vi and ed to determine the shell to start up when you escape to the shell or execute a shell command. It's also used by the shell on startup to determine if it should run restricted. This determination is made based upon whether the letter "r" appears in the name of the shell

The shell assigns default values to IFS, MAILCHECK, PATH, PS1, and PS2, on login. HOME and MAIL are set to default values by the login program.

Parameter Substitution

In the simplest case, the value of a parameter can be accessed by preceding the parameter with a dollar sign ($). Table A-3 summarizes the different types of parameter substitution that can be performed. Parameter substitution is performed by the shell before file name substitution and before the command line is divided into arguments.

TABLE A-3. Parameter substitution

Parameter	Meaning
$parameter or ${parameter}	Substitute the value of parameter
${parameter:−value}	Substitute the value of parameter if it's non-null; otherwise, substitute value
${parameter:=value}	Substitute the value of parameter if it's non-null; otherwise, substitute value and also assign it to parameter
${parameter:?value}	Substitute the value of parameter if it's non-null; otherwise, write value to standard error and exit. If value is omitted, then write parameter: parameter null or not set instead
${parameter:+value}	Substitute value if parameter is non-null; otherwise, substitute nothing

◆ Quoting ◆

There are four different types of quote characters that are recognized. These are summarized in Table A-4.

TABLE A-4. Summary of quote characters

Quote	Description
`'...'`	Removes special meaning of all enclosed characters
`"..."`	Removes special meaning of all enclosed characters except $, `, and \
`\c`	Removes special meaning of character *c* that follows; inside double quotes removes special meaning of $, `, ", newline, and \ that follows, but is otherwise not interpreted; used for line continuation if appears as last character on line (newline is removed)
`` `command` ``	Executes *command* and inserts standard output at that point

♦ File Name Substitution ♦

After parameter substitution (and command substitution) is performed on the command line, the shell looks for the special characters `*`, `?`, and `[`. If they're not quoted, then the shell searches the current directory, or another directory if preceded by a `/`, and substitutes the names of all files that match (these names are first alphabetized by the shell). If no match is found, then the characters remain untouched.

Note that file names beginning with a `.` must be explicitly matched (so `echo *` won't display your hidden files; `echo .*` will).

The file name substitution characters are summarized in Table A-5.

TABLE A-5. File name substitution characters

Character(s)	Meaning
`?`	Matches any single character
`*`	Matches zero or more characters
`[chars]`	Matches any single character in *chars*; the format c_1–c_2 can be used to match any character in the range c_1 through c_2, inclusive (e.g., `[A-Z]` will match any uppercase letter)
`[!chars]`	Matches any single character *not* in *chars*; a range of characters may be specified as above

◆ I/O Redirection ◆

When scanning the command line, the shell looks for the special redirection characters < and >. If found, they are processed and removed (with any associated arguments) from the command line. Table A-6 summarizes the different types of I/O redirection that the shell supports.

TABLE A-6. I/O redirection

Construct	Meaning
< *file*	Redirect standard input from *file*
> *file*	Redirect standard output to *file*; *file* is created if it doesn't exist and zeroed if it does
>> *file*	Like >, only output is appended to *file* if it already exists
<< *word*	Redirect standard input from lines that follow up until a line containing just *word*; parameter substitution occurs on the lines, and back-quoted commands are executed and the backslash character interpreted; if any character in *word* is quoted, then none of this processing occurs and the lines are passed through unaltered; if *word* is preceded by a –, then leading tabs on the lines are removed
<& *digit*	Standard input is redirected from the file associated with file descriptor *digit*
>& *digit*	Standard output is redirected to the file associated with file descriptor *digit*
<&–	Standard input is closed
>&–	Standard output is closed

Note that file name substitution is not performed on *file*. Any of the constructs listed in the first column of the table may be preceded by a file descriptor number to have the same effect on the file associated with that file descriptor.

The file descriptor 0 is associated with standard input, 1 with standard output, and 2 with standard error.

◆ Exported Variables and Subshell Execution ◆

Commands other than the shell's built-in commands are normally executed in a "new" shell, called a *subshell*. Subshells cannot change the values of variables in the parent shell, and they can only access variables from the parent shell that were *exported* to them—either implicitly or explicitly—by the parent. If the subshell changes the value of one of these variables and wants to have its own subshells know about it, then it must explicitly export the variable before executing the subshell.

When the subshell finishes execution, any variables that it may have set are inaccessible by the parent. You should note that redirected `while`, `until`, `for`, `if`, and `case` commands get executed as pseudo-subshells.

The (. . .) Construct

If one or more commands are placed inside parentheses, then those commands will be executed in a subshell.

The { . . . ; } Construct

If one or more commands are placed inside curly braces, then those commands will be executed by the *current* shell.

With this construct and the (. . .) construct, I/O can be redirected and piped into and out of the set of enclosed commands, and the set can be sent to the background for execution by placing an `&` at the end. As an example,

```
(prog1; prog2; prog3) 2>errors &
```

submits the three listed programs to the background for execution, with standard error from all three programs redirected to the file `errors`.

More on Keyword Parameters

A keyword parameter can be placed into the environment of a command by preceding the command name with the assignment to the parameter on the command line, as in

```
PHONEBOOK=$HOME/misc/phone rolo
```

Here the variable PHONEBOOK will be assigned the indicated value and then placed in `rolo`'s environment. The environment of the current shell remains unchanged, as if

```
(PHONEBOOK=$HOME/misc/phone; export PHONEBOOK; rolo)
```

had been executed intead.

◆ Functions ◆

Functions take the following form:

> *name* () { *command; command; ... command;* }

where *name* is the name of the function that is defined to the current shell (functions can't be exported). The function definition can span as many lines as necessary. A `return` command can be executed to cause execution of the function to be terminated without also terminating the shell (see the `return` command description).

As an example,

```
nf () { ls | wc -l; }
```

defines a function called `nf` to count the number of files in your current directory.

◆ Command Summary ◆

This section summarizes the shell's built-in commands. These commands are organized alphabetically for easy reference.

The : Command

> *General Format:*   :

This is essentially a *null* command. It is frequently used to satisfy the requirement that a command appear.

> *Example*

```
if who | grep jack > /dev/null
then
        :
else
        echo "jack's not logged in"
fi
```

The : command returns an exit status of zero.

The . Command

General Format: .   *file*

The "dot" command causes the indicated *file* to be read and executed by the shell, *just as if the lines from the file were typed at that point.* Note that *file* does *not* have to be executable, only readable. Also, the shell uses the PATH variable to find *file*.

Example

  . progdefs   *Execute commands in* progdefs

The above command causes the shell to search the current PATH for the file progdefs. When it finds it, it reads and executes the commands from the file.

    Note that since *file* is not executed by a subshell, variables set and/or changed within *file* remain in effect after execution of the commands in *file* is complete.

The break Command

General Format: break

Execution of this command causes execution of the innermost for, while, or until loop to be immediately terminated. Execution continues with the commands that immediately follow the loop.

    If the format

        break *n*

is used, where *n* is an integer greater than or equal to 1, then execution of the *n* innermost loops is automatically terminated.

The case Command

General Format:

```
case value in
        pat₁ )   command
                 command
                 . . .
                 command ; ;
        pat₂ )   command
                 command
```

```
               . . .
               command;;
         . . .
pat_n )   command
          command
          . . .
          command;;
   esac
```

The word *value* is successively compared against pat_1, pat_2, ..., pat_n until a match is found. The commands that appear immediately after the matching pattern are then executed until a double semicolon (;;) is encountered. At that point, execution of the `case` is terminated.

If no pattern matches *value,* then none of the commands inside the case are executed. The pattern `*` matches *anything,* and is often used as the last pattern in a `case` as the "catchall" case.

The shell metacharacters `*` (match zero or more characters), `?` (match any single character), and `[...]` (match any single character enclosed between the brackets) can be used in patterns. The character `|` can be used to specify a logical ORing of two patterns, as in

$$pat_1 \mid pat_2$$

which means to match either pat_1 or pat_2.

Examples

```
case $1 in
     -l)   lopt=TRUE;;
     -w)   wopt=TRUE;;
     -c)   copt=TRUE;;
      *)   echo "Unknown option";;
esac

case $choice in
     [1-9]) valid=TRUE;;
         *) echo "Please choose a number from 1-9";;
esac
```

The cd Command

General Format: cd *directory*

Execution of this command causes the shell to make *directory* the current directory. If *directory* is omitted, then the shell makes the directory specified in the `HOME` variable the current directory.

   If the shell variable `CDPATH` is null, then *directory* must be a full directory path (e.g., `/usr/steve/documents`) or relative to the current directory (e.g., `documents, ../pat`).

   If `CDPATH` is non-null and *directory* is not a full path, then the shell searches the colon-delimited directory list in `CDPATH` for a directory containing *directory*.

Examples

`$ cd documents/memos`	*Change to* documents/memos *directory*
`$ cd`	*Change to* HOME *directory*

The `continue` command

General Format: `continue`

Execution of this command from within a `for`, `while`, or `until` loop causes any commands that follow the `continue` to be skipped. Execution of the loop then continues as normal.

   If the format

```
continue n
```

is used, then the commands within the *n* innermost loops are skipped. Execution of the loops then continue as normal.

The `echo` Command

General Format: `echo` *args*

This command causes *args* to be written to standard output. Each word from *args* is delimited by a blank space. A newline character is written at the end. If *args* is omitted, then the effect is to simply skip a line. If the format

```
echo -n args
```

is used, then a terminating newline character is not written to standard output.

   Certain backslashed characters have a special meaning to `echo` as shown in Table A-7.

TABLE A-7. echo escape characters

Character	Prints
\b	Backspace
\c	The line without a terminating newline
\f	Formfeed
\n	Newline
\r	Carriage return
\t	Tab character
\\	Backslash character
\nnn	The character whose ASCII value is nnn, where nnn is a one- to three-digit octal number that starts with a zero.

Remember to quote these characters so that the echo command interprets them and not the shell.

Examples

```
$ echo *                          List all files in the current directory
bin docs mail misc src
$ echo                            Skip a line

$ echo 'X\tY'                     Print X and Y, separated by a tab
X       Y
$ echo "\n\nSales Report"         Skip two lines before displaying Sales Report


Sales Report
$ echo "Wake up!!\007"            Print message and beep terminal (CTRL-G)
Wake up!!
$
```

The eval Command

General Format: `eval args`

Execution of this command causes the shell to evaluate *args* and then execute the results. This is useful for causing the shell to effectively "double-scan" a command line.

Example

```
$ x='abc def'
$ y='$x'                          Assign $x to y
$ echo $y
$x
$ eval echo $y
abc def
$
```

The exec Command

General Format: `exec command args`

When the shell executes the `exec` command, it initiates execution of the specified *command* with the indicated arguments. Unlike other commands that are executed as a new process, *command replaces* the current process (i.e., no new process is created). Once *command* starts execution, there is no return to the program that initiated the `exec`.

If just I/O redirection is specified, then the input and/or output for the shell is accordingly redirected.

Examples

```
exec /usr/lbin/ksh        Replace current process with ksh
exec < datafile           Reassign standard input to datafile
```

The exit Command

General Format: `exit n`

Execution of `exit` causes the current shell program to be immediately terminated. The exit status of the program is the value of the integer *n*, if supplied. If *n* is not supplied, then the exit status is that of the last command executed prior to the `exit`.

An exit status of zero is used by convention to indicate "success," and nonzero to indicate "failure" (such as an error condition). This convention is used by the shell in evaluation of conditions for `if`, `while`, and `until` commands, and with the `&&` and `||` constructs.

Examples

```
who | grep $user >/dev/null
exit                        Exit with status of last grep

exit 1                      Exit with status of 1

if finduser                 If finduser returns an exit status of zero then...
then
    . . .
fi
```

You should note that executing `exit` from a login shell has the effect of logging you off.

The **export** Command

General Format: `export` *variables*

The `export` command tells the shell that the indicated variables are to be marked as exported; i.e., their values are to be passed down to subshells. Inherited exported variables must be re-exported to pass a modified value to a subshell.

`export` with no arguments causes the shell to write a list of the exported variables explicitly exported by the current shell to standard output.

Examples

```
export PATH PS1
export dbhome x1 y1 date
```

The `for` Command

General Format:

```
for var in word₁ word₂ ... wordₙ
do
        command
        command
        . . .
done
```

Execution of this command causes the commands enclosed between the `do` and `done` to be executed as many times as there are words listed after the `in`.

The first time through the loop, the first word—$word_1$—is assigned to the variable *var* and the commands between the `do` and `done` executed. The second time through the loop, the second word listed—$word_2$—is assigned to *var* and the commands in the loop executed again. This process continues until the last variable in the list—$word_n$—is assigned to *var* and the commands between the `do` and `done` executed. At that point, execution of the `for` loop is terminated. Execution then continues with the command that immediately follows the `done`.

The special format

```
for var
do
    . . .
done
```

indicates that the positional parameters `"$1"`, `"$2"`, ... are to be used in the list and is equivalent to

```
for var in "$@"
do
    . . .
done
```

Example

```
# nroff all of the files in the current directory

for file in *
do
        nroff -Tlp $file | lp
done
```

The `getopts` Command

General Format: `getopts` *options var*

This command processes command line arguments. *options* is a list of valid single letter options. If any letter in *options* is followed by a `:`, then that option takes a following argument on the command line, which must be separated from the option by at least one whitespace character.

Each time `getopts` is called, it processes the next command line argument. If a valid option is found, `getopt` stores the matching option letter inside the specified variable *var* and returns a zero exit status.

If an invalid option is specified (that is, one not listed in *options*), then `getopts` stores a `?` inside *var* and returns with a zero exit status. It also writes an error message to standard error.

If an option takes a following argument, then `getopts` stores the matching option letter inside *var* and stores the following command line argument inside the special variable `OPTARG`. If no arguments are left on the command line, `getopts` stores a `?` inside *var* and writes an error message to standard error.

If no more options remain on the command line (that is, if the next command line argument does not begin with a `-`), then `getopts` returns a nonzero exit status.

The special variable `OPTIND` is also used by `getopts`. It is initially set to 1, and is adjusted each time `getopts` returns to indicate the number of the *next* command line argument to be processed.

The argument `--` can be placed on the command line to specify the end of the command line arguments.

`getopts` supports stacked arguments, as in

```
repx -iau
```

which is equivalent to

```
repx -i -a -u
```

Options that take following arguments may not be stacked. The complete set of rules for command line syntax is specified in the `intro(1)` section to the *UNIX User's Reference Manual*.

If the format

```
getopts options var args
```

is used, `getotps` parses the arguments specified by *args* instead of the command line arguments.

Example

```
usage="Usage: foo [-r] [-o outfile] infile"

while getopts  ro: opt
do
        case "$var"
        in
                r) rflag=1;;
                o) oflag=1
                   ofile=$OPTARG;;
              \?) echo "$usage"
                   exit 1;;
        esac
done

if [ $OPTIND -gt $# ]
then
        echo "Needs input file!"
        echo "$usage"
        exit 2
fi

shift `expr $OPTIND - 1`
ifile=$1
  ...
```

The hash Command

General Format: hash *commands*

This command tells the shell to look for the specified *commands* and to remember what directories they are located in. If *commands* is not specified, then a list of the hashed commands is displayed.

If the format

```
            hash -r commands
```

is used, then the shell removes the listed *commands* from its hash list. Next time any of those commands is executed, the shell will use its normal search methods to find the command. If *commands* is omitted, then *all* commands are removed from the hash list.

Examples

```
hash rolo whoq          Add rolo and whoq to hash list
hash                    Print hash list
hash -r rolo whoq       Remove rolo and whoq from hash list
```

The **if** Command

General Format:

```
if    command_t
then
        command
        command
        ...
fi
```

command_t is executed and its exit status tested. If it is zero, then the commands that follow up to the `fi` are executed. Otherwise, the commands that follow up to the `fi` are skipped.

Example

```
if grep $sys sysnames > /dev/null
then
        echo "$sys is a valid system name"
fi
```

If the `grep` returns an exit status of zero (which it will if it finds `$sys` in the file `sysnames`), then the `echo` command will be executed; otherwise it will be skipped.

The built-in command `test` is often used as the command following the `if`.

Example

```
if [ $# -eq 0 ]
then
        echo "Usage: $0 [-l] file ..."
        exit 1
fi
```

An `else` clause can be added to the `if` to be executed if the command returns a nonzero exit status. In this case, the general format of the `if` becomes

```
if   command_t
then
            command
            command
            . . .
else
            command
            command
            . . .
fi
```

If *command_t* returns an exit status of zero, then the commands that follow up to the else will be executed, and the commands between the else and the fi skipped. Otherwise, command_t returns a nonzero exit status and the commands between the then and the else will be skipped and the commands between the else and the fi executed.

Example

```
if [ -z "$line" ]
then
        echo "I couldn't find $name"
else
        echo "$line"
fi
```

In the above example, if line has zero length, then the echo command that displays the message I couldn't find $name is executed; otherwise the echo command that displays the value of line is executed.

A final format of the if command is useful when more than a two-way decision has to be made. Its general format is

```
if   command_1
then
            command
            command
            . . .
elif   command_2
then
            command
            command
            . . .
. . .
elif   command_n
then
```

```
                command
                command
                . . .

        else
                command
                command
                . . .

        fi
```

$command_1$, $command_2$, ..., $command_n$ are evaluated in order until one of the commands returns an exit status of zero, at which point the commands that immediately follow the `then` (up to another `elif`, `else`, or `fi`) are executed. If none of the commands returns an exit status of zero, then the commands listed after the `else` (if present) will be executed.

Example

```
if [ "$choice" = a ]
then
        add $*
elif [ "$choice" = d ]
then
        delete $*
elif [ "$choice" = l ]
then
        list
else
        echo "Bad choice!"
        error=TRUE
fi
```

The newgrp Command

General Format: `newgrp` *group*

This command changes your real group id (GID) to *group*. If no argument is specified, then it changes you back to your default group.

Examples

```
newgrp shbook            Change to group shbook
newgrp                   Change back to default group
```

If a password is associated with the new group, then you will be prompted to enter it. Otherwise, you must be listed as a valid member of the group (in /etc/group) for you to newgrp to it.

The pwd Command

General Format: pwd

This command tells the shell to print your working directory, which is written to standard output.

Examples

```
$ pwd
/usr/steve/documents/memos
$ cd
$ pwd
/usr/steve
$
```

The read Command

General Format: read *vars*

This command causes the shell to read a line from standard input and assign successive whitespace-delimited words from the line to the variables *vars*. If fewer variables are listed than there are words on the line, then the excess words are stored in the last variable.

Specifying just one variable has the effect of reading and assigning an entire line to the variable.

The exit status of read is zero unless an end-of-file condition is encountered.

Examples

```
$ read hours mins
10 19
$ echo "$hours:$mins"
10:19
$ read num rest
39 East 12th Street, New York City 10003
$ echo "$num\n$rest"
39
East 12th Street, New York City 10003
```

```
$ read line
     Here      is an entire          line \r
$ echo "$line"
Here     is an entire        line r
$
```

Note in the last example that any leading whitespace characters get "eaten" by the shell when read. You can change IFS if this poses a problem.

Also note that backslash characters get interpreted by the shell when you read the line, and any that make it through (double backslashes will get through as a single backslash) will get interpreted by echo if you display the value of the variable.

The readonly Command

General Format: readonly *vars*

This command tells the shell that the listed variables cannot be assigned values. If you subsequently try to assign a value to the variable, the shell will issue an error message.

readonly variables are useful for ensuring that you don't accidentally overwrite the value of a variable. They're also good for ensuring that other people using a shell program can't change the values of particular variables (e.g., their HOME directory or their PATH). The readonly attribute is not passed down to subshells.

readonly with no arguments prints a list of your readonly variables.

Example

```
$ DB=/usr/steve/database            Assign value to DB
$ readonly DB                       Make it read-only
$ DB=foo                            Try to assign it a value
DB: is read-only                    Error message from the shell
$ echo $DB                          But can still access its value
/usr/steve/database
$
```

The return Command

General Format: return *n*

This command causes the shell to stop execution of the current function and immediately return to the caller with an exit status of *n*. If *n* is omitted, then the exit status returned is that of the command executed immediately prior to the return.

The **set** Command

General Format: set *options args*

This command is used to turn on or off options as specified by *options*. It is also used to set positional parameters, as specified by *args*.

Each single letter option in *options* is enabled if the option is preceded by a minus sign (–), or disabled if preceded by a plus sign (+). Options can be grouped, as in

    set -fx

which enables the f and x options.

Options that can be selected are summarized in Table A-8.

TABLE A-8. set options

Option	Meaning
--	Don't treat subsequent args preceded by a – as options
-a	Automatically export all variables that are subsequently defined or modified
-e	Exit if any command that gets executed has a nonzero exit status
-f	Disable file name generation
-h	Remember the locations of commands used in functions when the functions are defined (see hash command)
-k	Process arguments of the form *keyword=value* that appear anywhere on the command line (not just before the command) and place them in the environment of the command
-n	Read commands without executing them (useful for checking for balanced do...dones, and if...fis)
-t	Exit after executing one command
-u	Issue an error if a variable is referenced without having been assigned a value or if a positional parameter is referenced without having been set
-v	Print each shell command line as it is read
-x	Print each command and its arguments as it is executed, preceded by a +

The shell variable `$-` contains the current options setting.

Each word that is listed in *args* is set to the positional parameters `$1`, `$2`, ..., respectively. If the first word might start with a minus sign, then it's safer to specify the `--` option to `set` to avoid interpretation of that value.

If *args* is supplied, then the variable `$#` will be set to the number of parameters assigned after execution of the command.

Examples

`set -vx`	*Print all command lines as they are read, and each command and its arguments as it is executed*
`set +x`	*Turn off command trace*
`set "$name" "$address" "$phone"`	*Set `$1` to `$name`, `$2` to `$address`, and `$3` to `$phone`*
`set -- -1`	*Set `$1` to −1*

The `shift` Command

General Format: `shift`

This command causes the positional parameters `$1`, `$2`, ..., `$n` to be "shifted left" one place. That is, `$2` is assigned to `$1`, `$3` to `$2`, ..., and `$n` to `$n-1`. `$#` is adjusted accordingly.

If the format

```
shift n
```

is used instead, then the shift is to the left *n* places.

Examples

```
$ set a b c d
$ echo "$#\n$*"
4
a b c d
$ shift
$ echo "$#\n$*"
3
b c d
$ shift 2
$ echo "$#\n$*"
1
d
$
```

The test Command

General Format:

         test   *condition*
    or
         [*condition*   ]

The shell evaluates *condition* and if the result of the evaluation is *TRUE*, returns a zero exit status. If the result of the evaluation is *FALSE*, then a nonzero exit status is returned. If the format [*condition*] is used, then a space must appear immediately after the [and before the].

   condition is composed of one or more operators as shown in Table A-9. The -a operator has higher precedence than the -o operator. In any case, parentheses can be used to group subexpressions. Just remember that the parentheses are significant to the shell and so must be quoted. Operators and operands (including parentheses) must be delimited by one or more spaces so that test sees them as separate arguments.

   test is often used to test conditions in an if, while, or until command.

Examples

```
# see if perms is executable

if test -x /etc/perms
then
        . . .
fi
```

```
# see if it's a directory or a normal file that's readable

if [ -d $file -o \( -f $file -a -r $file \) ]
then
        . . .
fi
```

TABLE A-9. `test` operators

Operator	Returns TRUE (zero exit status) if
File Operators	
-b *file*	*file* is a block special file
-c *file*	*file* is a character special file
-d *file*	*file* is a directory
-f *file*	*file* is an ordinary file
-g *file*	*file* has its set group id (SGID) bit set
-k *file*	*file* has its sticky bit set
-p *file*	*file* is a named pipe
-r *file*	*file* is readable by the process
-s *file*	*file* has nonzero length
-t *fd*	*fd* is open file descriptor associated with a terminal (1 is default)
-u *file*	*file* has its set user id (SUID) bit set
-w *file*	*file* is writable by the process
-x *file*	*file* is executable
String Operators	
string	*string* is not null
-n *string*	*string* is not null (and *string* must be seen by `test`)
-z *string*	*string* is null (and *string* must be seen by `test`)
$string_1$ = $string_2$	$string_1$ is identical to $string_2$
$string_1$!= $string_2$	$string_1$ is *not* identical to $string_2$
Integer Comparison Operators	
int_1 -eq int_2	int_1 is equal to int_2
int_1 -ge int_2	int_1 is greater than or equal to int_2
int_1 -gt int_2	int_1 is greater than int_2
int_1 -le int_2	int_1 is less than or equal to int_2
int_1 -lt int_2	int_1 is less than int_2
int_1 -ne int_2	int_1 is not equal to int_2
Boolean Operators	
! *expr*	*expr* is *FALSE*; otherwise returns *TRUE*
$expr_1$ -a $expr_2$	$expr_1$ is *TRUE* and $expr_2$ is *TRUE*
$expr_1$ -o $expr_2$	$expr_1$ is *TRUE* or $expr_2$ is *TRUE*

The `times` Command

General Format: `times`

Execution of this command causes the shell to write to standard output the total amount of time that has been used by processes run by the shell. Two numbers are listed: first the accumulated user time, then the accumulated system time.

Note that `times` does not report the time used by built-in commands.

Example

```
$ times                          Print time used by processes
1m5s 2m9s              1 min., 5 secs. user time, 2 mins., 9 secs. system time
$
```

The `trap` Command

General Format: `trap` *commands signals*

This command tells the shell to execute *commands* whenever it receives one of the signals listed in *signals*.

`trap` with no arguments prints a list of the current trap assignments.

If the first argument is the null string, as in

```
        trap   ""   signals
```

then the signals in *signals* will be ignored when received by the shell.

If the format

```
        trap    signals
```

is used, then processing of each signal listed in *signals* is reset to the default action.

Examples

```
trap "echo hangup >> $ERRFILE; exit" 2    Log message and exit on hangup
trap "rm $TMPFILE; exit" 1 2 15        remove $TMPFILE on signals 1, 2, or 15
trap "" 2                              Ignore interrupts
trap 2                                 Reset default processing of interrupts
```

Table A-10 lists values that can be specified in the signal list.

TABLE A-10. Signal numbers for `trap`

Signal	Generated for
0	Exit from the shell
1	Hangup
2	Interrupt (e.g., `Delete` key)
3	Quit
4	Illegal instruction
5	Trace trap
6	IOT instruction
7	EMT instruction
8	Floating point exception
10	Bus error
12	Bad argument to a system call
13	Write to a pipe without a process to read it
14	Alarm timeout
15	Software termination signal (sent by `kill` by default)

The shell scans *commands* when the `trap` command is encountered and again when one of the listed signals is received. This means, for example, that when the shell encounters the command

```
trap "echo $count lines processed >> $LOGFILE; exit" 1 2 15
```

it will substitute the value of `count` at that point, and *not when one of the signals is received*. You can get the value of `count` substituted when one of the signals is received if you instead enclose the commands in single quotes:

```
trap 'echo $count lines processed >> $LOGFILE; exit' 1 2 15
```

The `type` Command

General Format: `type`   *commands*

This command prints information about the indicated *commands*, including the directory that each command can be found in.

Examples

```
$ type troff echo
troff is /usr/bin/troff
echo is a shell builtin
$
```

The ulimit Command

General Format: ulimit *size*

This command tells the shell to set the maximum size of files that can be written by child processes to *size* blocks.

If *size* is not specified, the current setting is printed. If a value of zero is displayed, then no limit has been set.

```
$ ulimit
0                              No limit set
$ ulimit 1000                  Set limit to 1000 blocks
$ ulimit
1000
$
```

No limit set
Set limit to 1000 blocks

The umask Command

General Format: umask   *mask*

umask sets the default file creation mask to *mask*. Files that are subsequently created are ANDed with this mask to determine the mode of the file.

umask with no arguments prints the current mask.

Examples

```
$ umask                        Print current mask
0002                           No write to others
$ umask 022                    No write to group either
$
```

Print current mask
No write to others
No write to group either

The unset Command

General Format: `unset   names`

This causes the shell to erase definitions of the variables or functions listed in *names*. The following variables cannot be specified: `IFS`, `MAILCHECK`, `PATH`, `PS1,` and `PS2`.

Example

`unset dblist files`   *Remove definitions of* `dblist` *and* `files`

The until Command

General Format:

```
      until   command_t
      do
              command
              command
              . . .
      done
```

command$_t$ is executed and its exit status tested. If it is nonzero, then the commands enclosed between the do and done are executed. Then *command$_t$* is executed again and its status tested. If it is nonzero, then the commands between the do and done are once again executed. Execution of *command$_t$* and subsequent execution of the commands between the do and done continues until *command$_t$* returns a zero exit status, at which point the loop is terminated. Execution then continues with the command that follows the done.

Note that since *command$_t$* gets evaluated immediately upon entry into the loop that the commands between the do and done may never be executed if it returns a zero exit status the first time.

Example

```
# sleep for 60 seconds until jack logs on

until who | grep jack >/dev/null
do
        sleep 60
done

echo jack has logged on
```

The above loop will continue until the grep returns a zero exit status (i.e., finds jack in who's output). At that point, the loop will be terminated and the echo command that follows executed.

The wait Command

General Format: wait *n*

This command causes the shell to suspend its execution until process *n* finishes executing. If *n* is not supplied, then the shell waits for all child processes to finish executing.

wait is useful for waiting for processes to finish that have been sent to the background for execution.

Example

```
sort large_file > sorted_file &      sort in the background
    ...                              Continue processing
wait                                 Now wait for sort to finish
plotdata sorted_file
```

The variable $! can be used to obtain the process number of the last process sent to the background.

The while Command

General Format:
```
            while   command_t
            do
                    command
                    command
                    . . .
            done
```

command$_t$ is executed and its exit status tested. If it is zero, then the commands enclosed between the do and done are executed. Then *command*$_t$ is executed again and its status tested. If it is zero, then the commands between the do and done are once again executed. Execution of *command*$_t$ and subsequent execution of the commands between the do and done continues until *command*$_t$ returns a nonzero exit status, at which point the loop is terminated. Execution then continues with the command that follows the done.

Note that since *command*$_t$ gets evaluated immediately upon entry into the loop that the commands between the do and done may never be executed if it returns a nonzero exit status the first time.

Example

```
# fill up the rest of the buffer with blank lines

while [ $lines -le $maxlines ]
do
        echo >> $BUFFER
        lines=`expr $lines + 1`
done
```

B

Korn Shell Summary

This appendix summarizes the main features of the Korn shell. Features that are only available on systems that support job control (Berkeley UNIX 4.1 and later and System V Release 3 and later) are marked with a *.

◆ Startup ◆

If the shell is started with exec, and the first character of the command name (argument 0) is a dash (–), then the shell will first execute the commands in /etc/profile and in the file .profile in the user's home directory. The shell can be given the same options on the command line as can be specified with the set command. In addition, the following options can be specified:

–c *commands*	*commands* are executed.
–i	The shell is interactive. Signals 2, 3, and 15 are ignored.
–r	A restricted shell is started.
–s	Commands are read from standard input.

◆ Commands ◆

The general format of a command typed to the shell is

    command arguments

where *command* is the name of the program to be executed, and *arguments* are its arguments. The command name and the arguments are delimited by *whitespace* characters, normally the space, tab, and newline characters (changing the variable IFS will affect this).

Multiple commands can be typed on the same line if they're separated by semicolons (;).

Every command that gets executed returns a number known as the *exit status*; zero is used to indicate success, and nonzero failure.

The pipe symbol | can be used to connect the standard output from one command to the standard input of another, as in

```
who | wc -l
```

The exit status is that of the last command in the pipeline.

If the command sequence is terminated by an ampersand character (&), then it is run asynchronously in the background. The shell displays the process number of the command at the terminal.

Typing of a command can continue to the next line if the last character on the line is a backslash character (\).

The characters && cause the command that follows to be executed only if the preceding command returns a zero exit status. The characters || cause the command that follows to be executed only if the preceding command returns a nonzero exit status. As an example, in

```
who | grep "fred" > /dev/null  &&  echo "fred's logged on"
```

the echo is executed only if the grep returns a zero exit status.

◆ Comments ◆

If a word begins with the character #, then the shell treats the remainder of the line as a comment and simply ignores it.

◆ Shell Variables ◆

There are three different "types" of shell variables, also known as *parameters*: *keyword* parameters, *positional* parameters, and special shell parameters.

Keyword Parameters

A keyword parameter name must start with an alphabetic or underscore (_) character, and can be followed by any number of alphanumeric or underscore characters. Values are assigned to keyword parameters by writing *variable=value variable=value ...*

File name substitution is not performed on *value*.

Positional Parameters

Whenever a shell program is executed the name of the program is assigned to the variable $0, and the arguments typed on the command line to the variables $1, $2, ..., respectively. Positional parameters can also be assigned values with the set command. Parameters beyond $9 can be explicitly referenced as ${nn} (see **Parameter Substitution**).

Other Special Parameters

The special shell parameters are summarized in Table B-1.

TABLE B-1. Special parameter variables

Parameter	Meaning
$#	The number of arguments passed to the program; or the number of parameters set by executing the set statement
$*	Collectively references all of the positional parameters as $1, $2, ...
$@	Same as $*, except when double-quoted ("$@") collectively references all of the positional parameters as "$1", "$2", ...
$0	The name of the program being executed
$$	The process id number of the program being executed
$!	The process id number of the last program sent to the background for execution
$?	The exit status of the last command not executed in the background
$-	The current options in effect (see the set statement)

In addition to these parameters, the shell has some other variables that it uses. These variables are summarized in Table B-2.

TABLE B-2. Other variables used by the shell

Variable	Meaning
COLUMNS	The width of your terminal in columns. Used for `select` lists and the edit window of the line editor modes. If not set, 80 is used.
CDPATH	The directories to be searched whenever `cd` is executed without a full path as argument
EDITOR	If the `VISUAL` is not set and `EDITOR`'s value ends in `emacs`, `gmacs`, or `vi`, the corresponding line edit mode is turned on.
FCEDIT	The editor used by `fc`. If not set, `/bin/ed` is used.
FPATH	The list of directories to search to autoload functions.
HISTFILE	If set when the Korn shell starts up, it specifies a file to be used to store the command history. If not set or if the file isn't writable, `$HOME/.sh_history` is used.
HISTSIZE	If set when the Korn shell starts up, it specifies the number of previously entered commands accessible for editing.
HOME	The directory that `cd` changes to when no argument is supplied
IFS	The Internal Field Separator characters; used by the shell to delimit words for the `read` and `set` commands, when substituting the output from a back-quoted command, and when performing parameter substituton. Normally, it contains the three characters space, horizontal tab, and newline
LINES	The height of your terminal in lines. Used for `select` lists. If not set, 24 is used.
MAIL	The name of a file that the shell will periodically check for the arrival of mail. If new mail arrives, then the shell will display its `You have mail` message. *See also* MAILCHECK *and* MAILPATH
MAILCHECK	The number of seconds specifying how often the shell is to check for the arrival of mail in the file in `MAIL` or in the files listed in `MAILPATH`. The default is 600. A value of 0 causes the shell to check before displaying each command prompt
MAILPATH	A list of files to be checked for the arrival of mail. Each file is delimited by a colon, and can be followed by a question mark (?) and a message to be displayed when mail arrives in the indicated file (`You have mail in` *file* is the default). The variable `$_` is set to the name of the file that changed.
PATH	A colon delimited list of directories to be searched when the shell needs to find a command to be executed. The current directory is specified as `::` (if it heads the list, `:` suffices)
PS1	The primary command prompt, normally "$ "
PS2	The secondary command prompt, normally "> "
PS3	Prompt used by the `select` built-in command. The default is #?.

PS4	Prompt used during execution trace (-x option to shell or set -x). Default is +.
SHACCT	The name of a file that the shell will use to write accounting information for commands that it executes. This information can later be analyzed using the acctcom command (see your *UNIX System Administrator's Manual* for details)
SHELL	The name of the shell (e.g. /bin/sh). This variable is used by vi and ed to determine the shell to start up when you escape to the shell or execute a shell command. It's also used by the shell on startup to determine if it should run restricted. This determination is made based upon whether the letter "r" appears in the name of the shell
TMOUT	If greater than zero, the shell will automatically exit after TMOUT seconds of inactivity. The message shell time out in 60 seconds is first printed, and if RETURN isn't entered within 60 seconds, the shell exits. If TMOUT is zero or unset, this feature is disabled. The Korn shell can be compiled so that TMOUT cannot be assigned a value greater than a maximum and cannot be set to zero.
VISUAL	If its value ends in emacs, gmacs, or vi, the corresponding line edit mode is turned on.

Built-in Shell Variables

The following variables are automatically set by the Korn shell:

_	The last argument of the previous command.
ERRNO	The error number of the last failed system call.
LINENO	The current line number.
OLDPWD	The previous working directory.
PPID	The process number of the parent process.
PWD	The current working directory.
SECONDS	The number of seconds since shell startup.
RANDOM	A random number, changed every time it is referenced. The random number sequence may be initialized by assigning it an integer value.
REPLY	Used by select and read when no variable is specified.

Parameter Substitution

In the simplest case, the value of a parameter can be accessed by preceding the parameter with a dollar sign ($). Table B-3 summarizes the different types of parameter substitution that can be performed. Parameter substitution is performed by the shell before file name substitution and before the command line is divided into arguments.

TABLE B-3. Parameter substitution

Parameter	Meaning
$parameter or ${parameter}	Substitute the value of *parameter*
${parameter:-value}	Substitute the value of *parameter* if it's non-null; otherwise, substitute *value*
${parameter:=value}	Substitute the value of *parameter* if it's non-null; otherwise, substitute *value* and also assign it to *parameter*
${parameter:?value}	Substitute the value of *parameter* if it's non-null; otherwise, write *value* to standard error and exit. If *value* is omitted, then write *parameter*: `parameter null or not set` instead
${parameter:+value}	Substitute *value* if *parameter* is non-null; otherwise, substitute nothing
${#parameter}	Substitute the length of *parameter*. If *parameter* is *, substitute the number of positional parameters (equivalent to $#).
${#array[*]} ${#array[@]}	Substitute the number of elements in *array*.
${parameter#pattern}	Substitute the value of *parameter* with *pattern* removed from the left side. The smallest portion of the contents of *parameter* matching *pattern* is removed. Shell file name substitution characters (*, ?, [. . .], !, !, and @) may be used in *pattern*.
${parameter##pattern}	Same as #*pattern* except the largest matching pattern is removed.
${parameter%pattern}	Same as #*pattern* except *pattern* is removed from the right side.
${parameter%%pattern}	Same as ##*pattern* except *pattern* is removed from the right side.

Arrays

The Korn shell supports one-dimensional arrays of up to 512 elements. Arrays are indexed by subscripts, a [followed by an arithmetic expression (see the `let` command description), followed by a]. Subscripts may range from zero to 511. Using an array name without a subscript is the same as a reference to element zero. All elements of an array may be referenced with the subscript [*].

When array elements are substituted, you must use the $ {*variable*} construct, e.g.,

```
echo ${arr[5]}
```

Inside a `let` command, The dollar signs and curly braces are not necessary:

```
(( x[10] = x[9] + x[8] ))
```

♦ Command Re-entry ♦

The Korn shell keeps a list, or history, of recently entered commands. The number of commands available is determined by the `HISTSIZE` variable (default 128), and the file in which the history is kept is determined by the `HISTFILE` variable (default `$HOME/.sh_history`). Because the command history is stored in a file, these commands are available after you log off and back on.
There are three ways you can access the command history in the Korn shell.

The `fc` Command

The Korn shell built-in command `fc` allows you to run an editor on one or more commands in the command history. When the edited command(s) is written and you leave the editor, the edited version of the command(s) is executed. The editor is determined by the `FCEDIT` variable (default `/bin/ed`). The `-e` option may be used with `fc` to specify the editor instead of `FCEDIT`.
A simple editing capability is built-in to the `fc` command: if the editor specified to the `-e` option is `-`, then an argument of the form

old=new

may be used to change the first occurrence of the string *old* to the string *new* in the command(s) to be re-executed.

`vi` Line Edit Mode

The Korn shell has a built-in implementation of the `vi` screen editor, scaled down to work on single lines. When `vi` mode is turned on, you are by default placed in a state similar to `vi`'s *input* mode. Commands can be typed just the same as when `vi` mode is off. At any time, however, you can hit the `ESC` key to be placed in *edit* mode. At this point, most `vi` commands will be interpreted by the Korn shell. The current command line can be edited, as can any of the lines in the command history. A `RETURN` at any point in either command or input mode will cause the command being edited to be executed.

If the width of the command line is larger than the variable COLUMNS (default 80) minus two, only a portion of the line is displayed, and one of the characters >, <, or * is placed on the far-right side of the screen, signifying that the line is truncated on the right, left, or both sides, respectively. If a cursor motion moves the cursor past the last character displayed on the right or left, the line is repositioned with the cursor in the middle of the screen.

Table B-4 lists all of the editing commands in vi mode, Note: *count* is any integer and may be omitted.

TABLE B-4. vi editing commands

Input Mode Commands	
Command	Meaning
erase	(Erase character, usually *CTRL-h* or #); delete previous character
CTRL-w	Delete the previous blank-separated word
kill	(Line kill character, normally *CTRL-u* or @); delete the entire current line
eof	(End-of-file character, normally *CTRL-d*); terminate the shell if the current line is empty
CTRL-v	Quote next character; editing characters and the erase and kill characters may be entered in a command line or in a search string if preceded by a *CTRL-v*
\	Escape the next *erase* or *kill* character
CTRL-j	Execute the current line
CTRL-m	Execute the current line
RETURN	Execute the current line

Edit Mode Commands	
Command	Meaning
[count]k	Get previous command from history
[count]-	Get previous command from history
[count]j	Get next command from history
[count]+	Get next command from history
[count]G	Get the command number *count* from history; the default is the least recently entered command
/string	Search history for the most recent command containing *string*; if *string* is null, the previous string will be used (*string* is terminated by a RETURN or a *CTRL-j*); if *string* begins with ^, search for line beginning with *string*
?string	Same as / except that the search will be for the least recent command
n	Repeat the last / or ? command

N	Repeat the last / or ? command but reverse the direction of the search
[*count*]l	Move cursor right one character
[*count*]w	Move cursor right one alphanumeric word
[*count*]W	Move cursor right to next blank-separated word
[*count*]e	Move cursor to end of word
[*count*]E	Move cursor to end of current blank-separated word
[*count*]h	Move cursor left one character
[*count*]b	Move cursor left one word
[*count*]B	Move cursor left to previous blank-separated word
0	Move cursor to start of line
^	Move cursor to first nonblank character
$	Move cursor to end of line
[*count*] |	Move cursor to column *count*; 1 is default
[*count*]f*c*	Move cursor right to character *c*
[*count*]F*c*	Move cursor left to character *c*
[*count*]t*c*	Same as f*c* followed by h
[*count*]T*c*	Same as F*c* followed by l
;	Repeats the last f, F, t, or T command
,	Reverse of ;
a	Enter input mode and enter text after the current character
A	Append text to the end of the line; same as $a
[*count*]c*motion*	Delete current character through character specified by *motion*
c[*count*]*motion*	and enter input mode; if *motion* is c, the entire line is deleted
C	Delete current character through end of line and enter input mode
S	Same as cc
[*count*]d*motion*	Delete current character through the character specified by
d[*count*]*motion*	*motion*; if *motion* is d, the entire line is deleted
D	Delete current character through the end of line; same as d$
i	Enter input mode and insert text before the current character
I	Enter input mode and insert text before the first word on the line
[*count*]P	Place the previous text modification before the cursor
[*count*]p	Place the previous text modification after the cursor
[*count*]y*motion*	Copy current character through character specified by *motion*
y[*count*]*motion*	into buffer used by p and P; if *motion* is y, the entire line is copied
Y	Copy current character through the end of line; same as y$
R	Enter input mode and overwrite characters on the line
[*count*]r*c*	Replace the current character with *c*
[*count*]x	Delete current character
[*count*]X	Delete preceding character
[*count*].	Repeat the previous text modification command
~	Invert the case of the current character and advance the cursor

[count]_	Append the *count* word from the previous command and enter input mode; the last word is the default
*	Attempt file name generation on the current word; if a match is found, replace the current word with the match and enter input mode
=	List files that begin with current word
\	Complete pathname of current word; if current word is a directory, append a /; if current word is a file, append a space
u	Undo the last text modification command
U	Restore the current line to its original state
@*letter*	Soft function key — if an alias of the name _*letter* is defined, its value will be inserted on the line
[count]v	Executes the command `fc -e ${VISUAL:-${EDITOR:-vi}}` *count*; if *count* is omitted, the current line is used
CTRL-l	Linefeed and print current line
CTRL-j	Execute the current line
CTRL-m	Execute the current line
RETURN	Execute the current line
#	same as `I#RETURN`

emacs and gmacs Line Edit Modes

Like vi mode, these modes implement a one-line editor that simulates the emacs and gmacs screen editors. These modes are the same except for the CTRL-*t* command. emacs mode is turned on via the emacs argument to set -o, and gmacs mode is turned on via the gmacs argument. In these modes, you are always in input mode. The lines are truncated in these editing modes in the same manner as vi mode.

Table B-5 lists all of the editing commands in emacs mode.

TABLE B-5. emacs editing commands

Command	Meaning
CTRL-p	Get previous command from history
CTRL-n	Get next command from history
ESC <	Get the oldest command from history
ESC >	Get the most recently executed command from history
CTRL-r string	Search history for the most recent command line containing *string*; if a parameter of zero is given, search for the least recent command (*string* is terminated by a RETURN or CTRL-j); if *string* begins with ^, search for line beginning with *string*
CTRL-f	Move cursor right one character
ESC f	Move cursor right one word
CTRL-b	Move cursor left one character
ESC b	Move cursor left one word
CTRL-a	Move cursor to start of line
CTRL-e	Move cursor to end of line
ESC char	Move cursor to character *char*
CTRL-xCTRL-x	Exchange cursor and mark
CTRL-d	Delete current character
erase char	(erase character, usually # or CTRL-h), delete previous character
ESC d	Delete current word
ESC CTRL-h	Delete previous word
ESC h	Delete previous word
ESC CTRL-?	Delete previous word
ESC DELETE	Delete previous word (if the interrupt character is DELETE, then this command won't work)
kill	(Line kill character, normally CTRL-u or @); delete the entire current line
kill kill	from now on *kill* causes a line feed
CTRL-k	Delete from the cursor to the end of the line; if given a parameter of zero then delete from the start of line to the cursor
CTRL-w	Delete from the cursor to the mark
CTRL-y	Restore last item removed from line
CTRL-t	Transpose current character with next character in *emacs* mode, or transpose two previous characters in *gmacs* mode
CTRL-c	Capitalize current character and advance cursor
ESC C	Capitalize current word and advance cursor
ESC l	Convert current word to lowercase and advance cursor
CTRL-l	Linefeed and print current line
CTRL-@	(Null character) set mark
ESC space	Set mark

ESC p	Push the region from the cursor to the mark on the stack
CTRL-j	Execute the current line
CTRL-m	Execute the current line
RETURN	Execute the current line
CTRL-o	Operate — execute the current line and get the line after the current line from the history
eof	(End-of-file character, normally CTRL-d); terminate the shell if the current line is empty
ESC digits	digits is the parameter to the next command; the commands that accept a parameter are CTRL-f, CTRL-b, erase, CTRL-d, CTRL-k, CTRL-r, CTRL-p, and CTRL-n
ESC letter	Soft function key — if an alias of the name _letter is defined, its value will be inserted on the line; the letter cannot be one of the above commands beginning with ESC
ESC _ ESC .	The last argument of the previous command is inserted at the current cursor position
ESC *	Attempt file name generation on the current word
ESC =	List files that begin with current word
ESC ESC	Complete pathname of current word; if current word is a directory, append a /; if current word is a file, append a space
CTRL-u	Multiply parameter of next command by 4
\	quote next character; editing characters, erase, kill, and interrupt characters may be entered in a command line or in a search string if preceded by a \
CTRL-v	Display version of the shell

♦ Quoting ♦

There are four different types of quote characters that are recognized. These are summarized in Table B-6.

TABLE B-6. Summary of quote characters

Quote	Description
'...'	Removes special meaning of all enclosed characters
"..."	Removes special meaning of all enclosed characters except $, ', and \
\c	Removes special meaning of character c that follows; inside double quotes removes special meaning of $, ', ", newline, and \ that follows, but is otherwise not interpreted; used for line continuation if appears as last character on line (newline is removed)
`command`	Executes command and inserts standard output at that point

Command Substitution

The form $(...) may be used instead of `...` for command substitution. Unlike `...`, the command is executed by the shell as-is, reducing the need for complex quoting techniques. Nesting is permitted.

The command substitution `< file` is equivalent to and faster than `cat file`. Command substitution of built-in commands that do not perform redirection is done without creating a separate process.

◆ File Name Substitution ◆

After parameter substitution (and command substitution) is performed on the command line, the Korn shell looks for the special characters *, ?, [, !, +, and @. If they're not quoted, then the shell searches the current directory, or another directory if preceded by a /, and substitutes the names of all files that match (these names are first alphabetized by the shell). If no match is found, then the characters remain untouched.

Note that file names beginning with a . must be explicitly matched (so echo * won't display your hidden files; echo .* will).

The file name substitution characters are summarized in Table B-7.

TABLE B-7. File name substitution characters

Character(s)	Meaning
?	Matches any single character
*	Matches zero or more characters
[*chars*]	Matches any single character in *chars*; the format c_1-c_2 can be used to match any character in the range c_1 through c_2, inclusive (e.g., [A-Z] will match any uppercase letter)
[!*chars*]	Matches any single character *not* in *chars*; a range of characters may be specified as above
?(*pattern*)	Matches zero or one occurence of *pattern*
@(*pattern*)	Matches exactly one occurence of *pattern*
*(*pattern*)	Matches zero or more occurences of *pattern*
+(*pattern*)	Matches one or more occurences of *pattern*
!(*pattern*)	Matches strings not containing *pattern*

pattern (inside parentheses) may contain other patterns separated by vertical bars (|), signifying that a match can be made against any of the patterns.

♦ I/O Redirection ♦

When scanning the command line, the shell looks for the special redirection characters < and >. If found, they are processed and removed (with any associated arguments) from the command line. Table B-8 summarizes the different types of I/O redirection that the shell supports.

TABLE B-8. I/O redirection

Construct	Meaning
< *file*	Redirect standard input from *file*
> *file*	Redirect standard output to *file*; *file* is created if it doesn't exist and zeroed if it does; if the `noclobber` option to set is on, and the file exists, an error message is displayed and no redirection is performed
>| *file*	Redirect standard output to *file*; *file* is created if it doesn't exist and zeroed if it does; the `noclobber` option to set is ignored
>> *file*	Like >, only output is appended to *file* if it already exists
<< *word*	Redirect standard input from lines that follow up until a line containing just *word*; parameter substitution occurs on the lines, and back-quoted commands are executed and the backslash character interpreted; if any character in *word* is quoted, then none of this processing occurs and the lines are passed through unaltered; if *word* is preceded by a –, then leading tabs on the lines are removed
<& *digit*	Standard input is redirected from the file associated with file descriptor *digit*
>& *digit*	Standard output is redirected to the file associated with file descriptor *digit*
<&–	Standard input is closed
>&–	Standard output is closed
<> *file*	Open *file* for both reading and writing
<&p	Use coprocess for input; see **Coprocesses**
>&p	Use coprocess for output; see **Coprocesses**

Note that file name substitution is not performed on *file*. Any of the constructs listed in the first column of the table may be preceded by a file descriptor number to have the same effect on the file associated with that file descriptor.

The file descriptor 0 is associated with standard input, 1 with standard output, and 2 with standard error.

◆ Exported Variables and Subshell Execution ◆

Commands other than the shell's built-in commands are normally executed in a "new" shell, called a *subshell*. Subshells cannot change the values of variables in the parent shell, and they can only access variables from the parent shell that were *exported* to them—either implicitly or explicitly—by the parent. If the sub-shell changes the value of one of these variables and wants to have its own sub-shells know about it, then it must explicitly export the variable before executing the subshell.

When the subshell finishes execution, any variables that it may have set are inaccessible by the parent. Note that, unlike the Bourne shell, redirected while, until, for, if, and case commands in the Korn shell are not executed as subshells.

The (...) Construct

If one or more commands are placed inside parentheses, then those commands will be executed in a subshell.

The { ...; } Construct

If one or more commands are placed inside curly braces, then those commands will be executed by the *current* shell.

With this construct and the (...) construct, I/O can be redirected and piped into and out of the set of enclosed commands, and the set can be sent to the background for execution by placing an & at the end. As an example,

```
(prog1; prog2; prog3) 2>errors &
```

submits the three listed programs to the background for execution, with standard error from all three programs redirected to the file errors.

More on Keyword Parameters

A keyword parameter can be placed into the environment of a command by preceding the command name with the assignment to the parameter on the command line, as in

```
PHONEBOOK=$HOME/misc/phone rolo
```

Here the variable PHONEBOOK will be assigned the indicated value and then placed in rolo's environment. The environment of the current shell remains unchanged, as if

```
(PHONEBOOK=$HOME/misc/phone; export PHONEBOOK; rolo)
```

had been executed intead.

◆ Functions ◆

Functions take the following forms:

```
function name { command; command; ... command; }
name () { command; command; ... command; }
```

where *name* is the name of the function that is defined to the current shell (functions can be exported with `typeset -fx`). The function definition can span as many lines as necessary. A `return` command can be executed to cause execution of the function to be terminated without also terminating the shell (see the `return` command description).

As an example,

```
function nf { ls | wc -l; }
```

defines a function called `nf` to count the number of files in your current directory.

Autoloading Functions

When a function is declared with the `autoload` alias or the `typeset -fu` command, it is tagged as undefined. When it is first used, the directories listed in the `FPATH` variable are searched for a file whose name matches the function name. The shell executes this file in the current execution environment (as if it were executed with the dot command) and then executes the function, which is presumable defined somewhere within the file. Subsequent calls to the function simply execute the function.

Differences With the Bourne Shell

Except for a few differences, functions behave the same in both the System V, Release 3 Bourne shell and the Korn shell. The following list gives all the differences between the two:

- The Bourne shell doesn't implement the `function` *name* format for function definitions.

- Traps set in a Korn shell function are local to that function and are reset to their previous values when the function returns. Traps set in a Bourne shell function remain in effect when the function returns.

- An exit trap (0) set in a Korn shell function will be activated when a `return` is executed. In the Bourne shell, an exit trap set in a function will change the value of the current exit trap and will be executed when the shell program exits.

- By default, shell variables within functions are global. This is true for both the Bourne shell and the Korn shell; however, the Korn shell provides for local variables within functions.

- Korn shell functions can be exported to subshells.

- An error in a Korn shell function aborts the function and returns to the calling program; an error in a Bourne shell function aborts the calling program.

- Bourne shell functions are stored with variables, so a `set` will list all variables and functions, and an `unset` *function* will remove *function*; a variable and a function cannot have the same name. In the Korn shell, functions are stored separately and are not listed by the `set` command; functions are removed by using `unset` with the `-f` option. A function and a variable may share the same name.

- The `-h` option to the Bourne shell `set` command causes commands in functions to be added to the hash list when the function is defined. The Korn shell has no comparable option, and all commands in functions are added to the tracked command alias list when the function is executed; this is the default in the Bourne shell as well.

- `$0` in a Korn shell function contains the name of the function.

♦ Job Control ♦

Shell Jobs

Every command sequence run in the background is assigned a job number, starting at one. The lowest available number not in use is assigned. A job may be referred to with a `%` followed by the job number, a `+`, `-`, `%`, `?`, or the first few letters of the pipeline. The following built-in commands may be given a job as an argument: `kill`, `fg*`, `bg*`, and `wait`. The special conventions `%+` and `%-` refer to the current and previous jobs, respectively; `%%` also refers to the current job. The current job is the most recent job placed in the background or the job running in the foreground*. The previous job is the previous current job. The convention `%`*string* refers to the job whose name begins with *string*; `%?`*string* refers to the job whose name contains *string*. The `jobs` command may be used to list the status of all currently running jobs.

If the `monitor` option of the `set` command is turned on, the shell will print a message when each job finishes. If you still have jobs when you try to exit the shell, a message will be printed to alert you of this. If you immediately try to exit again, the shell will exit.

Stopping Jobs*

If the Korn shell is running on a system with job control, and the `monitor` option of the `set` command is turned on, then jobs that are running in the foreground may be placed in the background and vice versa. A *CTRL*-z will stop the current job. The `bg` command puts a stopped job in the background. The `fg` command brings a background or stopped job to the foreground.

Whenever a job in the background attempts to read from the terminal, it is stopped until it is brought to the foreground. Output from background jobs normally comes to the terminal on Berkeley systems. If `stty tostop` is executed on Berkeley UNIX, then output from background jobs is disabled, and a job writing to the terminal is stopped until it is brought to the foreground. This is the only mode of operation on System V, Release 3. When the shell exits, all stopped jobs are killed.

♦ Other Features ♦

Coprocesses

A *pipeline* (command line) may be terminated with a `|&`. This causes asynchronous execution of the preceding pipeline (just like `&`), except that the standard input and standard output of the pipeline are redirected to a two-way pipe managed by the shell. This is called a *coprocess*. The coprocess can be read from using the `-p` option to `read`, and it can be written to using the `-p` option to `print`. The standard input and standard output of the coprocess can be reassigned to file descriptors of another pipeline with `>&p` and `<&p`, respectively, or to the shell's file descriptors with `exec`. Once the standard input of a coprocess has been reassigned, another coprocess can be started.

Example

```
$ who | cut -c1-8 |&
$ read -p name
$ echo $name
root
$ read -p name
$ echo $name
pat
$ cat <&p
steve
root
lev
$
```

Tilde Substitution

Each word and shell variable on a command line is checked to see if it begins with an unquoted ~. If it does, then the rest of the word or variable up to a / is considered a login name and is looked up in /etc/passwd. If that user exists, his home directory replaces the ~ and his login name. If that user doesn't exist, the text is unchanged. A ~ by itself or followed by a / is replaced by the HOME variable, and a ~ followed by a – or a + is replaced by the OLDPWD and PWD variables, respectively.

Command Tracking

Both the Korn shell and the System V, Release 3 Bourne shell have command tracking. When a command is entered and the PATH is searched for that command, the shell remembers where that command was found so that the next time the command is invoked, the PATH isn't searched; instead, the remembered path name is used. The Bourne shell implements this with an internal table of commands. The Korn shell implements this using its aliasing capability. The first time a command is invoked, the Korn shell creates an alias (or tracked alias) with the same name as the command, assigning the full path name of the command to the alias.

In the Bourne shell, this feature is called *hashing*, and it is always turned on. In the Korn shell, this feature is called tracked aliasing, and it can be turned on or off with the trackall option to the set -o command; by default, it is turned off. If a command is moved to another directory in the PATH after it has been found, the Bourne shell will still be able to find it; the Korn shell will not. The command's alias must be removed with the unalias command to force the shell to create a new alias for it.

New Conditional Testing

The [[command can be used for testing instead of test and [. Its format is

[[*test expression*]]

where *test expressions* can be any of the conditional expressions that test uses as well as parentheses for overriding precedence, && for logical ANDing of test expressions, || for logical ORing of test expressions, or > and < for testing strings. Strings can also be tested against patterns with the = and != conditionals.

♦ Command Summary ♦

The following commands are built-in to the Korn shell.

The : Command

General Format: :

This is essentially a *null* command. It is frequently used to satisfy the requirement that a command appear.

Example

```
if who | grep jack > /dev/null
then
        :
else
        echo "jack's not logged in"
fi
```

The : command returns an exit status of zero.

The . Command

General Format: . *file*

The "dot" command causes the indicated *file* to be read and executed by the
shell, *just as if the lines from the file were typed at that point.* Note that *file* does *not*
have to be executable, only readable. Also, the shell uses the PATH variable to
find *file.*

Example

```
. progdefs                  Execute commands in progdefs
```

The above command causes the shell to search the current PATH for the file
progdefs. When it finds it, it reads and executes the commands from the file.

Note that since *file* is not executed by a subshell, variables set and/or
changed within *file* remain in effect after execution of the commands in *file* is
complete.

The `alias` Command

General Format: `alias` *name=string* [*name=string* ...]

The `alias` command assigns *string* to the alias *name*. Whenever *name* is used as a command, the Korn shell substitutes *string*, performing command-line substitution after *string* is in place.

Examples

```
alias ll='ls -l'
alias dir='basename `pwd`'
```

If an alias ends with a blank, the word following the alias is also checked to see if it's an alias.

The format

```
                 alias name
```

causes the alias for *name* to be printed out.

The `-x` option causes an alias to be exported. Exported aliases are defined across subshells, i.e., shell programs will be able to access exported aliases, but a separate invocation of the Korn shell will not.

Examples

```
alias -x dir='basename `pwd`'
alias -x ll teg
```

The format

```
                 alias -t name
```

creates a "tracked alias." The tracked alias is the full path to *name* that is derived by searching the PATH for *name*. Whenever the PATH is changed, all tracked aliases are undefined.

The following aliases are compiled into the Korn shell:

```
autoload='typeset -fu'
echo='print -'
false='let 0'
function='typeset -f'
hash='alias -t'
history='fc -l'
integer='typeset -i'
nohup='nohup '
```

```
pwd='print - $PWD'
r='fc -e -'
true=':'
type='whence -v'
```

alias with no arguments lists all aliases; alias -x lists all exported aliases; alias -t lists all tracked aliases.

alias returns an exit status of zero unless a *name* is given (as in alias *name*) for which no alias has been defined.

The autoload Command

autoload is an alias for typeset -fu. It is used to specify functions that are to be loaded in the first time they are used.

The bg Command*

General Format: bg %*n*

Job *n* is put into the background. If no argument is given, the current job is put into the background.

Example

```
bg %2
```

The break Command

General Format: break

Execution of this command causes execution of the innermost for, while, or until loop to be immediately terminated. Execution continues with the commands that immediately follow the loop.

If the format

```
break n
```

is used, where *n* is an integer greater than or equal to 1, then execution of the *n* innermost loops is automatically terminated.

The case Command

General Format:

```
case value in
        pat₁ )    command
                  command
                  . . .
                  command;;
        pat₂ )    command
                  command
                  . . .
                  command;;
        . . .
        patₙ )    command
                  command
                  . . .
                  command;;
esac
```

The word *value* is successively compared against pat_1, pat_2, ..., pat_n until a match is found. The commands that appear immediately after the matching pattern are then executed until a double semicolon (;;) is encountered. At that point, execution of the case is terminated.

If no pattern matches *value*, then none of the commands inside the case are executed. The pattern * matches *anything*, and is often used as the last pattern in a case as the "catchall" case.

The shell metacharacters * (match zero or more characters), ? (match any single character), and [...] (match any single character enclosed between the brackets) can be used in patterns. The character | can be used to specify a logical ORing of two patterns, as in

pat_1 | pat_2

which means to match either pat_1 or pat_2.

Examples

```
case $1 in
        -l)    lopt=TRUE;;
        -w)    wopt=TRUE;;
        -c)    copt=TRUE;;
         *)    echo "Unknown option";;
esac
```

```
case $choice in
    [1-9]) valid=TRUE;;
        *) echo "Please choose a number from 1-9";;
esac
```

The Korn shell allows an optional (in front of case patterns, e.g.,

```
case $i in
        (-a)
                print -a option
                break;
        (-b)
                print -b option
                break;
esac
```

This allows case statements inside $(...) without quoting the) after each pattern.

The cd Command

General Format: cd *directory*

Execution of this command causes the shell to make *directory* the current directory. If *directory* is omitted, then the shell makes the directory specified in the HOME variable the current directory.

If the shell variable CDPATH is null, then *directory* must be a full directory path (e.g., /usr/steve/documents) or relative to the current directory (e.g., documents, ../pat).

If CDPATH is non-null and *directory* is not a full path, then the shell searches the colon-delimited directory list in CDPATH for a directory containing *directory*.

Examples

$ **cd documents/memos**	*Change to* documents/memos *directory*
$ **cd**	*Change to* HOME *directory*

The Korn shell adds two new features to the cd command. An argument of – causes the Korn shell to make the previous directory the current directory. The path name of the new current directory is printed out.

The format

cd *old new*

causes cd to replace the first occurrence of *old* in the current directory path name with *new* and to change to that directory. The path name of the new current directory is printed out.

Examples

```
$ pwd
/usr/lib/uucp
$ cd /
$ cd -
/usr/lib/uucp
$ cd lib spool
/usr/spool/uucp
$
```

The cd command sets the shell variable PWD to the new current directory, and OLDPWD to the previous directory.

The continue command

General Format: continue

Execution of this command from within a for, while, or until loop causes any commands that follow the continue to be skipped. Execution of the loop then continues as normal.
     If the format

continue *n*

is used, then the commands within the *n* innermost loops are skipped. Execution of the loops then continues as normal.

The echo Command

In the Korn shell, echo is aliased to 'print -'. Note that print - is equivalent to the echo command built-in to the System V, Release 3 Bourne shell. See the print command for more details.

The **eval** Command

General Format: `eval` *args*

Execution of this command causes the shell to evaluate *args* and then execute the results. This is useful for causing the shell to effectively "double-scan" a command line.

Example

```
$ x='abc def'
$ y='$x'                        Assign $x to y
$ echo $y
$x
$ eval echo $y
abc def
$
```

The **exec** Command

General Format: `exec` *command args*

When the shell executes the `exec` command, it initiates execution of the specified *command* with the indicated arguments. Unlike other commands that are executed as a new process, *command replaces* the current process (i.e., no new process is created). Once *command* starts execution, there is no return to the program that initiated the `exec`.

If just I/O redirection is specified, then the input and/or output for the shell is accordingly redirected.

Examples

```
exec /usr/lbin/ksh           Replace current process with ksh
exec < datafile              Reassign standard input to datafile
```

The **exit** Command

General Format: `exit` *n*

Execution of `exit` causes the current shell program to be immediately terminated. The exit status of the program is the value of the integer *n*, if supplied.

If *n* is not supplied, then the exit status is that of the last command executed prior to the `exit`.

An exit status of zero is used by convention to indicate "success," and nonzero to indicate "failure" (such as an error condition). This convention is used by the shell in evaluation of conditions for `if`, `while`, and `until` commands, and with the `&&` and `||` constructs.

Examples

```
who | grep $user >/dev/null
exit                            Exit with status of last grep

exit 1                          Exit with status of 1

if finduser                     If finduser returns a zero exit status...
then
       ...
fi
```

You should note that executing `exit` from a login shell has the effect of logging you off.

The `export` Command

General Format: `export` *variables*

The `export` command tells the shell that the indicated variables are to be marked as exported; i.e., their values are to be passed down to subshells.

`export` with no arguments causes the shell to write a list of the exported variables explicitly exported by the current shell to standard output.

Examples

```
export PATH PS1
export dbhome x1 y1 date
```

Inherited environment variables that are changed are *automatically* re-exported. Recall that the Bourne shell requires that the variable be explicitly exported again for the change to be passed down to subshells.

Variables may be set when exported using the form

$$export \quad variable=value \ ...$$

So lines such as

```
PATH=$PATH:$HOME/bin; export PATH
CDPATH=:$HOME:/usr/spool/uucppublic; export CDPATH
```

can be rewritten as

```
export PATH=$PATH:$HOME/bin CDPATH=:$HOME:/usr/spool/uucppublic
```

The output of `export` with no arguments is a list of the exported variables and their values in the form

variable=value

as opposed to the Bourne shell, which lists just the names of the variables explicitly exported by the shell, preceded by `export`.

The `fc` Command

General Format: `fc -e` *editor* `-lnr` *first last*

The `fc` command is used to edit commands in the command history. A range of commands is specified from *first* to *last*, where *first* and *last* can be either command numbers or strings; a negative number is taken as an offset from the current command number; a string specifies the most recently entered command beginning with that string. The commands are read into the editor *editor* and executed upon exit from the editor. If no editor is specified, the value of the shell variable `FCEDIT` is used; if `FCEDIT` is not set, then `/bin/ed` is used.

The `-l` option lists the commands from *first* to *last* (i.e., an editor is not invoked). If the `-n` option is also selected, then these commands are not preceded by command numbers.

The `-r` option to `fc` reverses the order of the commands.

If *last* is not specified, then it defaults to *first*. If *first* is also not specified, then it defaults to the previous command for editing and to -16 for listing.

The format

`fc -e -` *old=new command*

causes the *command* (a number or string like *first*) to be re-executed after the string *old* in the command is replaced with *new*. If *command* isn't specified, the previous command is used, and if *old=new* isn't specified, the command is not changed.

Examples

`fc -l`	*List the last 16 commands*
`fc -e vi sed`	*Read the last* `sed` *command into* `vi`
`fc 100 110`	*Read commands 100 to 110 into* `$FCEDIT`
`fc -e -`	*Re-execute the previous command*
`fc -e - abc=def 104`	*Re-execute command 104, replacing* `abc` *with* `def`

The `fg` Command*

General Format: `fg %n`

Job n is brought to the foreground. If no argument is given, the current job is brought to the foreground.

Example

`fg %2`

The `for` Command

General Format:

```
for var in word₁ word₂ ... wordₙ
do
        command
        command
        . . .
done
```

Execution of this command causes the commands enclosed between the `do` and `done` to be executed as many times as there are words listed after the `in`.

The first time through the loop, the first word—*word₁*—is assigned to the variable *var* and the commands between the `do` and `done` executed. The second time through the loop, the second word listed—*word₂*—is assigned to *var* and the commands in the loop executed again. This process continues until the last variable in the list—*wordₙ*—is assigned to *var* and the commands between the `do` and `done` executed. At that point, execution of the `for` loop is terminated. Execution then continues with the command that immediately follows the `done`.

The special format

```
for var
do
     ...
done
```

indicates that the positional parameters "$1", "$2", ... are to be used in the list and is equivalent to

```
for var in "$@"
do
     ...
done
```

Example

```
# nroff all of the files in the current directory

for file in *
do
        nroff -Tlp $file | lp
done
```

The function Command

General Format: function *name* { *list* ; }

This defines the function *name* to the shell. For more details, see the heading **Functions** presented earlier in this Appendix.

The getopts Command

General Format: getopts *options var*

This command processes command line arguments. *options* is a list of valid single-gle letter options. If any letter in *options* is followed by a :, then that option takes a following argument on the command line, which must be separated from the option by at least one whitespace character.

Each time getopts is called, it processes the next command line argument. If a valid option is found, getopt stores the matching option letter inside the specified variable *var* and returns a zero exit status.

If an invalid option is specified (that is, one not listed in *options*), then getopts stores a ? inside *var* and returns with a zero exit status. It also writes an error message to standard error.

If an option takes a following argument, then getopts stores the matching option letter inside *var* and stores the following command line argument inside the special variable OPTARG. If no arguments are left on the command line, getopts stores a ? inside *var* and writes an error message to standard error.

If no more options remain on the command line (that is, if the next command line argument does not begin with a -), then getopts returns a nonzero exit status.

The special variable OPTIND is also used by getopts. It is initially set to 1, and is adjusted each time getopts returns to indicate the number of the *next* command line argument to be processed.

The argument -- can be placed on the command line to specify the end of the command line arguments.

getopts supports stacked arguments, as in

```
repx -iau
```

which is equivalent to

```
repx -i -a -u
```

Options that take following arguments may not be stacked. The complete set of rules for command line syntax is specified in the intro(1) section to the *UNIX User's Reference Manual*.

If the format

```
getopts options var args
```

is used, getotps parses the arguments specified by *args* instead of the command line arguments.

Example

```
usage="Usage: foo [-r] [-o outfile] infile"

while getopts  ro: opt
do
        case "$var"
        in
                r) rflag=1;;
                o) oflag=1
                   ofile=$OPTARG;;
                \?) echo "$usage"
```

```
                    exit 1;;
          esac
done

if [ $OPTIND -gt $# ]
then
          echo "Needs input file!"
          echo "$usage"
          exit 2
fi

shift `expr $OPTIND - 1`
ifile=$1
    ...
```

The `hash` Command

The `hash` command in the Korn shell is implemented as an alias to `'alias -t'`.

The `if` Command

General Format:

> if   *command*$_t$
> then
> > *command*
> > *command*
> > ...
> fi

command$_t$ is executed and its exit status tested. If it is zero, then the commands that follow up to the `fi` are executed. Otherwise, the commands that follow up to the `fi` are skipped.

Example

```
if grep $sys sysnames > /dev/null
then
          echo "$sys is a valid system name"
fi
```

If the `grep` returns an exit status of zero (which it will if it finds `$sys` in the file `sysnames`), then the `echo` command will be executed; otherwise it will be skipped.

The built-in command `test` is often used as the command following the `if`.

Example

```
if [ $# -eq 0 ]
then
        echo "Usage: $0 [-l] file ..."
        exit 1
fi
```

An `else` clause can be added to the `if` to be executed if the command returns a nonzero exit status. In this case, the general format of the `if` becomes

```
if   command_t
then
            command
            command
            . . .
else
            command
            command
            . . .
fi
```

If *command_t* returns an exit status of zero, then the commands that follow up to the `else` will be executed, and the commands between the `else` and the `fi` skipped. Otherwise, *command_t* returns a nonzero exit status and the commands between the `then` and the `else` will be skipped and the commands between the `else` and the `fi` executed.

Example

```
if [ -z "$line" ]
then
        echo "I couldn't find $name"
else
        echo "$line"
fi
```

In the above example, if `line` has zero length, then the `echo` command that displays the message `I couldn't find $name` is executed; otherwise the `echo` command that displays the value of `line` is executed.

A final format of the `if` command is useful when more than a two-way decision has to be made. Its general format is

```
if   command₁
then
            command
            command
            . . .
elif   command₂
then
            command
            command
            . . .
. . .
elif   commandₙ
then
            command
            command
            . . .
else
            command
            command
            . . .
fi
```

$command_1$, $command_2$, ..., $command_n$ are evaluated in order until one of the commands returns an exit status of zero, at which point the commands that immediately follow the `then` (up to another `elif`, `else`, or `fi`) are executed. If none of the commands returns an exit status of zero, then the commands listed after the `else` (if present) will be executed.

Example

```
if [ "$choice" = a ]
then
        add $*
elif [ "$choice" = d ]
then
        delete $*
elif [ "$choice" = l ]
then
        list
else
        echo "Bad choice!"
        error=TRUE
fi
```

The jobs Command

General Format: jobs

The list of active jobs is printed. If the -l option is specified, process ids are listed as well. If the -p option is specified, only process ids are listed.

Example

```
$ sleep 100 &
[1]       1104
$ jobs
[1] +  Running                    sleep 100 &
$
```

The kill Command

General Format: kill -*signal process*

The kill command sends the signal *signal* to the process *process*, where *process* is a process or job number, and *signal* is a number or one of the signal names specified in /usr/include/sys/signal.h (minus the SIG prefix):

HUP	1	hangup
INT	2	interrupt
QUIT	3	quit
ILL	4	illegal instruction
TRAP	5	trace trap
IOT	6	IOT instruction
EMT	7	EMT instruction
FPE	8	floating point exception
KILL	9	kill
BUS	10	bus error
SEGV	11	segmentation violation
SYS	12	bad argument to system call
PIPE	13	write on a pipe with no one to read it
ALRM	14	alarm clock
TERM	15	software termination signal from kill
USR1	16	user-defined signal 1
USR2	17	user-defined signal 2
CLD	18	death of a child
PWR	19	power-fail restart

`kill -l` lists these names.

If *signal* isn't specified, TERM is used.

Examples

```
kill -9 1234
kill HUP %2
kill %1
```

The `let` Command

General Format: `let` *expressions*
                   ((*expressions*))

The `let` command evaluates integer arithmetic *expressions*. *expressions* can contain constants, shell variables (which don't have to be preceded by dollar signs), and operators. The operators, in order of decreasing precedence, are:

-	unary minus
! ~	logical negation, bitwise NOT
* / %	multiplication, division, remainder
+ -	addition, subtraction
<< >>	left shift, right shift
<= >= < >	comparison
== !=	equal, not equal
&	bitwise and
^	bitwise exclusive or
|	bitwise or
&&	logical and
||	logical or
=	assignment

Parentheses may be used to override operator precedence.

The exit status is zero (true) if the last expression is nonzero and one (false) if the last expression is zero.

Examples

```
let y=22*33
let "z = y * y / (y - 1)" "x = y + 1"

if let "y % 12"
then
        echo "y mod 12 != 0"
else
        echo "y mod 12 == 0"
fi
```

Note that quotes must be used if blanks are in the expression. The last example uses the exit status from `let` to perform an arithmetic test.

The format

$$((\textit{expression}))$$

is the same as the format

$$\texttt{let }\textit{"expression"}$$

The `newgrp` Command

General Format: `newgrp` *group*

This command changes your real group id (GID) to *group*. If no argument is specified, then it changes you back to your default group.

Examples

newgrp shbook	*Change to group* shbook
newgrp	*Change back to default group*

If a password is associated with the new group, then you will be prompted to enter it. Otherwise, you must be listed as a valid member of the group (in `/etc/group`) for you to `newgrp` to it.

The `print` Command

General Format: `print` *-options args*

`print` is the Korn shell output command. It can replace `echo` in both System V and Berkeley UNIX. The escape sequences of the System V echo command are interpreted; also, the sequence \a prints a bell. Valid options are

−	Ignore all options that might follow
−n	Do not put a newline at the end of the line
−r	Ignore echo escape sequences
−R	Same as −r plus ignore all options except −n
−s	Put *args* in the history file
−u*n*	Write output to file descriptor *n* (default 1)
−p	Write output to process spawned with │&.

Examples

```
print - "this is a test"        Same as Sys V echo
print -R -n "no newline"        Same as V7 & BSD echo
print -s "vi echo.c"            Put into the history file
```

The pwd Command

General Format: pwd

This command tells the shell to print your working directory, which is written to standard output.

Examples

```
$ pwd
/usr/steve/documents/memos
$ cd
$ pwd
/usr/steve
$
```

The read Command

General Format: read −*options var1*?*prompt var2 ...*

This command causes the shell to read a line from standard input and assign successive whitespace-delimited words from the line to the variables *vars*. If fewer variables are listed than there are words on the line, then the excess words are stored in the last variable.

If *prompt?* is specified, *prompt* is displayed to the user as a prompt.
Valid options are:

-r	Don't treat trailing \ as line continuation
-s	Put input line in the history file
-u*n*	Read input from file descriptor *n* (default 0)
-p	Read from output of process spawned with |&.

Specifying just one variable has the effect of reading and assigning an entire line to the variable. If no variables are listed, the line that is read is stored inside the variable REPLY.

The exit status of read is zero unless an end of file condition is encountered.

Examples

```
$ read hours mins
10 19
$ echo "$hours:$mins"
10:19
$ read num rest
39 East 12th Street, New York City 10003
$ echo "$num\n$rest"
39
East 12th Street, New York City 10003
$ read line
       Here     is an entire          line \r
$ echo "$line"
Here     is an entire          line r
$ read file?"tell me "
tell me edit.c
$ read -r raw
abc\ndef\t
$ echo $raw
abc\ndef\t
$ read
this is a test
$ echo $REPLY
this is a test
$
```

Note in the third example that any leading whitespace characters get "eaten" by the shell when read. You can change IFS if this poses a problem.

Also note that backslash characters get interpreted by the shell when you read the line, and any that make it through (double backslashes will get through as a single backslash) will get interpreted by echo if you display the value of the variable.

The **readonly** Command

General Format: `readonly` *vars*

This command tells the shell that the listed variables cannot be assigned values. If you subsequently try to assign a value to the variable, the shell will issue an error message.

Variables may be set when made read only using the form

`readonly` *variable=value ...*

So lines such as

```
PATH=$PATH:$HOME/bin; readonly PATH
```

can be rewritten as

```
readonly PATH=$PATH:$HOME/bin
```

`readonly` variables are useful for ensuring that you don't accidentally overwrite the value of a variable. They're also good for ensuring that other people using a shell program can't change the values of particular variables (e.g., their HOME directory or their PATH). The readonly attribute is not passed down to subshells.

`readonly` with no arguments prints a list of your readonly variables.

Example

```
$ DB=/usr/steve/database        Assign value to DB
$ readonly DB                   Make it read-only
$ DB=foo                        Try to assign it a value
DB: is read-only                Error message from the shell
$ echo $DB                      But can still access its value
/usr/steve/database
$
```

The **return** Command

General Format: `return` *n*

This command causes the shell to stop execution of the current function and immediately return to the caller with an exit status of *n*. If *n* is omitted, then the exit status returned is that of the command executed immediately prior to the `return`.

When `return` is executed in a Korn shell function, if the exit trap (0) is set inside the function, it is executed before returning to the calling program; in the Bourne shell, the exit trap isn't executed until the main program exits.

The `select` Command

General Format:

```
select var in word₁ word₂ ... wordₙ
do
        command
        command
        . . .
done
```

This command is useful for displaying a menu to the user.   `select` prints each *word*, preceded by its relative number in the list (1 through *n*), on standard error. The variable `PS3` is then printed as the prompt, and a line is read from standard input and assigned to the variable `REPLY`. If the line begins with one of the numbers 1 through *n*, then *var* is set to the corresponding *word* from the list. If the line begins with anything else, *var* is set null. In either case, the commands between the `do` and the `done` are then executed. If the line is blank, then the menu is redisplayed. The `LINES` and `COLUMNS` variables are used to determine the layout of the menu.

After execution of the commands, the user is prompted for another selection. This continues until an end of file is encountered, or a `break`, `exit`, or `return` is executed from inside the loop.

The special format

```
select var
do
        . . .
done
```

indicates that the positional parameters `"$1"`, `"$2"`, ... are to be used as the *words*.

Example

```
PS3="Please select one of the above: "

select choice in Lookup Add Remove Change List Exit
do
        case "$choice"
        in
                Lookup) ...;;
                Add    ) ...;;
                Remove) ...;;
                Change) ...;;
                List   ) ...;;
                Exit   ) exit 0;;
                *      ) echo "Bad choice";;
        esac
done
```

The set Command

General Format: set *options args*

This command is used to turn on or off options as specified by *options*. It is also used to set positional parameters, as specified by *args*.

Each single letter option in *options* is enabled if the option is preceded by a minus sign (–), or disabled if preceded by a plus sign (+). Options can be grouped, as in

```
set -fx
```

which enables the f and x options.

Options that can be selected are summarized in Table B-9.

TABLE B-9. set options

Option	Meaning
`--`	Don't treat subsequent args preceded by a – as options
	If there are no arguments, the positional parameters are unset
`+A` *arr*	Assign specified values to array *arr*
`-A` *arr*	Same as +A but unset *arr* first
`-a`	Automatically export all variables that are subsequently defined or modified
`-e`	Exit if any command that gets executed has a nonzero exit status. The ERR trap is executed before exiting
`-f`	Disable file name generation
`-h`	Each command that is found in the PATH becomes a tracked alias
`-k`	Process arguments of the form *keyword=value* that appear anywhere on the command line (not just before the command) and place them in the environment of the command
`-m`	Turn on the job monitor
`-n`	Read commands without executing them (useful for checking for balanced do...dones, and if...fis)
`-o` *m*	Turn on mode *m* (see Table B-10)
`-p`	Turn on privileged mode
`-s`	Sort the positional parameters
`-t`	Exit after executing one command
`-u`	Issue an error if a variable is referenced without having been assigned a value or if a positional parameter is referenced without having been set
`-v`	Print each shell command line as it is read
`-x`	Print each command and its arguments as it is executed, preceded by a +

Korn shell modes are turned on or off by using the −o and +o options, respectively, followed by an option name. These options are summarized in Table B-10.

TABLE B-10. Korn shell modes

Mode	Meaning
allexport	same as -a
bgnice	run background jobs at lower priority
errexit	same as -e
emacs	the in-line editor is set to emacs
gmacs	the in-line editor is set to gmacs
ignoreeof	the exit command must be used to leave the shell
keyword	same as -k
markdirs	directory names from file name expansion end in /
monitor	same as -m
noclobber	don't truncate existing files when redirecting output
noexec	same as -n
noglob	same as -f
nolog	don't put function definitions in the history
nounset	same as -u
privileged	same as -p
trackall	same as -h
verbose	same as -v
vi	the in-line editor is set to vi
viraw	process each character as it is typed in vi mode
xtrace	same as -x

The command set -o without any following options has the effect of listing all Korn shell modes and their settings.

The shell variable $- contains the current options setting.

Each word that is listed in *args* is set to the positional parameters $1, $2, ..., respectively. If the first word might start with a minus sign, then it's safer to specify the -- option to set to avoid interpretation of that value.

If *args* is supplied, then the variable $# will be set to the number of parameters assigned after execution of the command.

Examples

```
set -vx                              Print all command lines as they are read, and each
                                     command and its arguments as it is executed
set +x                               Turn off command trace
set "$name" "$address" "$phone"      Set $1 to $name, $2 to $address, and
                                     $3 to $phone
set -- -1                            Set $1 to -1
set -o vi                            Turn on vi mode
set +o verbose -o noglob             Turn verbose mode off, noglob on
```

The Korn shell expands and prints the PS4 variable before every line when xtrace mode is turned on. By default this variable is set to +, producing the same output as the Bourne shell.

The shift Command

General Format: shift

This command causes the positional parameters $1, $2, ..., $n to be "shifted left" one place. That is, $2 is assigned to $1, $3 to $2, ..., and $n to $n-1. $# is adjusted accordingly.

If the format

shift *n*

is used instead, then the shift is to the left *n* places.

Examples

```
$ set a b c d
$ echo "$#\n$*"
4
a b c d
$ shift
$ echo "$#\n$*"
3
b c d
$ shift 2
$ echo "$#\n$*"
1
d
$
```

The test Command

General Format:

test   *condition*

   or

[*condition*   ]

The shell evaluates *condition* and if the result of the evaluation is *TRUE*, returns a zero exit status. If the result of the evaluation is *FALSE*, then a nonzero exit status is returned. If the format [*condition*] is used, then a space must appear immediately after the [and before the].

   condition is composed of one or more operators as shown in Table B-11.

   The -a operator has higher precedence than the -o operator. In any case, parentheses can be used to group subexpressions. Just remember that the parentheses are significant to the shell and so must be quoted. Operators and operands (including parentheses) must be delimited by one or more spaces so that test sees them as separate arguments.

   test is often used to test conditions in an if, while, or until command.

Examples

```
# see if perms is executable

if test -x /etc/perms
then
        ...
fi



# see if it's a directory or a normal file that's readable

if [ -d $file -o \( -f $file -a -r $file \) ]
then
        ...
fi
```

The Korn shell test command allows any arithmetic expression with the integer comparison operators (-eq, -ge, -gt, -le, -lt, and -ne).

TABLE B-11. test operators

Operator	Returns TRUE (zero exit status) if
File Operators	
-b *file*	*file* is a block special file
-c *file*	*file* is a character special file
-d *file*	*file* is a directory
-f *file*	*file* is an ordinary file
-g *file*	*file* has its set group id (SGID) bit set
-G *file*	*file*'s group is the effective group id
-k *file*	*file* has its sticky bit set
-L *file*	*file* is a symbolic link (link across file systems)
-O *file*	*file*'s owner is the effective user id
-p *file*	*file* is a named pipe
-r *file*	*file* is readable by the process
-s *file*	*file* has nonzero length
-S *file*	*file* is a socket
-t *fd*	*fd* is open file descriptor associated with a terminal (1 is default)
-u *file*	*file* has its set user id (SUID) bit set
-w *file*	*file* is writable by the process
-x *file*	*file* is executable
file1 -ef *file2*	*file1* and *file2* are linked
file1 -nt *file2*	*file1* is newer than *file2*
file1 -ot *file2*	*file1* is older than *file2*
String Operators	
string	*string* is not null
-n *string*	*string* is not null (*string* must be seen by test)
-z *string*	*string* is null (*string* must be seen by test)
$string_1$ = $string_2$	$string_1$ is identical to $string_2$
$string_1$!= $string_2$	$string_1$ is *not* identical to $string_2$
Integer Comparison Operators	
int_1 -eq int_2	int_1 is equal to int_2
int_1 -ge int_2	int_1 is greater than or equal to int_2
int_1 -gt int_2	int_1 is greater than int_2
int_1 -le int_2	int_1 is less than or equal to int_2
int_1 -lt int_2	int_1 is less than int_2
int_1 -ne int_2	int_1 is not equal to int_2
Boolean Operators	
! *expr*	*expr* is FALSE; otherwise returns TRUE
$expr_1$ -a $expr_2$	$expr_1$ is TRUE and $expr_2$ is TRUE
$expr_1$ -o $expr_2$	$expr_1$ is TRUE or $expr_2$ is TRUE

Examples

```
if test "x + y" -gt 100
then
      ...
fi

if [ "x - 1" -eq "(y + 1) / 3" ]
then
      ...
fi
```

The `time` Command

General Format: `time` *pipeline*

The *pipeline* is executed and the real, user, and system times are printed out to the nearest hundredth of a second. Note that the `/bin/time` command will only list the time of the first command in a pipeline, and the `time` built-in will list the time of the *entire* pipeline. `time` will also list the times of other built-in commands.

Example

```
$ time ps
   PID TTY TIME COMMAND
    28 02  0:38 ksh
   602 02  3:50 vi
   647 02  0:03 ps


real    0m11.45s
user    0m0.90s
sys     0m2.15s
$ time pwd
/usr/src/cmd

real    0m0.05s
user    0m0.05s
sys     0m0.00s
```

The `times` Command

General Format: `times`

Execution of this command causes the shell to write to standard output the total amount of time that has been used by the shell and processes run by the shell. Two numbers are listed for each: first the accumulated user time, then the accumulated system time.

Example

```
$ times
0m0.30s  0m0.85s
0m0.64s  0m1.98s
$
```

The `trap` Command

General Format: `trap` *commands signals*

This command tells the shell to execute *commands* whenever it receives one of the signals listed in *signals*. Either the signal name or number may be used (see the **kill** command for a list of signal names and numbers).

Two new names, ERR and DEBUG, have been added. ERR is triggered whenever a command has a nonzero exit code; DEBUG is triggered after every command is executed. These names are not passed to functions. All traps are local to functions.

`trap` with no arguments prints a list of the current trap assignments.

If the first argument is the null string, as in

> `trap   ""   ` *signals*

then the signals in *signals* will be ignored when received by the shell.

If the format

> `trap   ` *signals*

is used, then processing of each signal listed in *signals* is reset to the default action.

Examples

`trap "echo hangup >> $ERRFILE; exit" 2` *Log message and exit on hangup*

```
trap "rm $TMPFILE; exit" 1 2 15        remove $TMPFILE on signals 1, 2, or 15
trap "" 2                              Ignore interrupts
trap 2                                 Reset default processing of interrupts"
```

The shell scans *commands* when the trap command is encountered and again when one of the listed signals is received. This means, for example, that when the shell encounters the command

```
trap "echo $count lines processed >> $LOGFILE; exit" 1 2 15
```

it will substitute the value of count at that point, and *not when one of the signals is received*. You can get the value of count substituted when one of the signals is received if you instead enclose the commands in single quotes:

```
trap 'echo $count lines processed >> $LOGFILE; exit' 1 2 15
```

The type Command

The Korn shell type command is an alias for 'whence -v'. Its output is similar to the Bourne shell's type command; it also lists aliases and reserved words.

Examples

```
$ type who
who is /bin/who
$ type for
for is a reserved word
$ type cd
cd is a shell builtin
$ type funx1
funx1 is a function
$ type nu
nu is an alias for who | wc -l
$
```

The typeset Command

General Format: typeset *options var=value*   [*var=value ...*]

This command assigns *value* to the shell variable *var*. The variable's type is determined by *options*. Variables typeset inside functions are local; the old variables' type and value (if any) are restored when the function returns.

Table B-12 describes the options available to typeset. Note that when *options* are preceded with a –, the type is turned on and when preceded with a +, the type is turned off. When invoked without *variables*, typeset lists all variables of the type specified by the *options*; – causes the variables and their values to be printed, and + causes just the variable names to be printed. When used by itself, typeset lists all set parameters along with their type.

Examples

typeset -i num1 num2	num1 *and* num2 *are integers*
typeset -Lu left=ABCDEF	*Left justified, width=6, uppercase*
typeset +r PWD	*Turn off read-only on* PWD
typeset -r	*List all read-only variables*

The ulimit Command

General Format: ulimit *options size*

This command tells the shell to set maximum limits on processes it runs. Valid options are:

-a	display all limits
-c *size*	limit core dumps to *size* blocks
-d *size*	limit the data size (of executables) to *size* blocks
-f *size*	limit the size of files to *size* blocks (default)
-m *size*	limit the size of physical memory to *size* K bytes
-s *size*	limit the size of the stack area to *size* K bytes
-t *secs*	limit process execution time to *secs* seconds

The umask Command

General Format: umask *mask*

umask sets the default file creation mask to *mask*. Files that are subsequently created are ANDed with this mask to determine the mode of the file.
umask with no arguments prints the current mask.

Examples

$ **umask**	*Print current mask*
0002	*No write to others*
$ **umask 022**	*No write to group either*
$	

TABLE B-12. typeset options

Option	Meaning
-H	Map UNIX file names to host file names (only on non-UNIX systems).
-L*n*	Left justify and strip leading blanks. If *n* is specified and nonzero, set the width of *var* to *n*; otherwise, the width is that of the first assignment to *var*. Subsequent assignments to *var* will be blank-padded or truncated to fit. If the -z option is also set, leading zeros will be stripped. The -R option is automatically turned off.
-R*n*	Right justify and strip trailing blanks. If *n* is specified and nonzero, set the width of *var* to *n*; otherwise, the width is that of the first assignment to *var*. Subsequent assignments to *var* will be blank-padded (on the left) or truncated (on the right) to fit. The -L option is automatically turned off.
-Z*n*	If the -L option has not been set, right justify and strip trailing blanks. If *n* is specified and nonzero, set the width of *var* to *n*; otherwise, the width is the width of the first assignment to *var*. If the first nonblank character is a digit, *var* will be zero-padded (on the left) or truncated (on the right) to fit; otherwise, *var* will be blank-padded or truncated to fit.
-f	*var* is a function name. No assignments may be made, and the only other valid flags are x, u, and t. x exports the function, u makes the function name undefined so it will be subsequently autoloaded on its first invocation, and t turns on the xtrace option for the function (see set).
+f	List function names.
-i*n*	*var* is defined as an integer variable. If *n* is specified and nonzero, it is the base the variable will evaluate to in parameter substitutions; otherwise, the base is determined from the base of the first assignment to *var*. Built-in arithmetic is faster with integer variables.
-l	Convert uppercase characters to lowercase. The -u option is automatically turned off.
-r	*var* is made read-only.
-t	*var* is tagged. This option is unused by the shell and may be set or unset by the user.
-u	Convert lowercase characters to uppercase. The -l option is automatically turned off.
-x	*var* is exported.

The unalias Command

General Format: `unalias` *names*

The aliases *names* are removed from the alias list.

The unset Command

General Format: `unset [-f]` *names*

This causes the shell to erase definitions of the variables or (if `-f` is specified) functions listed in *names*. The following variables cannot be specified: `IFS`, `MAILCHECK`, `PATH`, `PS1`, and `PS2`.

Example

unset dblist files   *Remove definitions of* `dblist` *and* `files`

The until Command

General Format:
```
until   command_t
do
        command
        command
        . . .
done
```

$command_t$ is executed and its exit status tested. If it is nonzero, then the commands enclosed between the `do` and `done` are executed. Then $command_t$ is executed again and its status tested. If it is nonzero, then the commands between the `do` and `done` are once again executed. Execution of $command_t$ and subsequent execution of the commands between the `do` and `done` continues until $command_t$ returns a zero exit status, at which point the loop is terminated. Execution then continues with the command that follows the `done`.

Note that since $command_t$ gets evaluated immediately upon entry into the loop, the commands between the `do` and `done` may never be executed if it returns a zero exit status the first time.

Example

```
# sleep for 60 seconds until jack logs on
```

```
until who | grep jack >/dev/null
do
        sleep 60
done

echo jack has logged on
```

The above loop will continue until the grep returns a zero exit status (i.e., finds jack in who's output). At that point, the loop will be terminated and the echo command that follows executed.

The wait Command

General Format: wait *n*

This command causes the shell to suspend its execution until process *n* finishes executing. If *n* is not supplied, then the shell waits for all child processes to finish executing. *n* may be a process number or a job number (see **Job Control**).

wait is useful for waiting for processes to finish that have been sent to the background for execution.

Example

```
sort large_file > sorted_file &     Send sort to the background
    ...                             Continue processing
wait                                Now wait for sort to finish
plotdata sorted_file
```

The variable $! can be used to obtain the process number of the last process sent to the background.

The Korn shell allows you to specify a job number instead of a process number, as in

```
wait %2
```

The whence Command

General Format: whence *commands*

The whence command prints out how *commands* would be interpreted if typed in. If a command has an alias, the value of the alias is printed out; if it is a built-in or function, the command name is printed out; otherwise, the PATH is searched, and the full path name is printed out.

The -v option can be used to get a more detailed description of *commands*. Note that the Korn shell has a built-in alias called type that is defined as whence -v.

The while Command

General Format:

```
while    command_t
do
         command
         command
         . . .
done
```

command$_t$ is executed and its exit status tested. If it is zero, then the commands enclosed between the do and done are executed. Then *command$_t$* is executed again and its status tested. If it is zero, then the commands between the do and done are once again executed. Execution of *command$_t$* and subsequent execution of the commands between the do and done continues until *command$_t$* returns a nonzero exit status, at which point the loop is terminated. Execution then continues with the command that follows the done.

Note that since *command$_t$* gets evaluated immediately upon entry into the loop, the commands between the do and done may never be executed if it returns a nonzero exit status the first time.

Example

```
# fill up the rest of the buffer with blank lines

while [ $lines -le $maxlines ]
do
        echo >> $BUFFER
        lines=`expr $lines + 1`
done
```

For More Information

There are many sources of information on the UNIX system; however, we have selectively listed some titles here of particular value to shell programmers.

There is one reference that you cannot do without. This is the UNIX documentation for your particular version. It will give detailed descriptions on the syntax and various options for each of the commands. A complete set of UNIX documentation is available from Prentice Hall. This is the ten-volume set of standard System V, Release 3 produced by AT&T. The reference manuals (referred to as the "man pages" by UNIX users) are necessary for any serious use.

Papers marked with a † are printed in the Berkeley 4.3 *UNIX User's Supplementary Documents*, *UNIX Programmer's Supplementary Documents*, and *UNIX System Manager's Manual*, available from the USENIX Association, P.O. Box 2299, Berkeley, CA 94710.

Kornshell Command and Programming Language, Korn and Bolsky, Prentice Hall Englewood Cliffs, NJ, 1988.

Contains complete coverage of the Korn shell, coauthored by its creator.

The UNIX C Shell Field Guide, G. Anderson and P. Anderson, Prentice Hall, Englewood Cliffs, NJ 07632, 1986.

An in-depth reference to the C shell.

†"An introduction to the C shell," W. Joy.

An Introduction to the C shell and many of its commonly used commands.

†"SED—A Non-interactive Text Editor," L. E. McMahon.

A complete description of the sed editor.

The AWK Programming Language A.V. Aho, B. W. Kernighan, P. J. Weinberger, Addison-Wesley, Reading, MA 1988.

A complete description of the awk language.

The UNIX Programming Environment, B. W. Kernighan and R. Pike, Prentice Hall, Englewood Cliffs, NJ 07632, 1984.

An advanced UNIX programming book.

Index

Programming in C, Revised Edition

Stephen G. Kochan

This timely revision provides complete coverage of the C language, including language features and over 90 program examples. The comprehensive tutorial approach teaches the beginner how to write, compile, and execute programs and teaches the experienced programmer how to write applications using features unique to C.

Program examples include a step-by-step explanation of all the procedures involved. The book covers all the essentials of C, including program looping, decision-making, arrays, functions, structures, character strings, bit operations, enumerated data types, and ANSI C.

Topics covered include:

■ Introduction and Fundamentals
■ Writing a Program in C
■ Variables, Constants, Data Types, and Arithmetic Expressions
■ Program Looping
■ Making Decisions
■ Arrays
■ Functions
■ Structures
■ Character Strings
■ Pointers
■ Operations on Bits
■ The Preprocessor
■ Working with Larger Programs
■ Input and Output
■ Miscellaneous and Advanced Features

476 Pages, 7½ x 9¾, Softbound
ISBN: 0-672-48420-X
No. 48420, $24.95

Portability and the C Language

Rex Jaeschke

Portability, the feature that distinguishes C from other programming languages, is thoroughly defined and explained in this definitive reference work. The book primarily addresses the technical issues of designing and writing C programs that are to be compiled across a diverse number of hardware and operating system environments.

Organized around the ANSI C Standard, it explains the C preprocessor and the run-time library and tackles portability from a C language perspective, discussing implementation-specific issues as they arise.

Topics covered include:

■ Introduction and Overview
■ The Environment
■ Conversions, Expressions, Declarations, and Statements
■ The Preprocessor
■ Diagnostics, Character Handling, Errors
■ Numerical Limits and Localization
■ Mathematics, Non-Local Jumps, Signal Handling
■ Variable Arguments and Common Definitions
■ Input/Output, General Utilities, String Handling
■ Date and Time
■ Appendix: Keywords and Reserved Identifiers

400 Pages, 7½ x 9¾, Softbound
ISBN: 0-672-48428-5
No. 48428, $24.95

Advanced C: Tips and Techniques

Paul L. Anderson and Gail C. Anderson

This in-depth book on C looks at portability, execution efficiency, and programming application techniques. Examples and techniques are portable across today's popular operating systems, making it appropriate for professional programmers, applications developers, systems level engineers, and programming students.

Entire chapters are devoted to special areas of C such as debugging techniques, C's run-time environment, and arrays and pointers. Techniques for allocating storage for multidimensional arrays at run-time, working with complex C expression, and speeding up programs with multidimensional arrays are presented clearly with realistic examples that demonstrate the techniques.

Topics covered include:

■ C Refresher
■ The Run-Time Environment
■ An Array of Choices
■ A Closer Look at C
■ C Debugging Techniques
■ The Source Code for a Memory Object Allocator
■ New ANSI C Features
■ Appendices: Standard C Under UNIX System V, Microport System V/ATC, Microsoft C Under XENIX, Microsoft C Under DOS, Turbo C Under DOS

456 Pages, 7½ x 9¾, Softbound
ISBN: 0-672-48417-X
No. 48417, $24.95

Programming in ANSI C

Stephen G. Kochan

This comprehensive programming guide is the newest title in the Hayden Books C Library, written by the series editor Stephen G. Kochan. A tutorial in nature, the book teaches the beginner how to write, compile and execute programs even with no previous experience with C.

The book's clear, logical style provides a well-organized instruction to C with over 90 program examples covering all features of the language. It details such C essentials as program looping, decision making, arrays, functions, structures, character strings, bit operations, and enumerated data types. Examples are complete with step-by-step explanations of each procedure and routine involved as well as end-of-chapter excercises, making it ideally suited for classroom use.

Topics covered include:

■ Introduction and Fundamentals
■ Writing a Program in ANSI C
■ Variables, Data Types, and Arithmetic Expressions
■ Program Looping
■ Making Decisions
■ Arrays, Functions, Structures
■ Character Strings, Pointers
■ Operations on Bits
■ The Preprocessor
■ More on Data Types
■ Working with Larger Programs
■ Input and Output
■ Miscellaneous Features and Topics
■ Appendices: ANSI C Language Summary, The UNIX C Library, Compiling Programs Under UNIX, The Program LINT, The ASCII Character Set

450 Pages, 7½ x 9¾, Softbound
ISBN: 0-672-48408-0
No. 48408, $24.95

Visit your local book retailer or call
800-257-5755